Jørgen Hæstrup

Passage to Palestine

»In tribute to the name and memory of S. Ralph Cohen who served as officer and director of Thanks To Scandinavia until the time of his death on June 27, 1983.«

JØRGEN HÆSTRUP

Passage to Palestine

Young Jews in Denmark 1932-45

ODENSE UNIVERSITY PRESS

© Odense University Press 1983

Photoset by Syfoma Sats, Svendborg, Denmark

Printed by Special-Trykkeriet Viborg a-s, Denmark

Drawings by Inger Bjerg Poulsen

ISBN 87 7492 447 8

Thanks to Scandinavia, Inc.

The funding for the translation and publication of this book has been provided by THANKS TO SCANDINAVIA and the Danish Research Council for the Humanities, not only to honor the author, Dr. Jørgen Hæstrup for his activities in the wartime resistance, but also including his studies in the rescue of persons of the Jewish faith, and also for his vast contributions to the history of the war-time and pre-war periods.

Thanks To Scandinavia was founded in June of 1963 by Victor Borge and Richard Netter, and since that date has been providing scholarships to American universities and fellowships to doctors, nurses and others involved in health care at American medical centers, in appreciation of the singular acts of humanity and bravery of the people and governments of Denmark, Finland, Norway and Sweden who risked, and so many of whom lost their lives in saving persons of the Jewish faith from a fate which overwhelmed 6,000,000 others of the same faith – –

– – while serving as a reminder to the present and future generations of man's responsibility to fellow man.

Contributions and inquiries concerning this scholarship fund may be transmitted to:

Thanks To Scandinavia, Inc.
745 Fifth Avenue
New York, New York ~~10051~~ 10151
U.S.A.

CONTENTS

Introduction

During the 1930's Denmark received a considerable number of refugees from Central Europe, including the two groups accounted for in this book. From April 9th 1940 the stream of refugees came to an end. On that day Denmark was occupied by German forces after a sudden assault and a demand in the character of an ultimatum to the Danish Government to accept the occupation or take the consequences, of which bombardment of undefended towns was only one. Minor skirmishes occurred in the early hours of the morning, but a military defence was considered to be impossible owing to the country's geographical nature and because the great Western Powers had made it clear, that Denmark in case of German aggression could not expect any military aid. The German Government used the pretext, that the occupation had the character of »protection« and pleaded that Germany had no intention of contesting Danish neutrality, independence and integrity. This, of course, was an illusion, but yielding to the circumstances the Danish Government chose an attempt to bind the German Government to these assurances and to try a policy of negotiation, lasting more than 3 years. Such a policy of negotiation must necessarily lead to a long sequence of humiliating concessions, but on some fundamental issues the government insisted that no negotiation was possible. If Germany made demands on these major issues the government must break off all negotiation and resign. One such issue was the government's refusal to discuss or in any way take measures against the Jews living in Denmark

This political situation lasted until August 29th 1943, when the government had to resign after an unacceptable German ultimatum caused by a growing resistance movement in the country, creating widespread strikes, riots and sabotage acts etc.

The occupying power declared a state of martial law, and from that day on the Germans were free to introduce a large number of encroachments upon the rights of the population, including a lightning action against the Danish Jews on October 2th 1943. Thanks to some fortunate circumstances such as the Swedish Government's declared willingness to receive all Danish Jews and a warning from a German official, G.F. Duckwitz, in the German headquarter in »Dagmarhus« in Copenhagen, the action generally speaking failed.

People all over the country improvised an extensive aid to escapees and almost 8000 Jews reached safety in Sweden in all forms of illegal transports across the waters between Denmark and Sweden. 284, however, were arrested on the day of the action and 190 were apprehended during the following weeks during attempts to reach Sweden, and the arrested were taken to the KZ-camp, »Theresienstadt«. Of these 425 survived and were in April 1945 brought via Denmark to Sweden and freedom.

A contributory cause to the survival of almost 90% of the deported and a reason why they could be brought home in time was the fact, that Danish civil servants succeeded – also after August 29th 1943 – in maintaining a purely Danish administration without any German possibility of interfering in internal Danish matters. In co-operation with broad sectors of Danish society the central administration was thereby able to send »Red Cross« parcels to the deported and to prepare the rescue expedition in April 1945. In that expedition they worked closely together with the Swedish Count Bernadotte.

General map of Denmark.

Hechaluz immigration

Binjamin Slor

On 20 July 1933, the local newspaper of the Danish town of Kalundborg had a small paragraph with the following heading:

60 YOUNG JEWS TO CAMP AT BRØJ?

The paragraph stated that the estate manager of Brøj, near Saltbæksvig, had received a request some time before, from a Jewish merchant in Copenhagen, to house 60 young Jewish boys and girls, from the ages 14 to 17, who had been turned out of Germany by the Nazi government, and who after a stay of six weeks in Denmark intended to go on to the British mandate in Palestine. The paper could add that the agent had applied for and had been given the town council's permission for temporary billeting of this kind. The query in the heading remained, however, as the »merchant in Copenhagen« had also applied elsewhere, and the small paragraph concluded:

THE JEWS ARE NOT COMING.

»Late this afternoon we have learned that ... the Jews are not coming here. They have been billeted in Nærum boarding school.«

Adolf Hitler had become German Reich Chancellor on 30 January 1933, and Nazism was beginning to cast its shadow, also over Denmark. In the months up to July 1933, the Danish press had been full of reports on revolutionary developments in Germany, and of horrified denunciations of Nazi persecution including economic boycott of the Jewish population in Germany. There was no deeper knowledge of Nazism, and no one could foresee how long the movement would be able to remain in power in the neighbour country, plagued as it was by disturbances.

The Copenhagen merchant mentioned in the paragraph was the wine merchant Binjamin Slor, who was not sitting idle, in the face of the danger that was now looming over his fellow Jews. He was not alone in taking action. The Jewish community in Denmark started »The Committee of 4 May 1933« in aid of Jewish refugees in Denmark, and this committee collected a total of about three-quarters of a million crowns in

13

the years that followed, amongst other things to pay for a civic restaurant for Jewish and other refugees in Copenhagen. But Slor's action contained a special perspective and was the start of a piece of Danish-Jewish history of far-reaching importance for a group of about 1,450 Jews. During the next decade, these were to find a temporary, and for some, a final existence in Denmark.

Binjamin Slor was not unprepared when this task confronted him. He was born on 25 July 1892 in the little marshland hamlet of Petach Tikvah, about 14 kilometres north of Tel-Aviv. He belonged to the third generation of a family of Jewish immigrants. His grandfather had been a goldsmith in Dvinsk, in Latvia, but had emigrated in 1852 to Palestine, driven by strict Jewish piety, and his grandmother, who came from Bialystock in Russia, took the same path, with four small children. They were both Zionists, before the Zionist movement had taken on political form, and Slor was to grow up in an orthodox Jewish home, for which it was both a stark necessity and a religious duty to cultivate the soil and build Israel up as a home for the Jews. From his childhood he accepted it as a matter of course that the actual cultivation of the soil was a Jewish duty, and for Slor it was the obvious conclusion that physical strength and stamina were needed for the task.

In an interview given in 1962, he speaks of his grandfather, and the latter's reasons for emigration:

»He was a very religious man, who went to the synagogue three times a day . . . He read his Talmud and lived more in heaven than on earth. Every morning, before daybreak, he prayed the usual morning prayer and asked God to bring the Jews home to Jerusalem, home to Israel. For waking up – he did not trust the works of men such as clocks – he had a cock under his bed. When the cock crowed the third time, grandfather got up, and prayed. For many years he prayed the same prayer, and at night he dreamed the same dream of coming home, and God came to him in a dream and said: »Binjamin, you are to go to Israel and work as a religious Jew should.« A religious Jew should, amongst other things, cultivate his land and give a tithe to the poor. No Jew had been able to keep this commandment, as no country had allowed them to own land.«

At this call, with no personal persecution in his homeland, Latvia, the goldsmith went to Palestine with his wife and children. His relation to the soil and the physical demands which all reclamation must make in that meagre, poor land became part of Slor's inheritance, also encouraged by his grandmother who, with the same uncompromising religious feeling left her quite prosperous Russian home, to settle in the country where she felt that she belonged. To her husband, who asked her to return, she

14

wrote: »If I cannot live on the soil of Israel, I would rather be under the soil, but NEVER outside it.«

This conviction lived on in Slor's childhood home. His father was a farmer. He had managed to bring a plantation under cultivation. And he too was profoundly religious. And then, the boy from the Zionist home, the boy who was deeply engaged in the cultivation of the soil and physical development, and who throughout his life was a convinced Zionist, was to live that life as a wine merchant in Copenhagen. How did his career come to take on such a strange, unexpected form?

It was not his home that gave it this direction. His father wished the boy to be a rabbi, while he himself wished to be a farmer. Palestine could only become Israel, in his eyes, if the farmers could wrest the fertility from the miserly soil, which was latent in it, but which had been lost during the centuries of inefficient Turkish rule. To make the soil fertile necessitated hard work and physical training, and as an 18-year-old, with four comrades, Slor founded the sports organisation *Makkabi*, partly for the physical training's own sake, and partly because such an organisation could serve as camouflage for the shooting practice which was forbidden by the Turkish rulers, and which would be greatly needed in a Jewish colony, which had to arm itself against Arab attacks. The organisation grew, and one of Slor's memories from his youth is the competition in 1913 with teams from other Jewish settlements, which was won by his team from Petach Tikvah.

It was at that point, however, that he and his comrades realised that they badly needed serious training in gymnastics, and that one or several of them would have to obtain this. His comrades insisted that it was he who should go, and Slor decided, much against the wishes of his father, to go abroad with the intention of returning and training others as leaders of athletics. The plan was for him to go to the U.S.A. to qualify, but there was not much money, and as the ticket to Scandinavia was cheaper, the gymnastics country, Sweden, was chosen as his destination. His route was via Copenhagen, but as fate would have it, he there met the principal of a physical training college, K.A. Knudsen. The latter took care of him, and became his friend and teacher for life. Slor became the first foreigner, with K.A. Knudsen's help, to receive a training at the State Gymnastics Institute, and for periods he was taken into the Knudsen's home and gradually felt himself at home in Denmark. At the end of 1914, he tried to carry out his original plan and return to Palestine, but he got no further than Berlin. The First World War had broken out, and as Slor, who was a Turkish subject with a Turkish

Binjamin Slor.

passport, but hoped ardently for a British victory over Turkey, and had burned his Turkish passport, he landed in a German prison, where he spent seven months before being deported to Sweden. From there he went on to Denmark, where Knudsen and his family again looked after him, and helped him to obtain further training, for example at Ollerup Gymnastics High School.

Zionist Activity

The background for many years of Zionist activity was thus created. During the post-war years Slor managed to arrange for a large number of young gymnasts from Palestine to come to Denmark and receive gymnastic training, partly at the State Gymnastics Institute and partly at Ollerup Gymnastics High School, and this led still further. Through his high school connexions, Slor, who by this time had established himself as an importer of Israeli wine, made contact with farming circles, and through them with the Agricultural Travel Bureau, an office under the Royal Danish Agricultural Society. The bureau was started in 1912, one of its aims being to arrange for exchange of farming trainees between Denmark and a number of European countries. Here was the possibility to bring not only gymnastics students, but also Jewish agricultural trainees to Denmark. In the years up to 1933, Slor, in co-operation with the bureau and its secretary, Niels Siggaard, arranged for about fifteen Jewish agricultural pupils to be placed on farms in various parts of Sjælland, mostly in the neighbourhood of Copenhagen. Pupils could thus meet in Copenhagen on the Jewish holidays and spend the day together. Both then and later it would prove that there was a crying need for the young visitors to be able to get together with their co-religionists and discuss the Zionist problems, since they had to live far from their home country during their period of training. As Great Britain was the mandatory power for Palestine, this placing of pupils from Palestine came naturally within the Anglo-Danish agreement on exchange of agricultural trainees, regardless of the fact that the reciprocity which the agreement implied in theory could not be practised without a somewhat elastic interpretation.

Up to 1933, this work was loosely arranged, as occasion demanded, and there was no permanent organisation, but during those years Slor gained experience and contacts, which would prove extremely useful, when the crisis arose in 1933, with the Nazis' seizure of power in Germany and the fatal consequences which it brought to the German Jews.

Could one be born in Palestine and be an ardent Zionist, without residing permanently in his country of birth?

Slor could!

His practical and educational work brought him on repeated journeys to Palestine, and he must have felt that he was promoting the cause of Zionism by making full use of his Danish contacts, and in Denmark he found much of what he was seeking as a basis for his dream of Israel. Apart from the physical training culture he had first looked for, he found considerable knowledge of agriculture and horticulture, in all their aspects. He also found a social system which in many ways harmonised with the visions which he cherished of a coming Israel – felt most strongly when he was introduced into the Knudsen's home, almost as a son of the house. And it may be worth reminding ourselves, even if it is perhaps superflous, that Slor's birthplace was not a country but still only an area under British mandate, and an area to which access for Jewish immigrants was now eased, now closed. The Zionist Slor was to live his life in Denmark in the search for ways to realise a vision of the future.

60 Children in Transit

And it was Slor, with *»Jüdische Jugendhilfe E.V.«* in Berlin behind him, that was responsible for the application to the estate manager on Brøj. This German-Jewish organisation was an officially registered body, since »E.V.« stood for *Eingetragener Verein.* On 7 July 1933, Slor applied to the Ministry of Justice, with the request for a joint visa for the children. In this application he wrote:

»Jüdische Jugendhilfe E.V. has the object – because of the present conditions in Germany, which do not need further explanation – to transfer as many Jewish children as possible to Palestine. The first group of 60 children are to be transferred in the coming autumn, but as they are to live in a collective colony in Palestine, it is advisable for them, beforehand, to have the opportunity of living together. *Jüdische Jugendhilfe E.V.* has therefore thought of this taking place here in Denmark. The means required for their visit is available, but as it is necessary, nevertheless, to be very economical, I most respectfully beg the honourable ministry for a joint entry visa for them. It is intended that the children arrive here on about the 25th of this month, and remain for 6–8 weeks. I take the liberty of enclosing a list of the children, who are not German subjects, but are born and live in Germany.«

The next day, Slor followed this up with another note to the ministry, in which he stated that the Mosaic religious community in Denmark would be ready to supply all further information, as »the religious community also supports *Jüdische Jugendhilfe E.V.«* This support was both moral and economic, as the congregation had already started a subscription, to cover part of the expenses which it was already realised would be needed for a stream of refugees from Germany.

The intentions of the *Jüdische Jugendhilfe E.V.* were one thing, however. Quite another thing was what the attitude of the Danish authorities would be, as they had not committed themselves to any particular point of view in the sudden refugee problem. The Ministry of Justice immediately submitted the matter to the Alien Department of the State Police, which suggested the next day, that the request be granted, but »permission should probably only be given on condition that departure from here takes place for example on 10 September this year at the latest.« Transit of a fairly short duration was not a problem for the authorities. A more permanent immigration was another matter, on which the authorities took no decision as yet.

Hechaluz

Slor's contacts in Berlin were far from being limited to *Jüdische Jugendhilfe E.V.* He had parallel contact with the Zionist pioneer organisation »*Hechaluz*«, which from its headquarters in London and Berlin had already been working long before 1933 to provide Zionist-minded Jews with agricultural training, wherever possible in countries able to supply it until, after their training, they could go on to Palestine as pioneers in the work of cultivating the land. From April 1933, Slor became the organisation's intermediary in Copenhagen with the Agricultural Travel Bureau – a contact which would soon take on a more permanent organisational form and lead to a considerable volume of *Hechaluz* activities in Denmark.

The work started from Berlin. After Hitler's seizure of power, when it became clear that this would lead to violent measures towards the German Jews, a »*Reichvertretung der Juden in Deutschland*« was founded, a voluntary union of a number of large German Jewish organisations. Under this umbrella organisation, there was also »*Hechaluz*«, a Zionist Socialist youth movement, started in Russia after the First World War. The movement worked for the creation of a new social model in the Jewish settlements in Palestine and on the longer term, the creation of a Jewish state in the country. Its programme included the practical and theoretical training of young Jews, who should thus be prepared for »*Aliyah*« – a word which stands for climbing up to the holy land, and which became a Jewish expression for emigration to and settlement in Palestine. The movement was critical of the inappropriate social structure of Jewish society, where, particularly in Germany, there was a considerable over-representation of intellectuals, professional people and members of the service sector, whilst the leaders of *Hechaluz* – in view of the need to build up a Jewish homeland in Palestine and after a time also an Israeli state – had to place the greatest emphasis on practical training in farming, market gardening and the trades. If the miserly soil was to be made to yield, this could only be done with hard physical work, coupled with agricultural know-how. Another important characteristic was the stress on ideals of equality and fellowship, as they were practised in the Jewish kibbutzes, where the great majority of the kibbutz members, even in 1933, were former *Hechaluz* pupils; and just as many of the workers in the mandate had received their first schooling through the *Hechaluz* organisation's educational programme. For example, *Hechaluz* had set up a number of training centres in various places in Germany, where young Jews could collect before their actual training in one of a number of European countries, in preparation for possible immigration to Palestine.

While the movement laid decisive weight upon practical training, most of all in farming, it also tried as far as possible to supplement the pupils' training with lessons in Hebrew, Zionist ideology, Jewish history and general knowledge of Palestine. The members of the movement should not come to Palestine unprepared, and then be confronted with a pioneer period, with its hard work and unaccustomed social forms.

It almost goes without saying that the *Hechaluz* organisation's attention also had to be directed to Denmark as a suitable training country. The high standard of Danish farming was generally acknowledged, and the co-operative idea, particularly, was greatly developed, and harmonized ideally with the views held in these Zionist circles on building up a coming Jewish society in Palestine. Here, too, there was an organ which had possibilities for helping *Hechaluz* to sluice young Jews into Denmark for agricultural training. The organ was the Agricultural Travel Bureau. This had contact on the one side with the authorities, first of all with the Alien Department of the police, which could issue the necessary permits, and on the other side with the agricultural organisations and through them the extensive Danish agricultural circles. The bureau enjoyed the confidence of the authorities, and by this time had long experience in placing foreign agricultural trainees in Danish farm homes, in dairies, agricultural colleges or other institutions which could be of use to agricultural students.

During 1932, a copious correspondence developed between the bureau and the *Hechaluz* office in Berlin, since the Berlin office first wished to test the bureau's possibilities and willingness to help. The procedure in the beginning was that the office in Berlin requested the bureau to find training possibilities for the young people and also, in individual cases, itself obtained names and addresses of Danish farmers who were willing to receive a trainee. After this, the Agricultural Travel Bureau, in accord with the rule in force, took over the task of applying to the State police to obtain the necessary residence permits. The start, like most starts, was hesitant and questioning, until the members found a routine case treatment, which could then continue in a standard form.

As far as it went, the task of the bureau lay in a quite natural continuation of its usual work of finding training places in Denmark, possibly through exchange, where young Danish agricultural trainees also went abroad, mostly to England, but often as a one-sided Danish effort. The one-sidedness as regards a number of countries was necessarily pronounced, because the highly developed Danish agriculture had knowledge and methods to offer which did not exist in the exchange countries in question. In 1932 there was a question of placing trainees in Denmark from England, Estonia, Holland, India, Japan, Norway, Poland, Switzerland, Czechoslovakia, Germany and Austria, a list which in 1931 also included pupils from Finland, Latvia, Lithuania and Russia. The bureau thus had long and varied experience of receiving and placing hard-working trainees.

Jewish Trainees

In 1932, when the bureau had to add the category »Jewish trainees« to its register, it was entering upon a work of a somewhat different character from what it was used to in spite of all the previous variety. Apart from the humanitarian considerations, which were undeniably connected with this work, and which were in high degree to stamp Niels Siggaard's engagement in this cause, it was here a question of trainees who were not beforehand used to or in any way acquainted with farming conditions. The large majority came from urban environments, often from well-to-do homes, and for whom a training in commerce, or one of the professions or services had usually been their most natural future. They were youngsters who in answer to the Zionist urge or from political necessity had had to break with their homes, and all their surrounding milieu's traditional possibilities for education and career.

But added to this, there was the element that the Agricultural Travel Bureau normally arranged exchange of agricultural trainees between Denmark and other countries with which formal agreements had been made on exchange, whereas such a mutual exchange agreement could not be made between Denmark and a non-existent Jewish state. When, therefore, the *Hechaluz* in Berlin in May 1932 asked the bureau to obtain residence permits for a group of seven young Jews, the bureau had to reply that the State Police would first have to interview the homes referred to in Berlin, and investigate whether the conditions for exchange were present. In the given instance there was talk of a refusal, but on the special grounds that the farm homes offered all lay in the Danish-German frontier district. Neither then nor later would the authorities issue residence permits where there was a question of farming

Niels Siggaard.

homes in South Jutland. Indirectly, the refusal contained the opposite implication, that when this district was excepted and other conditions were favourable, the residence permits could be given.

This was also the interpretation that Niels Siggaard deduced from it. In the coming years he would make great efforts to find places and obtain the necessary permits, the latter usually going smoothly. The Aliens Department of the State Police had well-founded confidence in the bureau's judgement and put no obstacles in the way of the Jewish agricultural trainees' placing. His task was lightened to some extent by the fact that applications for German trainees came to a stop, generally speaking, after 1933, and in the years that followed, the bureau was able to bombard the State Police with hundreds of applications for residence permits for »German subject N.N.«, where the word »German« should nearly always be read as »Jewish«. Neither Siggaard nor the State Police were concerned with race or religion, and within the framework of the Danish-German exchange agreement, they could treat cases without regard to whether the names were Müller or Schmidt, or were Cohn, Goldstein, Hirsch or Levi. A special question was raised in March 1932 by the *Hechaluz* office concerning stateless Jews, but here the bureau could give the assurance: »As regards residence permits, it is unimportant whether the young agricultural trainees are German subjects or not,« and the bureau could give the further assurance that if it received the name and address of the farm, where the trainee in question would be, the bureau would take care of obtaining the necessary residence permits.

In 1932, the question was still one of individual cases, where the authorities, with justified confidence in Niels Siggaard, overlooked formal considerations and followed his recommendations. When the Agricultural Council in June 1932 inquired from the Agricultural Travel Bureau what the procedure actually was as regards the general exchange rules, Siggaard could reply on 16 June that there were agreements on exchange between Denmark and a number of other countries – in this case Yugoslavia – on condition that the agricultural trainees receive board and lodging, but no pay; that the trainees should take part in the current work; and that they should themselves be responsible for all expenses in connexion with travel to and from their place of training. Siggaard then continued his explanation:

»Practice had led to the exchange conditions mentioned becoming valid for all foreigners who wish to have places in this country. The State police demand a statement from the Agricultural Travel Bureau to the effect that the conditions for residence for the foreigners in question are the same as those laid down in the official agreement.«

In the coming years, Siggaard would willingly issue such statements for immigrating Jews from Germany, and later Austria, Poland and Czechoslovakia, as well as for stateless Jews. The practice mentioned was quite quietly established by him and with the understanding of the State Police and Danish legations and consulates in Germany and other lands affected. In the years up to 1940, roughly half the bureau's intensive work was to be concerned with the placing and further training of Jews entering Denmark from the south.

Bureaucracy, if it is properly managed, can be a blessing. Here the bureaucracy took the reins in a cause which was served best without too much attention being drawn to it.

On Danish Farms

During 1932, therefore, a little immigration had begun through direct correspondance between the two offices, but from April 1933 the applications from Meinickestrasse 10 in Berlin came to a stop, while Binjamin Slor acted thereafter as the Berlin office's contact in Copenhagen – the first time on 24 April, when the bureau can inform Slor that it has found training places for four young Jews, and now intends to ask

Map of Denmark showing the position of the place names mentioned in the text.

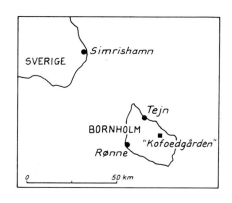

for permits from the State police. From then on, and clearly influenced by Hitler's seizure of power, the influx increases noticeably. The relatively few individual cases are replaced by applications for entry and places for young Jews, for example from 5–17 May, groups of 9 – 9 – 4 – 5 – 11 respectively. Fortunately, at the same time, it proved easy to find training places for the young people. While in 1932 there were traces of some hesitancy, engagement offers now arrived in a regular flow, so that there were plenty of places in the ensuing years, and the bureau often had to inform first one and then another home that trainees could not be allotted to them.

What the motive was for the many farm families that volunteered, throughout the country, cannot be covered in a single statement. The developments in Germany can have had their effect, and also the chance of obtaining cheap manpower can have contributed, but as it was a question of completely unskilled labour, humanitarian and political grounds have without doubt constituted a considerable part of the complex of motives. Reports from scores of former *Hechaluz* trainees make no secret of the fact that the work was hard and the life extremely Spartan, but many also emphasize that no more was demanded of them than of the farms' own men, with the farmers taking the lead. By far the most speak very warmly of the kind understanding that they met, which in many cases led to their feeling themselves adopted into the family, and decades later they keep up the connexion with their temporary Danish homes. That the transfer, from town life in Germany to life on a Danish farm in a Denmark in crisis, was hard and alienating, is obvious and understandable, but the deep gratitude expressed in by far the most of the reports on the humanity and support which the trainees usually met, was just as understandable, after their dreadful experiences in Germany.

At the beginning of the 30's, it was youngsters of a special stamp that arrived at the Danish farms and market gardens. Nazism had not yet quite unmasked its anti-Semitic threats and methods, and those who left in time and with foresight were chiefly radical Zionists. They had burned their boats behind them, and had said a final farewell to Jewish life in Europe and to the humiliations of the past. The trainees belonged to a new generation of Jews. With hope and pride they cherished a vision of the future, perhaps with the reunion of the family one day in Palestine or Israel, but at the worst without the lost generation, which had adapted itself and suffered so much persecution, and now once more faced a wave of pogroms. They did not shrink from hard work. On the contrary, they were inclined to seek out physical challenges in the fields and stables, and all the ballast of knowledge and strength, which the preliminary stage could give them. Their visit was only a station on the long road to Palestine, and young men of that stamp and with that attitude were not expecting riches or leisure in Denmark, let alone in Palestine. They were pioneers, with their gaze fixed on more far-flung, dangerous purposes. They had not come to the Danish station to settle down in a waiting room, but to await the signal for the next lap, and in the mean time to get wisdom and strength. Thus they contributed to advancing their cause and their descendants' cause.

The favourable developments increased when the news soon spread, that the young immigrants were keen, and had a positive attitude to their new work – information which the bureau passed on, again and again, to interested farmers. The following is just one example, in a letter of 22 July 1933 to a Danish market gardener:

»The Jewish trainees are clever and eager to learn, and they are under the strict control of a committee here in Copenhagen. It pays for the pupils' training, and is therefore extremely interested in their becoming skilled and reliable. If there is anything the matter with them, they are sent back to Germany. The trainees are to stay here for a year, so it will be necessary for the trainee to stay with you for a year, or at all events until the early summer 1934, as he must never be without a place up to November 1933 – all of this on condition that he is good.«

The Committee for the Jewish Agricultural Trainees

Now, therefore, Danish-Jewish co-operation had taken on a more permanent framework. Immediately after April 1933, Slor had allied himself with the book-seller Julius Margolinsky, who took over the practical side of the work, and writes of it:

» . . . as the pressure from outside increased enormously, the situation led to 120 being brought into the country after only 6 months, 92 *chawerim* (men trainees) and 28 *chawret* (women trainees) by the end of September 1933. Such considerable relief work for foreigners naturally demanded fixed organisational machinery. Neither within the community's administration nor in the Zionist circles in the country was there anyone who could take charge of the work, and as it was impossible, both technically and practically, for Binjamin Slor to cope with the work, I undertook the administration of the Danish *Hachscharah* (education) from the very start.«

Here we meet the committee to which Siggaard referred in the letter quoted above, and which became his principal contact on the Jewish side, while he himself took care of the contacts to the farmers' homes and to the State police. However, Siggaard's contact to the committee became, generally speaking, his contact with Margolinsky alone. Occasionally there is a letter to Slor after 1934 in his correspondance, but in the day-to-day work it was Margolinsky who looked after the connexion with the Agricultural Travel Bureau and through it with the Danish authorities. Margolinsky writes on this:

» . . . (I) found it unpractical, as the work developed considerably, to identify the Danish *Hachscharah* organisation with myself personally, and I therefore bought notepaper and various printed forms with the business name: THE COMMITTEE FOR JEWISH AGRICULTURAL TRAINEES. The committee was actually a 'one man show', however, as Binjamin Slor's activities were confined to certain negotiations with the *Reichvertretung* in Berlin, and with representatives of the Mosaic religious community in Copenhagen, regarding the financing of the *Hachscharah*.«

Julius Margolinsky, who was to be in charge of the practical side in an unbroken co-operation with Slor, was born in Copenhagen in 1895 Originally he had wanted to be a doctor, and began the study of medicine at Copenhagen University, but broke off and established himself as an antique book-seller, after the War becoming librarian of the Mosaic religious community's library. He was an ardent Zionist from his youth, and in 1925 watched the official opening ceremony of the Hebrew University in Jerusalem, with which he maintained a lively contact throughout his life. He was also active in the Jewish National Fund, the purpose of which was to acquire land in Palestine and make it suitable for cultivation. In the years 1933–43 his great capacity for work was devoted to the *Hechaluz* activities, but his sphere of interests was extensive. First of all he was engaged in Jewish history in general, and personal history in particular. His countless letters to *Hechaluz* trainees in the difficult years 1940–43 bear witness to his warm interest for each one of their problems and fates, usually encouraging, often admonishing and now and then fiercely rebuking. The Chief Rabbi, Bent Melchior, at his death in 1978 described his personality in, amongst others, the following words:

»In many ways Margo was an original, in the best meaning of the word – that is, an individualist who went his own way, never played to the gallery, but had an unfailing sense for judging a situation on the basis of a Jewish outlook, which was marked by humanity. He could appear dry and colourless at first sight, but in

Julius Margolinsky.
(Jerry Bergman fot.)

reality he was an ardent soul, and if one was at close quarters, his temperament and wit were sparkling.«

Slor's connexion with the Mosaic religious community became ever closer during the 1930's. Under the impression of developments in Germany, the Danish-Jewish community showed increasing interest in Zionist thinking, and at the election to the community's council in 1932, Slor was proposed though without being elected. He was elected, however, in 1937, an election which caused some perturbation in the community as an expression of the movement which was stirring in Danish-Jewish circles during that fateful decade. In the Jewish community in Denmark he was known as the moving spirit of Zionist activities in the country. It was he who in 1933 had the committee, which these activities required, set up, and although Margolinsky gradually took over most of the practical work, he never acted in decisive questions without Slor's guidance and advice, and Slor was always present in the decade following, when a case demanded an appeal to the authorities. Slor's home became a centre for the work, although the letters were actually written in the committee's office. His home was often packed with young *chawerim* in passage or during visits to Copenhagen.

When Siggaard could speak of the control kept on the agricultural pupils and their behaviour, this did not mean that this control was exercised chiefly from Copenhagen, although Slor and Margolinsky always had something to say on a case – in close co-operation with the

Agricultural Travel Bureau and the State Police particularly as regards the choice of suitable training places. The control was placed in the hands of the *Hechaluz* organisation in Germany, which by sifting in the normal way, and also by placing youngsters in transit camps in Germany, made sure that the pupils chosen really were motivated for agricultural training, and prepared to accept the conditions with which the work of construction in Palestine would confront them.

We hear of this in a letter of 26 November 1933, addressed to a farmer in the Faaborg district, who had applied to receive a pupil:

»Requests have been received for a number of Jewish trainees, who will be in the country ... None of the pupils have worked on farms before. The majority of them have had business training. Now they must be trained in agriculture in order to go to Palestine and take over a farm there. There is a world-wide union behind them, and the pupils usually behave well, as they are under the strict control of that union, which pays for their training. The pupils are mostly German subjects, the rest Polish.«

Similar letters went out at the same time to a great many farmers and market gardeners throughout the country, who were offering training places, but wished for further information. In the letters, the general economic and working conditions for exchange were stated. The most important was the decision that the trainees should take part in all the current farm work, and receive board and lodging, but no wages.

The description did not quite cover the situation. Quite a number of the young *chawerim*, who came to Denmark, had actually received preliminary training before they arrived, in one or several of the centres for agricultural training, which the *Hechaluz* had managed to set up in places in Germany. A number of reports mention short terms in these centres before the trainees had left for Denmark, and one of them could report on terms during 1936–38 on three such centres: first, Havelberg about 100 kilometres north of Berlin – a centre which was dissolved by the S.A.; then a 6 months term at a centre in Cologne, equipped as a kind of collective with a Jewish seminary for religious teachers, with classes in the Bible, the Talmud and synagogue singing; and finally a term at a centre in Gehringshof at Fulda. The pupil adds, however, »that it was nothing more than a waiting position for an emigration opportunity. In my case this was Denmark.«

How much or how little Siggaard knew of this work of preparation in Germany, can be left to conjecture. He never mentions it in his letters to the farmers, and always warns them that the trainees have no agricultural qualifications.

Some of the Hechaluz trainees had received preparatory instruction before coming to Denmark. The above picture is from »Landwerk Halbe«, c. 50 km south of Berlin.

Working Procedure

The procedure should now be clear. The motive force in the work lay with the *Hechaluz* office in Berlin, the committee in Copenhagen and the Agricultural Travel Bureau. Between them and the State police there existed an implied co-operation in solving problems that were best treated on the quiet and unnoticed. Margolinsky reports on the working procedure:

»The specific details of the work consisted in my receiving from *Hechaluz* in Berlin the names and the data referring to them, their type of passport and a short personal description of the *chawerim* wishing to be placed in Denmark. As a rule, with a personal visit to the Agricultural Bureau, I asked the latter to apply to the Ministry of Justice, to authorize the Danish legation in Berlin to issue a visa and work permit for six months for the *chawer* involved, as unpaid agricultural trainee with a farmer or a market gardener, with whom I had either been in personal contact or who was referred to me through the travel bureau. Through the local police, the conditions at the place of training were investigated, and if the working conditions were found satisfactory, after ten days' time I received a copy of the State Police's note to the legation in Berlin, and a couple of days after that, our *chawer* arrived in this country, where he was received by me, was equipped with the necessary working clothes and pocket money, and after receiving a briefing on the conditions in Denmark, the trainee in question travelled on to his place of work.«

This description needs only the addition that as the work progressed, it was often a pupil who had arrived earlier, who took over reception and briefing. He could often be better qualified to brief the new arrivals on the working conditions in general, and the local situation. A large number of the pupils did not pass through Copenhagen at all, on their way to their place of work. Others arrived without introduction or briefing: »The journey took place without any intermezzo at all, although the Danish travel bureau had issued a ticket: 'Berlin – Ebberup via Dalmose' (i.e. changing at Nykøbing, Falster, Næstved, Slagelse, Korsør, Nyborg, Odense and Tommerup). The bicycle I had with me ... brought me to my destination without much difficulty.«

Conditions of Pay

The decision that wages must not be paid was based on both general and special conditions. The decision was generally included in the agreements which, as mentioned, existed between Denmark and a number of other countries, and this generally valid decision was respected in the treatment of the individual case, which the Agricultural Travel Bureau used as regards the Jewish agricultural trainees, and which permitted the bureau to enter upon this work. The bureau guarded this principle, and Niels Siggaard opposed any alteration on this point, tooth and nail, although he neither sought to nor could prevent the individual farms from paying pocket money or gratuities to the pupils, and this took place according to attitude, possibilities and circumstances. Generally, however, the pupils were almost penniless, and a great many reports also tell of the lack of everything from toothpaste to cinema tickets, or pocket money for short trips to meet comrades.

But Siggaard opposed any thought of altering the principle of unpaid work. He was afraid that the whole idea of exchange, and with it the possibility of getting Jews into the country, would collapse if agreements were made for payment of wages in connexion with engagements. If this occurred, as there were sometimes signs that it would, on French, Dutch and Scandinavian proposals, one would immediately be faced with difficulties with trades unions with enormous unemployment.

There was a little money for the trainees, however, thanks to small contributions from abroad. During Slor's negotiations with the Jewish Joint Agency in London, an amount was granted of one dollar per trainee per month, to which was added small amounts for the administration expenses of the Zionist committee, and the Jewish community in Denmark also came to the help of the pupils. But Slor stuck tenaciously to the principle of unpaid work. He was well aware that it was a back door that he was holding open, and it was the word »training« that kept the door open.

After the Occupation in 1940, when arrangements were tightened up, one could foresee that the trainees' terms would last longer, while those who were now trained farmers became a really valuable work force, if they had not been before. Siggaard explained his viewpoint on this point in a letter of 29 August 1940 to the State police:

»The conditions were that the trainees should have board and lodging, but no pay for their work ... They should follow the customs of the country with regard to food, working hours and days off. On the other hand, steps should be taken so that their term should be as instructive as possible for them, for example, that they should have the opportunity to visit cattle shows, institutions and model farms in various parts of the country. The expenses of such excursions one expected the farmer to pay, if he considered the pupil's work to be worth more than the expenses of his board and lodging. As the majority of the trainees have come to the country poverty-stricken, it is understandable that they would like the farmers' 'presents' to be as large as possible, and to have a fixed engagement. The Agricultural Travel Bureau has reacted very strongly against the latter point, because it has always been a condition for exchange of agricultural pupils with other countries, that there must not be wage agreements, so that the pupils do not come in under the duties and rights of servants. The social services do not cover the foreign trainees, therefore, although it has been agreed that they have sickness insurance, when they are to remain in the country for 6 months or more.«

A strict Attitude

The bureau's attitude was strict, and the trainees have not found it easy to understand it, and impossible when circumstances forced prolonged visits on them. Several demanded wages, and several received them, as it transpires from their reports. But Siggaard fought for his exchange principle, also in the case of the Jews, where there was after all no question of exchange, but only a helping hand which could be given on account of a practice accepted by the authorities over a period of years. If one exceeded the framework of this practice, Siggaard was well aware that the authorities would be more than likely to object.

A parallel case illustrates that there was some truth in this. Here there was no accepted practice, and the authorities had to decide their position from bed rock.

On 4 October 1933, a barrister of the Supreme Court, C.B. Henriques, on behalf of the Mosaic religious community and »at the request of the committee which the religious community has established on account of the situation in Germany,« applied for residence and work permits for 20 young Jewish men, who wished to obtain a training in a trade in Denmark, and at the end of their training to emigrate to Palestine. Henriques pointed out that it was a case of chosen and well recommended young men, and that the Mosaic religious community would make itself responsible for all expenses and for the 20 leaving the country after their apprenticeships were completed, and he added: »The apprentices would only be placed with masters who make a statement that they engage the young man in question as an unpaid apprentice, and that the engagement will not cause dismissals or in any other way displace Danish manpower in the firm.« He added further that »it is intended to set up a collective home in Copenhagen for all the apprentices«, and that the community will also »request that permission may be given that up to 3 young German girls of Jewish birth may come here to take charge of the housekeeping, gratis.« The young people were divided between 7 smiths, 6 cabinet makers, 4 builders, 1 glazier, 1 house painter and 1 tiler.

In the conditions and requests the similarity with the agricultural trainees was obvious, and the matter was negligible in comparison with the c.200 agricultural pupils, who were in the country even at that stage. But the treatment and decision were certainly different. The case was sent to the Employment Directorate and the Ministry of Social Affairs for an opinion, and the reply came during November. The Employment Directorate would not oppose the application »if Danish manpower is not ousted and no dismissals take place«, while the Ministry of Social Affairs refused:

»Even if the engagement of those involved would not lead to dismissals of Danish manpower, in the opinion of the Ministry of Social Affairs, such engagement of unpaid workers would possibly mean that other employees are not engaged in the relevant firm. Considering that this situation cannot be controlled, and that for the country's own citizens it is extremely difficult to find places of employment for young people, the Ministry of Social Affairs cannot recommend that the desired permission should be given.«

With this, the refusal of the Ministry of Justice was announced.

This refusal was given at a time when no one could yet foresee the dimensions of the tragedy which awaited the German Jews, and it is in this light that one must also understand Siggaard's remark, quoted above, that in certain circumstances a trainee would be sent back to Germany, a decision which never seems to have been put into effect, except in a very few cases, where the pupil himself took the decision to go home. This was still conceivable during the very first years, but the possibility disappeared later, when emigrating Jews had their passports stamped with a »J« for »Jude«, which meant that re-entry into Germany was no longer possible. In 1933 it was generally known that the German Jews were in utmost need, threatened with economic boycott, persecution, coercive measures and injustice, but even in Jewish circles in Germany there were many who clung to the hope that the anti-Jewish measures could be a transitory phenomenon, and that they would hardly hit the old Jewish families, who had long been assimilated. There had been pogroms before, and the wave of pogroms must surely die down sooner or later, as had happened before. 1933 was after all earlier than the Nuremberg laws of 1935, earlier than the »Crystal Night« of 1938, and above all earlier than the »final solution« in 1942. It needed a more than perverse imagination, in 1933, to picture what was coming. It is on that background that the decision and the opinion given must be seen.

And yet, the young Jewish generation was breaking with the past. During 1933, the German *Hechaluz* department grew to c.15,000 youngsters who turned their backs on the idea of a quiet, assimilated existence, as Jews in a German society. This often took place in acute conflict with the older generation.

The Jews are welcome, now as before, to live in Germany

In a double feature article in the Danish national newspaper, »*Politiken*«, on 4 and 9 April 1933, the world-renowned German-Jewish journalist and politician, George Bernhard, chief editor for many years of »*Vossische Zeitung*«, delt in detail with the situation of the Jews in Germany in an attempt both to expose the situation and to explain the background for it. The articles made absolutely no secret of the Jews' actual desperate situation, and it described honestly all the persecutions, injustices and excesses to which the Jews were subjected. It was all there, from organised and unorganised boycott to exclusion and prohibitions of Jews in a large number of professions and on to regular cruelties: »Many people have been shot and beaten to death. Also refined cruelties have been used.«

And yet the German-Jewish writer tried to tone down the picture, and in particular he turned against the terror propaganda which was carried on from abroad against National Socialistic Germany, and which, in the writer's opinion, was not based on information from German Jews and, especially, had not done the cause any good: »Just because I wish to present the Jews' situation unadorned, and in conformity with the truth, I consider it my duty as a German and a Jew to counteract the widespread terror stories,« and the article continued: » . . .I still (hold) fast to my democratic convictions. But this does not stop me from hoping that my political opponents may achieve their purpose: to free Germany from its bitter need.« Elsewhere in the article he wrote that: »for the sake of justice it must yet be stated that everything that has occurred in Germany, up to the boycott of the Jews, speaks in favour of the Germans' moderation and of the National Socialist Party discipline«, and this party's discipline even gets some words of acknowledgement:

»But I also know cases where National Socialists, during tumults in front of Jewish shops, have made sure of the owners' safety. I know that National Socialist policemen, partly by force, have brought fanatical young members of the police reserves to their senses. In addition I know that the National Socialist storm trooper leaders have also protected Jewish personalities against the fury of undisciplined mobs.«

The article strongly emphasized that foreign terror propaganda had its roots more in anti-Germanism than in consideration of the German Jews, who, partly as the result of the propaganda, had had to suffer, although German Jews had not contributed with any deliberate participation in this propaganda. »The fact is that both Jewish and non-Jewish circles abroad have waded in on the well staged anti-German propaganda.« The German Bernhard thus believed that a reason for persecution of the Jews was the warped picture given abroad of the real situation, but the Jew Bernhard had to conclude his article with great bitterness. He complained once more of the »current tales of terror«.

»They WERE incorrect, and the wide dissemination they received is very much to be regretted. The Jews are welcome to live in Germany now as before. And unchallenged, if by that one means that they are neither killed nor beaten. But is that life? When one refuses them access to work, when with a cold system of proletarization one brings them to desperation, when one holds them down in constant fear that their passports will be taken from them, or that the newly introduced visa will be denied them or made difficult for them to obtain, how long will such a life be bearable?«

This very knowledgeable, sober analysis from one of Europe's most competent journalists in 1933, shortly after Hitler's seizure of power, could not, therefore, include a warning of the reality which lay ahead. The writer's objects were both to inform and to pour oil on the troubled waters, and they reflect both a hope for Germany and a faltering hope for the possibility for the German Jews to exist, if only the storm would subside. »The Jews are welcome to live in Germany, now as before« would turn out to be an invalid conclusion, but no one could have any idea, at that time, how invalid it would prove to be. When the Danish authorities could visualize the possibility of expulsion or refusal, in 1933, they could not know that such an action could be the equivalent of a death sentence. Here, posterity has no right to make an inflexible accusation, based upon knowledge which was not available at the time. In its attitude and actions the authorities and administration had to base their decisions on the facts of the time, and what one knew was bad enough, but not cruel enough.

Transit on British Certificates

When in spite of mass unemployment in Denmark. the Agricultural Travel Bureau could send its recommendations for residence permits to the State police, week after week, and in an ever-increasing stream, and regularly have the applications approved, one of the reasons for this was that there was no question of any permanent immigration to Denmark. What was proposed, in case after case, was a temporary stay at a place of training in Denmark, with a guarantee that after a shorter or longer training, the pupil could leave the country again, with Palestine or in a few cases other countries as his or her destination. This condition was absolute, and lay behind every one of the approvals, and to some extent it could be fulfilled. Whilst there was an economic crisis in the western world, Palestine was an area with economic progress, created by Jewish settlers, the supply of capital, and the Jewish colonizers' purposeful and technically skilful efforts to cultivate the land.

These colonists were actually *Hechaluz* trainees, to a large extent, and came from training centres in Germany or West European countries, such as Belgium, Denmark, France, Great Britain, Holland, Sweden and – until the Berlin-Rome axis was welded together – also Italy. It was a prerequisite for their and other Jews' immigration that Great Britain, the mandatory power for the area, permitted immigration, and issued certificates – certificates which both in the 1920's and 1930's were granted in considerable numbers.

Whilst the Jewish population in Palestine amounted to 83,000 persons in 1922, the number was almost doubled by 1930, and immigration with the required certificates would increase even more during the 1930's. For a period around 1930, the British government came into conflict, temporarily, with the Zionist organisation and the Jewish Agency, and suspended the issue of certificates for a time, but the restrictions were eased again by 1932, for one reason under the impression of events in Germany. After that, free entry was allowed for every agriculturalist, merchant or businessman, who had a minimum of £2,500 – later reduced to £1,000 – at his disposal. In addition, there was an annual quota for other immigrants, particularly such as could take over the agricultural work that was making the area fertile. In 1937, the Jewish population in the area had grown to 400,000 persons, and while in 1922 the Jews had only amounted to c.11% of the total population, their share in 1937 had increased to c.25%. This development gathered momentum up to the outbreak of the Second World War, which brought immigration to a stop.

The numbers of immigrants for the last 4 years up to the outbreak of war speak for themselves:

  1937: 12,475
  1938: 15,263
  1939: 18,433
  1940: 8,398

In implementing this immigration policy, the British were forced into a position where they were squeezed between their earlier promise to allow the establishment of a national home for the Jews in Palestine and violent Arab opposition to it. And yet Britain could not ignore her own promise, public pressure, or the fact that the Jewish immigrants brought a noticeable prosperity to the region. In a British White Book of 1931 on the latter point we read:

»The only organisations which have followed a consistent policy with regard to the development of agriculture have been the Jewish colonization organisations ... The Jewish colonists have all the advantages, such as capital, expertise and organisation have been able to give them. The remarkable progress is due to this and to the colonists' independent energy.«

Expertise, organisation and independent energy. That was indeed what characterized the activities which *Hechaluz* represented. The word means »pioneer«.

The British certificates, and with them the certainty that there was no question of final immigration to Denmark, but of transit, was a decisive element behind the activities of the Agricultural Travel Bureau, and the orderly way the cases were dealt with, which would soon be characteristic of its work. When a German-Jewish lawyer in Berlin in June 1933 approached the bureau to enquire as to the possibilities for his son, the reply was that young Jews, like all other foreigners, could stay in

Denmark as unpaid workmen. A request for this, however, must go through the *Hechaluz* office in Meinickestrasse 10 in Berlin, and from there via a committee in Copenhagen to the bureau's office, which would take the necessary steps to obtain work places and residence permits. It was the *Hechaluz* office which, through its choice out of a fixed quota. guaranteed that the necessary certificates were available when the time came.

When in August 1933 the Ministry of Justice enquired from the bureau as to the general provisions for exchange, and the special rules which were used in the case of Jewish trainees, Siggaard gave a detailed report on these rules and concluded:

»Incidentally, the office wishes to point out that a Jewish committee has been set up here in Copenhagen. It pays for the training of the Jewish pupils here, in agriculture, horticulture and domestic science, when pupils are engaged, and it guarantees their quality, and that the pupils leave the country when their term – one year – is over.«

Proof was given that the authorities could rely on this guarantee, when the first arrivals, at the end of their training in 1934, began to leave the country for Palestine with British certificates. Occasionally, a certificate was missing, and in that case *Hechaluz* made arrangements for the pupil to be transferred to a training place in another country; and occasionally, pupils from other countries came to Denmark to complete their training or to wait for a certificate. To keep pace with developments, the bureau and the committee applied for new residence permits at every departure, so that the Danish pool was constantly filled up. And the condition was still that the Berlin office, via its contact in London, could guarantee that certificates would be obtained, when the training term had run out. A letter to the State police on 18 April 1934 makes it clear that this condition was necessary: »The young man in question has been an agricultural trainee earlier, but at that time had not been accepted by the Jewish committee in Berlin, to go to Palestine. Now he has been accepted by the said committee on condition that he has had the full year's training in this country.« The bureau then recommended him and permission was given. The bureau applied for 6 months' residence permits regularly in all these cases, and the permits were later followed up with requests for prolongation for up to 1 year or 1½ years, depending amongst other things on the assessment of those in charge of the training place, as to further training being desirable, at an agricultural school, high school, dairy school, etc.

There was no lack of places in Denmark. Many letters went out from the bureau to Danish farms and market gardens, with such contents as the following, from 25 May 1935: »As there is still a long list of offers of places for Jewish pupils, and more offers than places, there cannot be any pupil for you this year.« The word »places« must be taken as »certificates«. It was their number which decided the size of the transit immigration.

Residence Permits

During 1933, the system had become established, and the procedure was fixed for the coming year. The bureau could confine itself to quite stereotype recommendations to the State police, without more motivation than the actual recommendation contained in the bureau's application: »The Agricultural Travel Bureau takes the liberty respectfully to request that there may be given a 6 month residence permit for German subject N.N. born a/b/19–. He is to be an unpaid agricultural trainee at Mr. X's farm at -town, near Y. It is requested that the permit be sent to the Danish legation in Berlin.« Now and then it was sent to the Danish consulate in Hamburg, and later other Danish agencies were included, but this was the only variation in these letters, almost formulas, which were both expected to be and were approved. The confidence between the bureau and the State police had become well rooted during the years of co-operation.

After that the pupils were scattered throughout the whole country, from Vendsyssel in the north over Mid-Jylland, Fyn and Sjælland, to Falster and Bornholm in the south. Only South-west Jylland and South Jylland do not appear with lists of village names, and here, as in all other instances, the State Police trusted Niels Siggaard, and with reason. A letter to a farmer in Rødding can serve as an example: »I have promised the State Police that I will not place foreign agricultural trainees in the South Jylland province, so that for that reason I am prevented from accepting your kind offer.«

And it was from Rødding that objections were raised against this special rule, when the High School Headmaster Hans Lund complained at South Jylland being excluded from taking part in a humanitarian task, but had to make the best of Siggaard's reply:

» . . . I have practised the ministerial injunction to the effect that foreign trainees can receive residence permits for terms at high schools and agricultural colleges in the South Jylland province . . . my feelings towards the Danish southern Jutlanders are still lively, even though I have noticed some of their bad habits. I will help them as far as my modest position allows, but I think that things being as they are, it is wisest and most considerate to maintain the injunction that foreign agricultural trainees must not be posted in the South Jylland province. To drag this subject out into the open for discussion would give the provocators wind in their sails and harm the Danish cause.«

The bureau was not angling after publicity.

The Extent of Immigration

How extensive, then, was immigration? Precise numbers cannot be given, for the sole reason that young, as well as older Jews were constantly arriving, independently of the Agricultural Travel Bureau and the Zionist Committee in Copenhagen – even though the bureau was always involved in the matter, as is clear from a number of letters, such as the following of 6 March 1936 to a Danish farmer:

»Every year, trainees are placed independently of the Agricultural Travel Bureau, but I always have something to do with such postings, in the sense that the State police always sends applications for residence permits for them here, for a statement as to whether residence permits can be issued nevertheless.«

The bureau also received a number of individual applications from Jews, who had come to Denmark independently of the established system, after having obtained training places privately. Here Siggaard was almost always ready to help, and those in question normally received word simply to send in their passports to the bureau, which would then obtain places and permits.

The question of help from the bureau only arose when it was a question of Jews who sought farm work. A number of Jewish fugitives came to the country, and to Copenhagen especially, in transit for a temporary stay with the hope of finding asylum in one country or another. This was the case, amongst others, for those who congregated temporarily around the Jewish civic restaurant in Copenhagen, where the clientele was somewhat mixed, as a ten-year old, stateless Jewish boy remembers:

»There were all kinds of people in the emigrant kitchen, most of them naturally Jews, but also political emigrants, and those who were both. There were religious and irreligious Jews, Marxists of every shade, those who followed the 2nd, 3rd, resp. 4th International, Social-Democrats, Stalinists, Trotskiists, Zionists, Assimilants, respectable citizens, social, asocial, schnorrers (i.e. with a good Jiddisch word, beggars) informers, i.e. people who informed on those of the emigrant comrades who kept themselves alive 'illegally', that is, without work permits, but there were absolutely no 'normal' people, living a normal life.«

Children's observations can be very sharp. They seem to have been so here – perceived with wondering eyes and edited later.

If quite precise numbers cannot be calculated, however, simply because the actual numbers still varied between entries and exits, it can be established approximately that the number of agricultural trainees up to the »Crystal Night« in November 1938 was about 200 a year. Margolinsky estimates that it was slightly higher, at c. 200–250, while Siggaard, in a fairly long report to the Head of Department, Vestbirk, in the Foreign Ministry, gives the number c. 200 as that estimated for the years 1934–36. The numbers remained relatively stable at that level, until the »Crystal Night« drastically changed them, with an immigration of about 120 in the course of a single month – an increase in the influx that from December 1938 continued into 1939, so that the total immigration from New Year 1939 to the outbreak of war on 1 September 1939 amounted to about 600. Siggaard, now as ever, was ready to receive all who could expect certificates, and ready to run the risk that these might fail to appear, in the increasingly tense international situation. Also where there was occasionally a question of transfer of *Hechaluz* trainees from other countries such as France and Italy, he was ready and willing to find training places and permits.

Transfers were altogether a very substantial part of the bureau's sphere of activity. A case was not solved, or never solved, simply because the pupil in question had entered the country and was placed in the training post intended for him or her. For many reasons, which could range from illness via disagreements to the pupil's wishes for further training or new posting near comrades – a wish that was always intense – there was a question of constantly moving the trainees to new farms, to high schools, agricultural colleges, dairies or other places of training, and the bureau had to keep up a running correspondance with the State Police, keeping them informed of changes of residence, and explaining the desirability or necessity of it. So day after day, notes whirred through the office to the State Police, to the farms, to schools and institutions, to Slor and Margolinsky, and to correspondents in Germany.

Co-operation was closest with Margolinsky, as it was chiefly he who, in the Copenhagen committee, looked after contact with the bureau. But whether Siggaard was contacting Margolinsky or occasionally Slor, it is clear from his countless letters, that he constantly threw himself into the work of promoting Jewish affairs. If certificates were not forthcoming for the Danish trainees after their term in Denmark expired, they had to be transferred to training places in other countries such as Yugoslavia and Great Britain. A large number could be sent to Sweden, after Slor's brother-in-law, the vetinerary surgeon Emil Glück, had had relief work established there on the lines of the Danish, although under somewhat different forms, such as a camp similar to a kibbutz. Contrariwise, it could happen that pupils, for example from Italy, obtained training places in Denmark.

Certificates were thus the bottle-neck of the work. However, the point never seems to have been reached where training places ran out in Denmark, and where the bureau had for that reason to say, »Stop«. The great increase in immigration after November 1938 thus brought no problems for the bureau, either in principle or practice, and undismayed at the intensification of the work, the staff found places when applications came in. In the whole period, Siggaard had such freedom of action that his positive attitude to those in need shines through his official, correct letters, which, however, never disclose directly what his feelings or private standpoint are in a cause which he sought unremittingly to promote. He writes to Margolinsky, for example, on 25 May 1934, that two trainees can quite well come to Denmark without waiting for their residence permits, as he will certainly get them once they have crossed the frontier. And he intervenes in April 1937 in a case where the State police have refused a prolongation of residence:

»After conversations with the State Police, I have understood that the reason why a residence permit . . . has been refused is that information on his possibilities for coming to Palestine have been inadequate. He does not belong to *Hechaluz* and so cannot obtain a certificate by that channel, but he can come to Palestine as a capitalist. He apparently has a fortune of £1,000. But it is not necessary for him to go to Palestine after his time in this country. The police are only interested in having a guarantee for his leaving the country again . . .«

and he adds some advice on the right procedure for dealing with the Danish bureaucracy.

44

In a number of cases, it happened that planned immigration to Denmark was annulled, because the young person in question had come direct to Palestine by a different route, before his documents were in order; or it could happen that an emigrant was forbidden to leave by the German authorities. In all such cases the committee and the bureau immediately took steps to have the places filled by other trainees, so that no possibility was overlooked, and in some cases, where a local chief of police according to the rules in force should have issued a prolongation of a permit but refused, Siggaard was quick to appeal against the refusal direct to the State Police, either with a request to reverse the chief's decision or to allow a postponement, so that a place could be found for the person in question in another country offering training.

Niels Siggaard

And who was this Niels Siggaard, who year after year sat unshakable in his office at Rolighedsvej 26, and without publicity about his work made himself a tool in the endeavour to rescue human lives in hundreds? For that was the fact. All the young Jews who reached the country were in one way or another in need. They had all been exposed to persecution of some kind, and they had all bidden an irrevocable farewell to parents and fatherland, language, culture and education. Several came direct from prison or concentration camps, interned there for the sole reason that they were of Jewish birth.

»I was born in Austria ... After 4 months in prison we came, with help from ... *Hechaluz* to Italy ... After 3 months we had to flee again (Rome-Berlin pact) ... and in November 1938 came to Denmark.« »Under the persecutions of the Jews ... the home (a children's home) was shut by the Gestapo, all boys over 16 years and I came to Dachau, my wife and the rest of the children were thrown out on the street. The Danish branch of *Hechaluz* had us brought ... to Denmark« »I was sent to K.Z. Sachsenhausen and set free after 3 weeks with the help of the factory. Every day – morning and evening – I had to report to the police ... In the middle of March 1939 ... I said Good-bye to my family and went with my fiancée to Hamburg ... At last the train brought me to Padborg. My fiancée was to come to Denmark a few days later, but I have never heard anything from her.« »I should have emigrated at the end of 1918, but experienced the 'Crystal Night' ... was taken, with my comrades, to K.Z. Buchenwald, where we lived through 2½ months' 'overture' to 'Holocaust'. Through Julius Margolinsky's approach to the

Danish authorities we received permits to work for a Danish farmer.« »On 10.11.38 (after the 'Crystal Night') to the concentration camp Dachau. Set free 8.12.38 after receiving Danish entry visa through the organisation 'Hechaluz' in Berlin.« »After 6 weeks in K.Z. Buchenwald ('Crystal Night') I came... to Fredensborg.«

It was for youngsters with this background or with the prospect of something similar or worse, that Niels Sigaard sat in his office and made sure of temporary residence in Denmark.

The brief, correct letters in the archives of the travel bureau disclose no more of the man Siggaard than that he had a practical touch in an intricate situation, that he was fearless when faced with difficulties and bureaucratic complications, and that he resolutely defended his and his office's rights. He was born in Gjellerup near Herning on 26 August 1878, and was thus 54 years old when he suddenly found himself involved in work which had perspectives far beyond the undramatic exchange of agricultural trainees, the arrangement of study terms and publication of pamphlets on agricultural matters. His father was a farmer and Siggaard was educated as a school teacher, with an extra term at a high school. In 1908, he took an agricultural diploma, was a teacher for three years at Ødum agricultural college, went on to take his matriculation examination in 1913, and then took his preliminary examination in philosophy. He then studied political economy from 1914–17. These studies went on parallel with a position as assistant at the Federation of Danish Agricultural Societies, and another in the State Seed Control. Siggaard was thus a very hard-working man, self-made and energetic, and with broad contacts with agricultural circles and with a number of their leaders. In 1921 he took over the daily leadership of the Agricultural Travel Bureau, with duties which he discharged with considerable independence, also when from 1932 he undertook to use the bureau as a convenient sluice for an exchange which was no exchange.

It was only in very rare border cases, when he felt that the bureau was on the point of exceeding its competence, that he asked his chief, the estate owner, Doctor K. Hasselbalch, President of the Royal Danish Agricultural Society, for advice and backing. It is clear from the few letters that the bureau now and then forwarded to his chief, that the latter was initiated in Siggaard's liberal interpretation of the expression »exchange«, when it was a question of transit of Jews from Central Europe, and that he also approved of this interpretation. But in the daily work, the bureau lived its life apart, and only very seldom were board meetings held. When the annual report was to be prepared, it was, for the sake of good order, presented for approval, but Siggaard took the daily decisions on his own responsibility and wrote his many letters in his own hand.

But a perusal of the thousands of letters which the bureau sent out in connexion with activities which doubled its work, does not tell us anything about the chief of the bureau except that he spared no pains to promote a cause which must have been very close to his heart. One would have to use a magnifying glass to find an instance where he has revealed the human being behind the official facade. It is clear, however, that his relations with Slor and Margolinsky were marked by great mutual confidence, even if the notes exchanged kept strictly to the correct and formal, and requests from the committee always brought an immediate and positive reaction from Siggaard. One single diminutive exposure, however, in all the correct sobriety, is worth mentioning. In a letter to the State police in November 1933, he gives his opinion on a case where two German Jews had applied for permanent residence in Denmark, with the intention of buying a farm. Siggaard refrains here from giving a vote in the case, as it lies outside the bureau's field, and he confines himself to pointing out the danger for the two Jews, as these had very little knowledge of farming, and »it is on account of the political situation in Germany that they have transferred to agriculture at all,« but one finds this sentence in the letter, nevertheless: »One will, however, believe that in this case, less weight should be given to the philanthropic than the economic.«

A philanthropic consideration! That slipped from his pen with a little glimpse into Siggaard's basis of decision, when he entered upon the work – a work which in October 1934 he still hoped would only be transitory. In 1934, Siggaard could know just as little as anyone else, what was coming. His basis for judgement was as slender as the average Dane's.

Discreet Administration

Another point which can illustrate Siggaard's administration is worth noting. In his annual report to the agricultural society, printed in »The Agricultural Magazine«, he normally omitted any mention of the Jewish immigration. It is only in the report for 1935 that there are a few words on it, with the stress on the educational element. In all other reports, the situation is covered with the terse remark that the majority of the trainees have come from Germany. In a narrower circle, such as an internal board meeting on 24 February 1937, with five participants, Siggaard once spoke a little more specifically. He explained – undeniably not quite correctly – that the exchanges with Germany in the first years after Hitler's seizure of power had stopped, and a new agreement of 1935 – according to which, contrary to all previous usage and on German demand, exchanges should take place on a »home to home« principle and with payment of wages – had not brought any results; and that the Agricultural Travel Bureau had requested that the demand for wages should be allowed to lapse, which had occurred.

Afterwards, however, Siggaard described what actually happened:

» . . . the placing of an increasing number of German Jewish pupils. It had begun in 1932 with a fixed number of 20. This number should also have been observed in 1933, but the bureau was requested by the authorities to assist in placing as large a number of Jewish trainees as the Jewish community could afford to support during training in this country. Since then the number has risen considerably, so that in the last years, it has been over 200. The Jewish pupils are hard-working and clever. Their places are glad of them. After a year's term in this country, they are to go to Palestine as colonists. The bureau has had nothing but satisfaction from the increase in work caused by the search for places for Jewish pupils. It is a little more difficult with the political refugees, of whom the bureau has placed some from Professor Aage Friis, who is secretary of the Relief Committee for Intellectual Refugees.«

These examples are the only exceptions to the golden rule of silence on the subject of the work, to which Margolinsky also refers: »In any case, there was seldom any mention in the home or foreign press of the Danish *Hachscharah*, as we did not want much publicity, on account of the political situation.« Incidentally, Siggaard did not mention either *Hechaluz* or the Zionist Committee in Copenhagen, in the report quoted above. In his report, the matter appeared as the natural continuation of the normal work of the bureau.

Unnoticed by the public, therefore, 1,450 young Jews came to Denmark in the years 1932–39 – in the first years somewhat spasmodically, partly owing to the starting days for agricultural workers (1 May and 1 November), but gradually in a constant stream. The initiative usually came from Berlin, but it could happen that Siggaard had a particularly suitable place available, in which case he applied to Margolinsky, to have it filled with a Jewish trainee. It could also occur that the Jewish trainees found suitable places in the districts where they were working, and sent news of this to Margolinsky, who could then propose these places. The

State Police, the bureau and the committeê all kept strict watch, to ensure that the places were suitable and the pupils were not made used of unduly. If it was found that everything was not as it should be, and if justified complaints were received from pupils, transfers were arranged to more suitable places. Now and then, local people with knowledge of the conditions intervened – sometimes the parson – and arranged for a desirable move.

In by far the most cases the procedure was that described earlier, and in most of these the »exchange« went smoothly. On the German side, obstacles were not generally put in the way of emigration, so long as the German authorities had made sure, with a »J« in the passport, that return was out of the question. In the 1930's, it was still in German interest simply to get rid of the country's undesired Jewish citizens or stateless Jewish persons in the country, and if this could take place by more or less voluntary emigration, the emigrants' subsequent fortunes were no longer a German question. As late as August 1939, when Germany had seized Czechoslovakia, the Consul-General Eigil Leth in Prague could report that he had had a conversation with the leader of the office for Jewish emigration from Austria and Czechoslovakia, the *Hauptsturmführer* Adolf Eichmann, and he had stated that one was aiming at »as far as possible to get rid of the Jews and get emigration going«. Their return was however conditional. If they could not go to their final destination, he would of course arrange that, on request from the consulate, they were allowed to return, but he then added a »dann werden sie hier eingesperrt«. In fact, therefore, a refusal – and a threatening refusal.

It happened occasionally that the bureau had to ask the police for residence permits for Jewish pupils in replacement for others »who have been prevented from leaving Germany«, and here the obstacle could be private matters or obstruction from the German authorities, or it could be that the original candidate for a place had gone to Palestine by another route than through Denmark.

It also occurred, occasionally, that immigration could be held up temporarily on economic grounds, and the bureau then informed the farmer in question and the local police authority that this was the reason for the trainee's non-arrival. »There has been some difficulty in getting the necessary currency for his journey granted, but now it seems to be going through, so that he can travel to this country in a few days. He is at present in Lithuania.« Or to the chief of police in the district: »X was announced about 1¾ months ago, but he has not been able to get the currency for his journey from Germany. Passport enclosed.« The last remark meant that now the pupil was coming. In a very few instances it happened that a pupil did not present himself at the place waiting for him, or that he was not strong enough – as Siggaard puts it – »to take his turn in the work«, and a couple of pupils from the earlier period gave up, and went home to Germany. In such cases, no one was able to intervene, but in the few quite unusual cases, where trainees lacked the necessary physical strength, the bureau, committee or Mosaic community tried to find solutions in the form of transfer to less heavy workplaces abroad.

Dispersing and Gathering

When the Jewish pupils came to Denmark, as mentioned already, they were dispersed throughout the whole country. Here it was a question of a repeated request from the Aliens Department of the State Police, that the pupils should be dispersed, at least to the extent that only one pupil be allotted to each farm, market garden, etc., and at the most two to an estate. Even married couples could be separated from each other: »I came to (a farm) near Bellinge, while my wife first went to a little farm in Bryllemark, but later was also moved to (Bellinge).« That was the principle on which Siggaard administered his organisation. This was, in fact, in full accord with his own ideas of procedure. He writes in June 1936 on this to the State Police:

»Would it not be a good idea if it became the practice to limit the number of foreign trainees on each estate to 2, so that speculation in cheap labour would be reduced. It seems, at least, to have had a good effect, since it was decided that there may be only one man or one woman pupil on each farm.«

This practice was roughly on a line with the wishes of Slor and Margolinsky. They found that the best training was obtained on the medium-sized farms, where it could be the most comprehensive, whilst the committee did not wish pupils to be placed on the larger estates, where the work was too specialized or on the very small farms, where the training possibilities must be considered limited.

It was a different matter that this very dispersal posed great problems for the trainees. It goes without saying that this was the case in the very few instances where a married couple arrived. Here one tried to place the man and wife near each other. But they were all hit by the necessary dispersal. No matter how single-minded the young trainees were, and no matter how determined to learn and adapt themselves to the unaccustomed type of work, and to bear the considerable privations, they were after all, in spite of all the kindness, exposed to a violent transplantation to a foreign language, foreign customs, a strange religion and strange people. Everything that met them was new and alien, and often physically hard – often to the limits of their endurance. They could often, and fortunately in most cases, feel welcome in these foreign surroundings, and especially, they could feel relieved to have escaped from the German hostility. But the fact was that were imigrants, without family, without fatherland, without anything whatever of home, and without certainty as to the more distant future. In such a situation, it must be of vital importance for them to have as much contact with others in the same situation as humanly possible. Comradeship must be their best compensation for the time being, and their only possibility, occasionally to feel themselves on home ground. Amongst their comrades they found not only similar ways of looking at the immediate problems and the possibility of discussing them, they also found there their only possibility of debating the Zionist view of life, which, in their temporary sojourn in a foreign land, must be the most important spiritual support on their pilgrimage towards a vision.

It was for that very reason that they were eager to find places in their neighbourhood for old and new comrades, and that they tried, as much as possible, to meet in groups, to be together, to talk, to discuss, and to make plans. When transfers occurred or new trainees arrived, they tried to the best of their ability to collect in groups, so that such meetings could take place, and cycle tours of many leagues were no hindrance. Nor was lack of bicycles: »We had the coldest winter in living memory, but walked 16 kilometres just the same, twice a week, to be together with 'our own'.« The meetings with »our own« were a vital necessity.

The following description from the Assens district is typical, and parallel to many similar accounts:

» . . . it was the practice that we, who had places, at the request of Copenhagen cycled around, looking for new places. Even though we often met with refusal, we were almost always kindly received. I have myself joined in getting hold of some, for example when we had to find places for 200 extra, who had been in Buchenwald after the Crystal Night. In the respective centres one keeps close contact with each other, and we actually lived together quite collectively, as much as could be done. The 'Ebberups' always met at the tea shop on the corner of Østergade and Nørregade in Assens . . . Later we managed to rent a room in

Ebberup ... and later again we frequented the 'confirmation room' at the parson's in Kærum, until we got a permanent place at the vicarage in Sandager, owned by the late Professor Løgstrup.«

The Trainees' internal Organisation

At the start of the immigration, when trainees were more scattered than was later the case, these meetings had to be quite improvised, and depended on local initiative, but from 1933, the pupils were already trying to meet in larger, geographically determined circles, with a first centre in the district around Hillerød and the next centre near Faxe. The idea behind these circles, which in the years that followed would lead to hundreds of transfers, was that it was only to the extent that the trainees could be kept more or less together, that the Zionist teaching and schooling could be maintained. And this was just as necessary, in the eyes of the *Hechaluz* organisation, as the technical training on the farms.

No sooner had a fairly large number of trainees arrived in Denmark during 1933, therefore, than the leaders in Berlin and Denmark took up the problem of forming circles with a central office for pupils. A first meeting took place on 10 June 1933, at Margolinsky's home, with the participation of about ten of the most Zionist-minded pupils. Here they had to confine themselves to discussion of organisational and technical conditions, such as passport questions, certificates, co-operation with the travel bureau, etc., but in that same month, the then leader of the German *Hechaluz*, Enzo Sereni, came to Denmark, to discuss the preparation of the Danish training programme, and he was back again in Denmark in August, to investigate the possibilities for supplementing the programmes with possible apprenticeships in a trade – an attempt which did not succeed. Here there was no travel bureau with exchange traditions to support its aims. In July a number of pupils from north Sjælland gathered at the Melchiors' in Vedbæk, and it was still necessary to keep the discussion to practical questions, in preparation for coming developments, which were estimated conservatively at an immigration of fifty pupils a year. Smaller centres were being established in Esrom, Fredensborg, Lillerød, Roskilde and Vipperup. The Jylland and Fyn pupils were largely cut off from participation in these discussions in a small inner circle.

Then, in September 1933, matters took a decisive turn. Up to this point, a number of technical and ideological groups had worked more or less independently of each other, but at a larger meeting of delegates it was now decided to found a »kibbutz-Alijah-Denmark«, and a concrete result of the co-operation between the groups was the establishment of a special »*Maskirut*« (a common board elected by the trainees), with its own office at Nørregade 20 in Copenhagen. The tasks of the office were multifarious: to seek to expand the Danish *Hachscharah* as much as possible; to take over the correspondance out to the circles, as they formed; to take care of foreign correspondance; to arrange tours and later seminars; to send out duplicated circulars; to answer letters from trainees and tackle their problems; and generally to try to raise the trainees' cultural level as much as possible, for example by purchase and circulation of literature. The office staff changed as the years passed. Older, experienced *Hechaluz* pupils could take part in the work periodically, while a few worked exclusively in the office. This was the case with the permanent secretary of the office, Magna Hartvig, who worked in the office for a number of years up to 1943, and it was also the case from 1940 with Bertl Grass, who became responsible for the organisational preparation of the movement's ideological and cultural work.

The central purpose for this *Hechaluz* office was quite clearly to maintain and as far as possible deepen their Zionist ideas for the trainees, who, scattered as they were on Danish farms, must be cut off from normal orientation in the special subjects and problems for which the Zionist movement stood. In a circular to the trainees, of September 1935, when a number of trainees had written to the *Maskirut* about their living conditions and situation, this purpose was stated emphatically. The circular noted with some regret that the trainees had concerned themselves in their letters solely with their momentary situation, and continued:

»But we must assess the overemphasis of your own personal life, and the neglect of political questions, as a lack. We must resist all political ignorance and form people who are socially inclined, into politically conscious people ... we shall only be able to solve our own problems when we learn to submit ourselves as links in a chain of collective consciousness.«

This *Maskirut* – or *Hechaluz* office, Nørregade 20, the name under which it appeared in the documents of the time – was from now on chosen by the most active of the trainees. The staff could change from year to year, but its attitude remained the same. The office was financed by contributions from the Danish-Jewish religious community, from the Jewish Agency in London, and later from smaller contributions from a common fund, a so-called »*Masser*«, from the pupils who could save a little of their pocket money, a kind of tax or collection, which they later tried to make obligatory. They were always short of money, and the office and its changing personnel had to live from hand to mouth.

Quite early, one, and later several visiting teachers *(Madrichim)* were appointed from this office. They either travelled about and visited the various circles, or took up residence in a particular district. The teachers were taken from the trainees' circles, from among the best qualified, often somewhat older trainees. The rule was two days of instruction a week, with lessons in Hebrew, Jewish history, and general conditions in Palestine. Those who lived farther away came on their bicycles, and the venues changed according to local conditions. The office became the trainees' contact organ. Its organisational adjustment to the system was difficult to define, during the first years. It had no actual authority. It took care of the ideological side of the trainees' lives, and became their link with the *Hechaluz* organisation in Berlin and London; it would also try to help trainees, after 1940, with practical problems such as change of place, and guidance in special situations.

But in the 1930's, the practical side of the work still lay in the hands of the Agricultural Travel Bureau, in co-operation with Slor and Margolinsky. No closer contact between the bureau and the office in Nørregade was established. Both offices had their special, limited spheres of activity, but now and then there was some contact. On 20 September 1937, Siggaard could write to the Danish Zionist Society at Nørregade 20 (one more designation, which was used before the name *Hechaluz* office became accepted) and give the office advice on the right procedure for a trainee who had wanted to change his training place, but had been refused by the State Police: »Perhaps it can change the decision, if you send a report to the State Police, from which it is clear that it is not (the pupil's fault), that he did not take up his place.« At that time, the office had hardly pushed itself into position in the established system, but in the course of the decade in which it existed, it would take on a more and more important function.

During the first years of immigration, in fact so long as immigration, and transit, lasted, the local meetings of comrades in smaller circles were the most important personal and intellectual breathing space in a hard working day. At first, it had been the decisive task for *Hechaluz*, the committee and the bureau, as well as for the Jewish communities which supported the work financially and practically at home and abroad, to bring the trainees to safety and to training places. In the longer term, however, there were other needs than material and security considerations, which must present themselves with increasing force. It was usual, in the first years, to collect as many trainees as possible in Copenhagen on the great Jewish holidays, and the young people were briefly lodged with Jewish families in greater Copenhagen. But for one thing this soon became impossible, with the rapidly increasing numbers of pupils, and for another, the pupils, who had a different background and a different and far more radical attitude from that of the Danish Jewish families, preferred to pass their scanty holidays and free days with their comrades in the *Hachscharah*, with whom they shared conditions and viewpoints. The visits to Copenhagen mostly came to an end and were replaced either by local gatherings or larger meetings at high schools or other meeting-places, where the subjects and heart of the lively, excited debates were the present employment situation, their chances for travelling on, the present political situation and, generally speaking, every kind of ideological viewpoint which surged among this Zionist-conscious group. This was nevertheless only a group brought together by external living conditions and the immediate situation, and far from being a homogenous circle, where it was a question of political views and beliefs, with ideas and attitudes covering a very wide spectrum.

At intervals, seminars were held with a qualified teaching staff and lecturers, sometimes coming from abroad, and this was a quite decisive part of the pupils' life that even though one must work hard in the fields and stables because hard work alone gave knowledge and physical strength, but built into existence there lay a need to supplement the hard toil with all kinds of cultural impulses. A good deal could be obtained in the surrounding Danish society, but the most important part must be fetched home from the trainees' own community. These were migrating beings, and the daily life in field or stable, or in the garden, was the temporary means by which they lived, but not what they lived for.

A divided Existence

It was these impulses that the trainees found, when they met as often as there was the slightest occasion for it, whether the year was 1933 – 1935 – 1937 – 1939 or 1941, and whether the group was large or small. Here it was not a question of ordinary agricultural trainees, for whom the future was settled and the training simply a straight path in their fathers' footsteps on safe home ground, but of a politically and spiritually rootless collection of young people, for whom all the future was uncertain and burdened with countless »ifs«. For them, cultural life, taken in its widest sense, was a crying need.

For the moment their existence was extremely divided. They all waited for the life-giving certificate and the offer of departure. »We sat on our suitcases«, as one of the pupils expressed it, with thanks for all the impulses he had received in Denmark. Up to the outbreak of the Second World War, the offer came to 1,000 of them, with 600 going direct from Denmark to Palestine, while 350 had to continue their training in other countries, while their wait for the certificate continued for a time, and about 50 reached temporary or final harbours in overseas countries, especially the U.S.A. For about 400 of them, however, the German Occupation of Denmark came in April 1940, and with it the end of all visible travelling possibilities, as one more omen that everything was uncertain.

Existence was also divided in another sense. On one side there was the place of training and its offer of temporary sanctuary and demand for physical presence and personal adjustments. On the other side there was a future under quite different skies, and with it a denial of the temptation to settle down. And the Danish offers could appear very varied. For just a few, their training places were a bad experience, until a new place was found – usually very quickly. Here the reaction could vary from quiet desperation to bitter defiance. For many their places were just a quite indifferent spot on the Danish map, where the trainee was drawn into the rhythm of the farm and faced with the monotonous everyday of a Danish farm, where there was little to enjoy and much to do – seldom in any unfriendly atmosphere, but even more seldom with any deeper understanding of the trainees' special personal needs. The redeeming point was that there could be something to learn. Still others, however – and they were the most numerous – found shelter and kindness in their new »home«, and in the highly developed farming circles even a certain superficial understanding of the trainees' Zionist attitudes, and their innermost desires and dreams. Where this last was the case, or would be the case, the stay in Denmark developed life-long friendships, which reached out into the future. The Danish home could then be a kind of compensation for the home in Germany which was lost for ever. But the division remained. The real home was to be built some time in the future.

The Break with the Family

A number of the pupils, but not all, could maintain a slender thread of communication for a short time with their German homes, through Red Cross letters, Christmas Cards, and, better still, some short letters of greetings. One trainee could report one or two telephone conversations. But then all communication ceased.

»Contact with my mother and sister via a single post card, after which they were deported to Auschwitz.« »My parents, who in 1942 had to share the fate of the majority of the remaining Jews in Germany.« »My parents who later perished in Auschwitz.« »Contact was broken off in December 1942. They were deported at that point.« »Through the Red Cross, I received a few letters from my family from the Warsaw ghetto where they had been deported from Nazi Germany. Contact by letter was broken off completely in February 1940.« »The contact with my family ... stopped abruptly in June 1942, when my parents were deported to a gas chamber in Poland.« »Contact with my parents until they were sent to a concentration camp in 1941.« »Contact with my mother up to her deportation to Minsk in 1941.« »Contact by letter was broken off, however, in 1942, when my parents, during a transport from Vienna to a labour camp near Minsk, together with 3000 other Jews ... were killed in a forest – the exact place is unknown.« »From my mother I received letters up to 1942. Then she was taken to one of Hitler's camps, where she died.« »With my family in Germany ... I had contact up to 1940.« »I had left my parents, and a month later they were sent to a concentration camp in Poland. A short time later, communication was broken off for ever.« »Contact by letter with my parents in Prague could be maintained up to their deportation to Theresienstadt in 1941 ... until they were sent on to the gas chambers.« »My only brother fell as a volunteer in the British Army, the rest of the family in Germany, over 24 people, all perished.« »No communication by letter with the free world and my family. From my dear grandfather I received the last letter of farewell from Prague in 1942, before he was deported to Theresienstadt and later Auschwitz.«

The first immigrants from the years in the 1930's had two hopes: To come to Palestine themselves, and later to be united with their families there. The latter hope was extinguished for the large majority of them.

Grievous Letters

And if any letters did come, they reported only sorrow and suffering. On 7 November 1941 – the eve of a deportation to Minsk – a mother wrote to her son in Denmark:

»My beloved child,
It can hardly have been so difficult for me, at any time before, to write a letter like this, now where it is a question of saying good-bye to you temporarily, my beloved child. The journey is very long, and we must make superhuman efforts, not to despair. Many friends . . . accompany us. Now we shall have to see whether we can write to each other, it is no use (sending) here . . . All this is too much to bear for a single human being, nerves will soon be unable to take any more. How painful for me, that now your letters too, which have always been a bright spot, will not come any more. But try, certainly, whether it perhaps may succeed all the same. The future lies so sadly before us, but in spite of all I will keep up my courage and go on being strong for your sakes. How much there is that our beloved, good father had been spared. We have always comforted ourselves by writing it – but now it has become a fact. He rests so quietly from all his torments, but now it is no longer possible to visit his resting-place, not even a photograph of it can be obtained. Let us constantly keep his dear memory in best remembrance. I am sure that you and Hans will do it. I have had some passport photos done, they are nothing special, but you have been glad of them, haven't you, my darling boy. Keep me, like your beloved father in your thoughts . . . It is now my greatest desire that you can stay with the good, kind people in Denmark, until everything is completely cleared up. Greet them now especially warmly and sincerely, and say how grateful I am for their goodness. My beloved child, keep on being good, industrious and single-minded, never disappoint me, for all my hopes and all my longing are for you two. Now you are well and will be able to do your work . . . Oh, now I will finish, my eyes are closing. God keep and protect you, my darling, good child. In sadness I embrace you and send you kisses without number. Your mother.«

It was not a temporary but a final farewell. In 1955, a German city court pronounced a statement of presumption of death for the widow, who on 8 November 1941 was reported to the national register as about to be deported to Minsk. Here all traces were obliterated.

One more letter shall tell of deep tragedy. It is written by a German Jewish couple, parents who in April 1941 were stranded in a concentration camp in France, and who by a roundabout way had learned that their son, after a stay in Denmark, had arrived safely in Palestine – a lot which never fell to the parents. Here too, it was a last sign of life, which did not come into the son's hands until after the War. The letter is addressed to the son's place of training in Denmark:

»Dear Hansen family . . . The main reason for these lines is that we wish to express to the Hansen family our deepest thanks for what you have taught our son Seppl. We understand that you have trained my son to be an able man, which in the faraway country will benefit his work. The Almighty must bring you your well-deserved reward, especially that you have been like real parents to my son, our Seppl has written it to us, and of your good treatment. As long as we live we shall never forget this of you . . . We have no relations abroad who can support us in our need. It is so bitter . . . Well, once more much thanksgiving for your good deed, and accept the sincerest greetings from your grateful family.«

As the letters ceased to arrive, and the families under the Nazi yoke disappeared, the Danish homes had to become their replacements, and in the experience of these homes we find every shade of light and shade, as well sober statements.

Memories from Days in Denmark

But let the young people from those days speak for themselves, with glimpses of their memories from Danish farming homes, still retained after 45 years have passed. They may perhaps see the past in a brighter light than when they experienced the harsh reality at close quarters. A layer of rationalisation after the event is obviously present, but still, the trainees are witnesses for the Crown, in a matter which they will never forget. The reality was too real for that.

The dark side is certainly represented:

»We did not get any wages . . . and were also dependent on the farmer's good-will. The reception in our new 'zu hause' was very miserable, as this farm was known far and wide as a bad one – the people could not get any Danish helpers, as they beat their servants and gave wretched food. It was the same with us. When both Hans and I were threatened with maltreatment, I rushed straight out of the house, and found refuge with . . . the then vicar . . . He and his wife arranged for us to get work with good people.«

This was not the end of the matter. As the new home did not include a farm, the two trainees, on demand from the police, had to find new places of work in the country, and found them:

»The time up to 9 April 1940 went fairly quietly, that is, we worked hard for the farmers, who had cheap labour in that way, but apart from that were very indifferent to our fate. Thanks to the solidarity in our group, we all survived happily and without psychological injury, through that time, without parents or other grown-ups who would have been able to give us support, when we needed it.«

Others also had to pass through a bad time:

»The term on the farm was a colossal upheaval . . . I had never done anything but go to school, and suddenly I had to be 'girl' on a farm, with all that includes. The first period was terrible, one didn't understand a word of what was said, had never eaten that kind of food, never seen a cow except in a picture, longed for home so much that I was going to pieces from it . . . but gradually one learned Danish, learned to work, got used to being there, became part of the little village, in a way. I can still remember that I was generally spoken of as Hans Jensen's 'Jewish girl'. And there was absolutely nothing discriminating in it. Just like 'the Co-operative's Ida', 'the carpenters's Poul', and 'them from the communal house' – one was just Hans Jensen's 'Jewish girl'. Then everyone knew who they were talking about.«

»My first place brought me to a family . . . who lived in a little house. I think they were extremely kind to me, but I couldn't communicate with them at all, they didn't know a word of German. I felt isolated, depressed, and I think I cried a lot. I missed my comrades.«

Here conditions altered, with a move to a different place:

» . . . I came to a farmer . . . and it was like coming home. Such wonderful people, as I have seldom met. Deeply rooted in their religion, culture and work, they showed so much understanding for my situation . . . I could gradually enter into their daily life, and the Danish language. Misunderstandings, simply as to language, were taken with good humour from both sides. I was never at any time exploited as to work«

Others, again, had toothing troubles after being placed incorrectly:

»My destination was a farm in (West Jylland) . . . the people were getting old, belonged to a very strict religious sect, and were neither able nor willing to communicate with me. My stay was not happy, therefore, as I was forced to work without wages or presents in a field which I was neither interested in nor suited to, as I was a typical town child.«

Here too, the conditions changed when the trainee came to the Technological Institute in Copenhagen:

»I was sent to a different farm... near Kalundborg. During that term I was fortunate enough to get permission to take part in a short course in farming machinery on the Technological Institute in Copenhagen, where I made good use of the extensive library to improve my limited knowledge of electronics... I would like to add, however, that I am very grateful to the Danish people... It was my own fault that I had a one-sided interest and was therefore completely unsuited to farming, and one could hardly expect that such an attitude could be understood by a man who had devoted his life to farming.«

And there were others who did not settle down at once:

»Was fetched by 'my' farmer to my first billet... where I only worked for 5 months, because the place was very unfortunate, both as regards the farmer and also because of the lack of contact with my comrades, who lived c. 30 kilometres away.«

Many took the situation with equanimity:

»I was the youngest, with 2 other farm hands, and was only put on cleaning, weeding and that sort of thing. When, after a couple of months, I could express myself well enough in Danish, I demanded to be put on the same work as the farm hands. When the farmer did not agree, I left the place in anger.«

Here it was difficult to get the work permit prolonged, but it was managed, and a new place was found. In a still later place, the trainee was galvanized:

»The farmer was encumbered with every imaginable bad characteristic. He was dirty, lazy, and as well as that a member of the Danish National Socialist Party. This did not worry me much, as here I was allowed to work independently... I left the place before time.«

A few trainees have quite neutral memories, and keep generally to unsentimental facts:

»The first place of work I had was a chicken farm... then I became a farm hand on a farm on Sjælland, and after that on 2 farms on Fyn. Since then I have only had contact with these places sporadically or not at all. I enjoyed the actual work and learning something about farming as the most important thing.« »Relations with the employer were correct, and I neither sought nor had direct family connexions.«
   »The Agricultural Travel Bureau found me a place... I was there for over a year. I took part in all the work but received no wages. Exactly according to the rules. They were really very kind. I lived in a cellar, with a Japanese and an English trainee.«

»Relations with these temporary employers were very individual. Some of the employers were very kind, others were indifferent.«

»Memories of my time in Denmark are varied, but it is probably right to say that the good memories outweigh the others.«

A number of neutral memories let fall a few appreciative words:

»The family ... was atypical for the farming community. The plantation was looked after, generally speaking, by a helper and me. At some time or other, the helper was dismissed. I was fairly 'trades-union-minded' and demanded wages, but received none. The family were friendly, however. I was drawn to some extent into their daily life.«

»I came to Haarby. It was a small farm of 25 tdr. (c. 50 acres). The conditions were excellent, but after 1½ years' stay. I changed my place, because I received higher wages. As a matter of fact, I was not supposed to have wages ... but most farmers gave us them, just the same. I have had good places, so that the relations between the farm family and me have been first class.«

»In spite of the unaccustomed and hard work which I sometimes had to do (many of us replaced a farm hand or a girl on the farm), I had to acknowledge – particularly on the background of what I had experienced in Germany – that conditions for us in Denmark must be comparable with a Paradise, even though I perhaps did not really appreciate it.«

»Apart from the heavy and unaccustomed work, I was very well off. I had special help from the young workers in the market garden, who stood by me in word and deed, and we were friends for many years.«

By far the most memories emphasize the bright side of their stay in Denmark, however. When the repeated remarks about the hard work, the lack of wages, the unaccustomed life and the need to meet their comrades often enough, are put aside, it is mostly grateful tones which stand out in the short outlines:

» ... from all sides among the common people, they met us with kindness. We hardly felt we were refugees.«

»I was kindly received by the family on the farm, stayed at that farm for 5 years and was ... a worker like all the others on the farm ... quite soon (after c. 2 years) I advanced to farm foreman, was quickly adopted as a popular village citizen, and enjoyed the greatest respect and understanding in every respect among the citizens of the village.«

»On the farm there was no one who could speak German, so we learned Danish in a short time, and were there for more than 2 years ... (later) we came to Sjælland ... The family was very much interested in our fate and in the Zionist idea of a Jewish state. There was a large library, and I was surprised at the high cultural level and the modern methods.«

»I felt myself quite at home, even if we did not understand each other, but after a couple of weeks we could already speak Danish, and I gradually taught myself with their help, to read and write good Danish. The connexion has been maintained through the years.«

»There is a great deal to tell about the unforgettable time in Denmark. I could fill a book ... I remained (with the family) for 1½ years. It should only have been 1 year but the certificate for Palestine did not arrive in time. I worked very hard on the farm, in the fields, with the cattle and also as maid in the house. A wonderful friendship developed with the family, and we still have contact with each other.«

» ... I was unpaid (I received 60 crowns a month) farming trainee ... I found many Danish friends, played football in the physical culture club, and was almost adopted by the country postman. I have kept in touch with these lovely people.«

»No one could speak German or English, and I was the first Jew in the whole district. I quickly learned to work – and it was hard – and I received 10 crowns in pocket money a month. The language I learned from 'my farmer' and 'my cowman'. It was of course 'peasant language' with a lot of swear words, that I learned, and many funny misunderstandings occurred ... On 9 November 1938, while we were drinking evening coffee, we listened to the radio news. And I could understand that something was said, which touched me personally (they were all looking at me). I could understand single words, which resembled German: for example, 'Frankfurt', 'all men', 'concentration camp'. They tried to explain to me, but it was no good. So I was told I should cycle with my cowman, and we came to the school. There I met the head teacher, and he and his family came to mean a great deal in my life in Denmark. He explained to me first of all about the radio news: the Crystal Night. And all men in Frankfurt were in concentration camps, that is to say, also my father. But the acquaintanceship with the teacher family became a deep friendship. I learned a great deal through them: the language, Danish songs, democracy, and so much besides ...«

»I was adopted into the family as the only girl. (The farmer) was German by birth ... so there were no language problems. I soon realised that I had been adopted in a splendid family. The family did everything to make things easier for me. We quickly established very close relations, and I really felt myself a child of the house. I later came to Fyn to a farming family. They were good people and received me with understanding. They taught me to milk and work in the fields. I thinned the beets and later helped to harvest them ... (I) moved to Horne where the family received me. They were older people, but again I realised I had got a good place. Farm work was not foreign to me. In the morning I milked as usual, and after breakfast I went into the fields with the sons. I learned to plough and work with the horse rake ...«

»They were splendid people. The village teacher could speak German and she came several times a day. The family took me to Rebild on 4 July, I was also with them in the Royal Theatre to plays. I was even invited to Copenhagen ... I came (later) to (the village of) Løgstrup. The family . . . was extremely intellectual and charming. Here I was a son of the house from the start . . .«

»From the first moment on Danish soil, yes, even on the deck of the Danish ferry, I felt confident and well. This in contrast to where I came from . . . My first reactions to Danish things was marked by slight interest. The reason was partly in the language – or the lack of anything particular to talk about, which interested both parties. The actual contact began . . . on Fyn. There I lived with some wonderful farming people . . . and their sincerity, gaiety, broke down the wall. With them I caught sight of this smiling genuineness in the midst of my shyness . . .«

»The reception on Bornholm was enormously cordial from everyone, perhaps especially the fishermen and their families . . . the fishermen were extremely Free Church, and treated us with kindness, hospitality, and with a strong desire that we then and for the rest of our lives should stay among them. Many boat-owners actually hoped to take us in as members of the family, by way of marriage and adoption . . .«

»I was met at the station by (the farmer) and driven in his car to the farm, where I was received most cordially by the whole family . . . after about 2 years I moved to another farm . . . and then to (yet another farm) . . . After that I came back to (the original farm) and was really regarded as a son of the family. A very warm relationship formed between us, and I have kept up the connexion with the family till today, with exchange of visits, correspondance and exchange of news of both the family and old Danish friends from my time on the farm.«

»I helped with the housework, but asked also to come out with them in the fields. 'Father' liked this, because his own daughter did not like working out of doors. We weeded and lifted the beets, threshed and also helped with the work in the garden . . . I have had contact with the family from that day to this. They were like a mother and father to me.«

Several expressed themselves laconically, but their meaning is clear:

»I had a lovely time. I helped in the house and on the farm, and often met my friends . . . The connexion with my 2 foster-homes was renewed after the War and maintained more or less for 36 years.«

»By the family I was received very kindly and warm-heartedly, and in a short time I was regarded and treated as a member of the family . . .«

»I came to a farm and can remember that everyone was very kind to me and I found many new friends . . .«

»I came to my foster-parents, who had a farm . . . Their reception of me was very cordial, and I felt very safe and at the same time very much relieved . . . I also had a fine contact with the neighbours . . . (they) could not speak German, and I could not speak Danish, but it went well, all the same, and I quickly learned Danish.«

These quotations are accounts, built on long remembrance of a time which burned itself fast. Perhaps time has softened the recollection of toil, uncertainty about their whole future, reverses in many places, and unhappy days. The writers have not been chosen with any other criterion than the sole one, that their present addresses have been traceable. Perhaps the writers are mostly those who have found it easiest to write, because most of them had a good deal to say. A mass of memories, which inspite of everything are painted mostly in bright colours, are rooted in the fact that it was probably the best and most enlightened farming families that volunteered with offers of places, and greater or lesser care and responsibility for the pupils. Many were really lucky in their places of work. But let the reports, with all reservations as to consideration of source material, speak for themselves. One of those who had a hard time, finishes his report from his home in Australia:

»I feel that the best part of my life was spent in Denmark, and that I feel myself more a Dane than an Australian. When anyone asks me, therefore, 'Where do you come from?' I always answer: 'Denmark!' because I know that when people ask this question, they don't really wish to know where you were born, but wish rather to decide your typical mentality. In that respect I love Denmark, feel Danish and never miss an opportunity to speak Danish and hear news from Denmark.«

On one point, the reports bear witness to solidarity with Denmark. Most write in Danish, many almost faultlessly.

In a Danish farming Environment

Even the best reception cannot change the fact that the adjustment to a Danish farming environment in the 1930's economic crisis was a great trial for them all. The physical demands which were made, with hardly any time of transition, often with only days' warning, looms large in the reminiscenses – also in those quoted. Through this remembered material we have a glimpse of the farming environment, which at that time could be both physically demanding and primitive. Let us hear what a young woman and a young man – both kindly received – have to say about it:

»As there were no modern conveniences on most of the farms – remember, labour was so cheap – this gave a lot of extra work. There was no electric light, only paraffin lamps, which had to be filled up often (and polished as well), no vacuum cleaner, only stoves, no chance for a bath, privies out of doors, no proper lavatories. And there was no water laid on, but wells – on washing day an indescribably heavy job pulling up the countless buckets. In the winter, unbearable cold, and the rod of the well was always covered with ice. The housewife, very very clever at everything – demanding a great deal of herself, but also of the help, in this case me. I didn't feel I LIVED during those years, it was a question of SURVIVING.«

»We drove into the farm courtyard, and I realised that this was my place of work. I was shown to a room in the house. There was straw in the bottom of the bed, and a heavy fustian quilt. I had no working clothes, and did not know how one behaved, when one had been taken in as a boy on a farm. I smartened myself up, carefully polished my shoes, and then I had to go out and be shown the cowstalls and the stable. It was worse when I saw their filthy backsides. It was a problem that I and the farmer could not talk to each other. I wanted to know where the lavatory was. It turned out to be an old-fashioned privy, and I could only use it the first few days, as it was meant for the women and children. The rest of us had to use the cowhouse, as I discovered when I saw a visiting veterinary surgeon squatting in the dung channel . . . I stayed for a long time on the farm. but then got a new place arranged . . . I did not have the physique to take the heavy work on the farms. I remember the very heavy sacks of corn, which had to be carried up on the loft by narrow ladders. My back felt as if it was broken after such a day's work. I had not many clothes to wear, so when it rained, and my clothes got wet, I had nothing to change into . . .«

A contemporary Description

Memories are one thing. A contemporary description another. Will a comparison of the reminiscences with contemporary reports change the picture? A *Hechaluz* trainee, soon after arriving in Denmark, in about 1938, has given his first impressions of the Danish farm where he was to work, until a Palestine certificate might arrive. Let this description, »My first days in Denmark« stand beside the remembered material.

The trainee describes his journey through Germany, and up through Jylland to Fredericia, and from there over to Fyn: »With great interest I looked out in passing at the fields, meadows and farms, as I was soon to work on such a farm myself.« The trainee thinks back to his preparatory camp in Germany and his experiences from there, and wonders: »But here in Denmark? Will the farm hands work much quicker than I? What does my farmer look like? Is he young, fat, thin, married, is he polite, is he educated?« His journey continues across Fyn, which the trainee has heard described as Denmark's garden. He observes the landscape and houses closely: »It really does give the effect of being a great garden, and in the colourful landscape, the pretty, clean houses lie, apparently scattered about at random.« And then the moment approaches:

»But now there is no more time for impressions of nature. At the next station I have to get out. Rather nervous, I collect my belongings and put them out in the corridor. Will anyone fetch me? Yes, just at that moment we run into the station, and two of my *chawerim* stand at the station, looking eagerly at the incoming train. A stone falls from my heart. I jumped down from the train. A brief, glad greeting. 'But where is the farmer?' 'He's waiting outside with his car.' A car, oh well, then he must be rich, I think to myself. We went out quickly through the station towards the exit. 'Goddag means Guten Tag, and Tak means Danke – you must make a note of those two words,' call one of the *chawerim* to me. Now we are outside. There is a car there, and it could actually go, as I found with some surprise later, but it must belong to rather an old vintage, as even I, a complete layman could see. My farmer, who was quite a young man, greeted me heartily. His wife and their 5-year-old Hans Ove had also come down to receive 'the German'. None of them spoke German, but as a start, my *chawerim*, who had already been in Denmark for 6 weeks, acted as interpreters. They talked to the farmer, perhaps mostly to show me in how short a time one could learn Danish, and they also satisfied my curiosity. They told me that the farm I was going to was a large. beautiful farm, and that the man was very decent and had wonderful horses. He had two farm hands, two maids, a cowman, and besides them, his parents lived on the farm. In the mean time, we had arrived. My *chawerim* had been right: a wonderful farm, big beautiful stables of red brick, and a small but very clean house. What a pleasure. The other *chawerim* from my group were also waiting for us there. Now came the welcome from the other inhabitants. The grandmother, in particular, seemed so kind that I immediately felt that I would soon feel at home. It was only the question of making myself understood, that was pathetic. But to begin with, I said 'Tak' and 'Goddag' alternately and laughed in a friendly but uncomprehending way at all the many greetings of welcome. After the ritual 'first visit coffee' we made a short tour through the house and farm. First my room. I must say, that after all the comfort I had seen up to then, I was rather disappointed. A bed, a chair, a table and 24 nails in the wall (I have counted them) – that was all. No cupboard, no possibilities for washing, nothing. But I dared not ask about it yet, and we went on to the horse stable. I was at once mollified. It was simply splendid. A light, roomy stable, such as I had never seen before. Seven enormous Belgian horses stood in there, and showed their docked tails and shining, polished rumps . . . I began to look forward to my future work, and yet I was rather uneasy. If those beasts should run away with me one day . . . I would have to make tremendous efforts, if I wanted to satisfy my man, here. And with some forebodings I lay down that evening to sleep. Could I manage it?«

Unavoidable Problems

As can be seen, problems could easily build up, out on the individual farms and market gardens in the provinces. Many were solved on the spot, but others were not. Whilst immigration and emigration took place, in those years, more or less according to the rules agreed in 1933, and while the central organs in Copenhagen were able to keep pace, approximately, with developments, it is clear from the material quoted that a good deal could go off the rails. One could and did make plans and preparations from Copenhagen, but then, a trifle, or some small detail could threaten to crush the hopes of an expectant Jew. For the individual, a trifle was never trifling, but always a new horror, piled on top of many previous horrors. For the organised bodies in Copenhagen, it was one complex of problems to obtain entry and residence permits, and a place somewhere in Denmark, but it was quite a different matter to make sure of, or simply to keep oneself informed on what the fate of the trainee was in his day-to-day life. Chance played a part, and humanity was mixed with stupidity and ineptitude. Many were able to help themselves, while others were not, or at least not without support from kind people in the locality or from comrades.

Problems arose especially and immeasurably, when the streams of immigrants increased enormously, from 1938, and when, a little later, immigration began of a large number of boys and girls of 14–16 years of age, 320 in all, who were not, as the earlier *Hechaluz* trainees had been, physically equipped and psychologically prepared for Danish farming conditions. The steady passage, which had been practised via the Agricultural Travel Bureau for a number of years, had now to be replaced by a more hectic activity, partly in the bureau, partly by other organisations, a situation we shall return to.

But it is a fact that some grip on developments could not but be lost; that in the bureau and elsewhere, hasty action had to be taken; and that advantage had to be taken of new and existing offers – also offers from training places lying outside Siggaard's personal acquaintance. Added to this, there were one or two fateful elements which complicated the situation still further. One of these was the lack of the required certificates, when Jews from Germany, and soon also from Austria and Czechoslovakia, as well as stateless Jews streamed out over Europe, wanting certificates which could not be obtained in nearly the number required. The other element appeared with the outbreak of war in September 1939, and then, and especially, with the German occupation of Denmark in April 1940. With that, practically all possibilities for emigration were blocked, and a completely new situation arose, with a breach of all the conditions which had existed and had been basic, when the passage of trainees had begun in 1932. These events placed the authorities and organisations in serious difficulties, but the young Jews, who were principally concerned, found themselves in an unhappy and threatened situation, which for some ended tragically.

But even if, up to 1938, trainee transit took place smoothly, as a general rule, in those years also, special problems could arise, requiring intervention and an elastic treatment of the cases in question. The greatest problems arose, as mentioned, in connexion with the pupils' need to be with their comrades. At first, Siggaard seems to have placed trainees according to the offers of places, and from his opinion as to which places were reasonably good. In the first quarter of 1934, one can note that the map of Denmark is pricked out with training places, from Thy to Bornholm, and a similar picture is to be seen for the second quarter of the same year. The number of village names run into scores. A place could look suitable from the bureau's office chair and from an agricultural point of view. The pupils soon pressed to obtain places which allowed them the best chance for what they had to consider just as essential, the vital intercourse with other Jews. And who does not understand the trainee, sitting in a remote spot up in Thy, with the nearest comrade near Skanderborg, and perhaps a friend near Maribo or in Slangerup. Even such an out-of-the-way place as Siø appears in the long list of village names.

The result was soon continuous transfers, sometimes on the advice and with the help of the bureau, sometimes on the pupils' own initiative, and their own visits to get hold of convenient places for their comrades. Siggaard seems to have understood this need, and have taken on the extra work with equanimity, and care for the best solution, and gradually it became usual to place trainees in areas which, at least with some good-will, could approach what was desirable – placing them in centres with such a reasonable distance between the training places that they could be reached on a bicycle, if the will was there.

The bicycle became just as acute a need as it was banal, and at first, a dictionary was also an essential. In July 1933, »*Jødisk Familieblad*« published the following appeal:

»As our readers will be aware, some young Jews from Germany (*chalutzim*) have been placed here in Denmark as unpaid trainees. Most of these *chalutzim* are without means, and the necessary money for their stay here is guaranteed by the committee which the religious community has set up. Many of the young people would be glad to have the loan of a bicycle, however, as long as they are in the country, and also dictionaries are much needed. If, therefore, any of this paper's readers could be willing to loan some bicycles and dictionaries, they will be helping a great need . . .«

The names, addresses and telephone numbers are then given of the leaders of the work, Slor and Margolinsky.

The announcement seems to give a clear impression of the Danish community's belief that the whole affair was probably just for the time being. The desperate character of the situation had not yet penetrated consciousness.

Training Possibilities

The many transfers did not only mean moving from district to district and from farm to farm. As the time for leaving the country was postponed, and especially when the War and the Occupation seemed to prohibit it in 1939–40, transfers came to mean transfers to training which went beyond what could be learned in the practical work on farms and market or nursery gardens. The list of such more specialized training courses is quite comprehensive, and also includes various specialized schools, such as Ahms Matriculation Cources, the Workers' High School in Roskilde, Ask High School, Askov High School, Beder Gardener School, Børkop High School, Dalum Agricultural School, Danebod High School, Haslev Trade School, Høng Small-holders School, Høng Trade School, Korinth Agricultural School, Kærhave Agricultural School, Lyngby Agricultural School, Ollerup Gymnastics High School, Ringsted Agricultural School, Rødding High School, Skårup Domestic Science School, Tune Agricultural School, Vinding Agricultural School and Uldum High School, besides which, individuals had the possibility of obtaining various forms of private teaching. Many of the trainees could also praticipate in Danish cultural life in the local village, local courses and evening school, as well as meetings in the assembly hall, with lectures etc. To a greater or lesser extent, the trainees thus acquired a wider knowledge of Danish cultural life and thinking, and the Danish political situation.

»I received an offer to come to Askov High School for three months . . . This was another upheaval for me, also as to language, as I spoke the Jylland dialect and was here confronted with a different Danish language. I got a great deal out of the term, amongst other things I learned to 'think' in Danish, and found many good human contacts.«

No Danish training could be compared, however, with the acquiring of knowledge which took place through the pupils' internal gatherings, whether these were connected with regular meeting activities, arranged locally, or with larger and more organized gatherings, where the subjects of meetings and seminars were connected with the trainees' special Zionist interests, and their immediate political problems and plans – to the extent that planning could be at all realistic for the groups, which depended entirely on decisions taken in offices far away from Denmark, and on international political developments! In the midst of Danish everyday life and their agricultural training, they had their internal situation to discuss, and if possible to take charge of. As immigrants to Denmark, they were caught in the Danish situation, particularly after the outbreak of war and then the Occupation, but in the midst of this, and dependent upon it, they formed an enclave in which they had to come to terms with their special situation. What should they do? In the short term? In the long term?

The many hundreds of transfers were registered in the Agricultural Travel Bureau, and through it by the State Police and local police chiefs, who received current information on places of residence and the reason for transfers, and none of this normally gave rise to difficulties in principle. But now and then, the bureau and the authorities were faced with cases which lay outside or on the edge of the bureau's competence, and the basis for decisions which the authorities had fixed as normative for immigration.

The Koefoed Farm

The cases in question are atypical and unimportant as far as numbers are concerned, but because they were atypical, they gave rise to a great deal more correspondance than the normal cases, and they illustrate both the bureau's good will – also in border cases – and the accuracy with which it dealt with its section of the immigration problem. Two of these cases arose partly from the decision that there might only be one trainee on each farm.

In November 1933, and the following months, a case of this kind appeared, when the State Police asked the bureau for a statement, with reference to the existence, noted by the police, of a colony of Jews living on the »Koefoed Farm« on the island of Bornholm. The bureau enquired from Slor/Margolinsky on the matter, and they in their turn enquired from the *Hechaluz* office in Berlin, but as transpires from the bureau's note of 28 December to the State Police, »in none of these places have they connexion with the immigration to Bornholm, towards which they are also somewhat sceptical.« The bureau, which meanwhile had investigated the situation via the local police, could give the information that at the moment there were 17 trainees at the »farm«, and that »this 'farm' is therefore more of a kind of boarding house«, and that the bureau believed that it would be difficult to find actual agricultural places for an extra number on the farms on Bornholm, »as the gentleman farms on Bornholm are small«. The bureau was favourably inclined and recommended residence permits« for the seven who can live and eat in the cowman house«, but also pointed out that it would be difficult to make a definite statement in the case, as this lay outside the normal rules for exchange – which was undeniably correct. Later, too, the bureau was asked about the case and recommended prolongation of residence, even though Siggaard stuck to the principle of dispersal and not placing in colonies. »The billeting must almost be considered an emigration colony, and it must probably be regarded as more desirable to have the many German emigrants distributed over different parts of the country.«

Here there was a question of an almost unique collective immigration, without contact to the *Hechaluz* organisation, or indeed in spite of it. The background was as follows: In May 1933, a German Jewish agronomist, Doctor Gutfeld, applied to a Doctor Fred Keibel, who as a young lawyer had an office in *Wirtschaftshilfe der jüdischen Gemeinde*, Berlin, and suggested that he collect a group of young Jews, who might be interested in a training in agriculture, and form a collective with a view to its later establishment in some foreign country, not necessarily Palestine. Keibel declared himself willing to collect such a group, and Gutfeld made himself responsible for finding a training area. He found this after a trip to Denmark, on Bornholm, where he, via a number of local contacts found the »Kofoed farm«, which is described by Doctor Keibel in the following words:

»The 'Kofoed farm' was especially suited to our purpose. It had been a much neglected farm. (The owner) had bought it chiefly on prestige grounds. He ran it with a very small skeleton staff, as he had to use his money to renew the herd. He was thus unable to engage more than a minimum of farm hands, for a number of years. But when the farm was brought back to its earlier footing, it could supply more work places for Danish farm workers than before.«

These words are added on the owner »He was known to be a very clever farmer and even able to give theoretical teaching. He could take on 20 trainees, 5 who could be put up on the farm, whilst the others could take over an empty house close by.« Added to all this, there was a German Jewish teacher, Doctor Prøschold, living in the neighbourhood. He had come to Bornholm in 1933 with a group of German Jewish holiday children (given free hospitality in Denmark) and then had settled on the island after difficulties with the Nazi regime. Together with his wife, he was willing to keep house for the immigrant group, and he could also, as a previous teacher in a workers' high school, take over the education of the group.

On this basis, in the autumn 1933, Doctor Keibel collected a group which arrived in Bornholm, where everything at first went well. 23 were housed on the Kofoed farm, and 7 were divided between other farms on the island, 2 of them on the farm next door. The State Police gave them a residence permit for 6 months, with instructions on how they could then apply for prolongation. In February, prolongation of residence was given to 1 August 1934, amongst others, on the recommendation of Siggaard, who was consulted in both cases. But after that, difficulties arose. The local trades union pointed out that a farm hand had been dismissed from the farm shortly before the arrival of the Jewish group, and apparently because of it. But even though the misunderstanding had been removed, and the trades union, after negotiations with the owner, stated that they had nothing against the group, and that they would inform the authorities to that effect, this special immigration came under the authorities' eagle eye. In July, when no decision had yet been taken on the matter, Professor Aage Friis, in his capacity as chairman of a committee for exiled intellectual workers, went to Bornholm to try to help the group, which actually lay outside the sphere of the organised *Hechaluz* immigration, but came at best partially within the domain which he had agreed to care for. On 25 July he wrote from Bornholm direct to Aage Svendsen, the Head of Department in the Ministry of Justice on the case:

»I have found out, here on Bornholm – also in conversation with the police authorities – about the 'wholly' or 'semi-' intellectual immigrants, who are staying here and studying agriculture under the leadership of, amongst others, Doctor Prøschold. Several of these people may come in under our committee, and they

73

speak to me about their future. There is great anxiety among them, because, so close to 1 August, they still have had no decision on their situation.«

Friis therefore appealed to the Minister to allow a prolongation until »after the harvest«, and two days later, the reply came in the form of a prolongation until 1 November,

During this transition period, the leaders of the group negotiated with an American Jewish »Organisation for Rehabilitation and Training« on the purchase of a farm in France, which was considered suitable for the continuation of the group's agricultural training. But the negotiations came to nothing, and contrary to the expectations of the group, that new groups would immigrate to Bornholm, it turned out that the authorities refused to give further permits for such collective placing. A deputation had already gone to negotiate on this with the Ministry of Justice in June 1934, but even though the ministry was informed that there was no objection on the part of the trades union, these negotiations gave no result, and the deputation could not obtain any explanation for the refusal. The reasons seems to have been the authorities' dislike of group placing.

As the residence permits ran out, the group was then scattered to the four winds – to Palestine, Australia, Rhodesia, England, Canada and U.S.A. According to a list in Doctor Prøschold's possession, this short wave of immigrants consisted of 29 persons of the ages of 17–34. One of them had previous training in horticulture. The rest came from typical urban occupations, grammar schools, students, merchants, lawyers and one doctor. Half of them came from Berlin, the rest from towns all over Germany. Doctor Prøschold remained on the island, alone. For a time he considered returning to Germany, but was warned seriously against it by a previous colleague who was living as an immigrant in France. During the 1930's he managed, with difficulty, to get prolongations of his residence permits, and he started a children's home on Bornholm, which, after the Occupation, had to be moved to Gilleleje, from where, in 1943, he had to escape to Sweden.

Orthodox Jews

In this case, internal Jewish differences played a part, and were also communicated to the Danish administration. There were no guarantees in this instance for later emigration with certificates, on which the authorities relied, and both this and also the undesired settlement in a colony, determined the dissolution of the group. A special case with some similarities but otherwise of a different type arose, when five orthodox Jews received permission from the authorities in 1933 to live together and eat at a farm near Skibstrup in North Sjælland, with one of the group, a Jewish lady, taking responsibility for the special preparation of food, and with the other four members of the group working as agricultural trainees on neighbouring farms, which let them observe the sabbath and the Jewish religious holidays. The arrangement continued throughout the year 1934, supported by Siggaard, who was here balancing rather near the edge of his framework for treating cases. The trainees were agricultural trainees, but could not, on religious grounds, be moved as was normal, to scattered farms.

In 1935, the problem increased somewhat, and gave rise to slightly more consideration of principle. The colony was then moved to a property in Aalsgaarde, supported financially by the Mosaic Religious Community, and the latter, represented by the Chief Rabbi, Doctor Friediger, pressed for the colony to be allowed to increase its personnel. In this situation, Siggaard turned, exceptionally, to his chief, the estate owner Doctor Hasselbalch, to consult with him on the statement to be made to the Ministry of Justice by the bureau:

»The Agricultural Travel Bureau has today received the documents regarding the boarding house for orthodox Jews in Aalsgaarde ... As well as these three new trainees, for whom the Chief Rabbi asks for residence permits, there are already six trainees in the rented house in Aalsgaarde, and the rabbi has said that he will send more trainees there, if residence permits are given to the three. I have asked him to wait before sending these applications, until we have decided whether such settlement in a colony comes under our sphere the exchange of agricultural trainees.«

Siggaard was himself prepared for a positive answer, but he did not neglect to point out why he felt some hesitancy:

»That I am a little hesitant about the matter is due to the fact that the bureau has twice had to decide its position – vis-à-vis the Foreign Ministry – regarding an exchange of Turkish agricultural trainees with Danish. The Danish Minister in Turkey was interested in having such an exchange started. On the bureau's side there was a good deal of hesitancy, both times ... and one recommended, as a necessary condition, that the trainees ate the farm's food, and followed the usual customs as regards religious holidays. If one now recommended exceptions in this respect for the Jews, one could hardly maintain (the opposite) for Mohamedans.«

The case was passed, although with a limitation as to numbers. On 8 July 1935, Siggaard could report the result to Hasselbalch:

»Last Saturday, it was reported in confidence that the Ministry of Justice, in consideration of various circumstances, which it is hoped are only of a short-lived character, had given permission to up to 12 orthodox Jewish agricultural trainees to be allowed to live and eat in the garden house mentioned. At the same time, the Ministry of Justice requested the bureau to keep a check that the number is not exceeded.«

The number does seem to have been slightly increased, however. A pupil reports »As I belonged to the religious wing, I could not eat at the peasants', and therefore lived with c. fifteen other religious *chaluzim* in Aalsgaarde, where we cooked our own food.«

Later, the colony moved to Smidstrup in North Sjælland, where, according to a report, the pupils »lived in a little 'Kibbutz', a dilapidated old farm – 8 farm workers and 2 girls – who took care of the housekeeping themselves. In the daytime we worked on the farms in the vicinity, but ate and slept at home. We did not work on the *shabbat*, but worked instead on Sundays«. The colony was maintained here to October 1943. The majority of the pupils who came to Denmark were not orthodox, and complied, as a rule, with Danish customs including Danish food. Some problems could arise as regards food, but were arranged normally on the spot in mutual understanding, and when children from Jewish homes began to come to Denmark from 1939, and in a few cases felt themselves bound by Jewish rules, the Chief Rabbi Friediger intervened, and informed them that they need not keep these rules in emergencies such as those in question.

Fishing Trainees

There was one more little colony to which the travel bureau became godfather. In February 1938, the bureau was asked to find places and residence permits for 8 Jewish fishing trainees, 6 men and 2 women, who wished to learn the trade on Bornholm. The application was in two senses on the periphery of the bureau's sphere of activity, as Siggaard did not have the same close contacts with the fishing trade as he had with farming, and as places in fishermen's homes were problematic, since they did not have the abundant room which was usual on the farms. The plan was also that the Mosaic Religious Community should rent a villa in Tejn for the purpose, and cover the expenses for it, and Siggaard supported it without hesitation, and even took the further step that on 1 March he recommended the State Police that »there is given these pupils a 12-month residence permit. If training requires a longer time, the question of prolongation can be taken up when the 12-month permit runs out«. It was now 1938, and Siggaard had reconciled himself to the idea of placing trainees in a colony, at least in a special case such as this.

The colony became a reality, though with only 5 men and 1 woman trainee, all attached to *Hechaluz*. They received an unusually cordial reception from the fishing population of the whole hamlet, and agricultural trainees also came to take part in fishing. The permit prolongation came, too, and the group stayed on Bornholm right to March 1943, where we shall later meet them in an unusual context. One of the young fishing trainees mentions that »Bornholm was the bright spot in all the misery of that period, a time when other human beings regarded us as human beings, and gave us real compensation for the time we had had to live through in Germany.«

The Danish Committee for exiled intellectual Workers

Occasional co-operation with Professor Aage Friis belong to the travel bureau's fringe area of work. As chairman of the Danish Committee for exiled intellectual Workers, he now and then asked for the bureau's help. The committee was started in the autumn 1933, by Professors Harald and Niels Bohr and Professor Aage Friis, with the latter as chairman. Siggaard was ready and willing to give help in answer to these requests, but the help had to be limited, as his possibilities only allowed for his placing the intellectual workers as agricultural trainees, on the current conditions, which could practically never be filled by refugees in this category. Attempts of this kind must almost inevitably miscarry, as will appear from just one single example of this kind. In 1934, at Friis's request, Siggaard had obtained a trial place for a refugee from this group on a Danish farm, but a year later he had to inform Friis that the attempt had failed:

» . . . he had received a residence permit up to 15/12/1935 as correspondent of a foreign newspaper. He has also left farming and has gone back to the profession where his academic education can be useful to him. I presume also that a residence permit can still be prolonged for him in this country, but I do not understand his decision to return to Germany in the present circumstances.«

At an early stage, Siggaard had no illusions as to the fate of Jews in Germany, and was ready to recommend residence prolongation, if quite special circumstances did not work against it.

Immigration is doubled

Up to March 1938, the great majority of trainees came from Germany, some of them stateless with residence in Germany. But in March 1938 came the Nazi seizure of power in Austria, the »*Anschluss*«, and a few months later, in September 1938, Germany's annexation of Sudeterland, the Czechoslovakian frontier area bordering on Germany. In March 1939, Germany's final march followed into Czechoslovakia itself, with the establishment of »the Protectorate, Bohemia and Moravia«. Austria became »Eastmark« and the name »Czechoslovakia« was crossed out of German consciousness with the stroke of a pen. With these events came a new wave of Jewish fugitives, first Austrian and then Czechoslovakian, the latter supplied with a special passport, the so-called »protectorate passport«.

Austria's and later Czechoslovakia's annexation created the purely technical problems for a short time, that the exchange agreement between Austria and Denmark ceased to exist, and even in April 1938, Siggaard had to inform a Danish farmer that Austrian trainees had not yet applied, but from August 1938, the stream of Austrian trainees began. The practice was begun that the Danish Legation in Berlin was authorized to visa the trainees' Austrian passports, until these could be replaced by a German passport. After that, the bureau kept to the Danish-German exchange agreement.

To these international political events was added the »Crystal Night« in November 1938. This was the culmination, up to then, of the anti-Semitic witch hunt, which had been whipped up during the 1930's by Nazi propaganda, when the party and the population, to order and after clear signals in the press and on the radio, went amok against the German

Jews. That night, which received its name from the tens of thousands of smashed windows, is briefly described in a Hitler biography by the English historian Alan Bullock, with the words:

»On 10 November, planned, systematic destruction of synagogues and Jewish businesses had already been organised all over Germany. At the same time, thousands of Jews were arrested, maltreated and taken to concentration camps. Fire service personnel were posted by the burning synagogues, with orders not to put out the fires, and they confined themselves to limiting the conflagration.«

In these few lines, Bullock does not mention the Jewish homes, but these did not go free. Several of the trainees directly mention the »Crystal Night«, in their accounts, as the immediate cause of their decision to leave the country, their parents, family and future, and seek refuge where refuge could be found. One trainee describes how, to avoid chicaneri against him as a Jew, he had become a student at an international school in Wiesbaden, and how he had gone home unsuspectingly to his parents in Cologne, after the »Crystal Night«, to find his father's shop shut for ever and his home razed to the ground, with all the furniture thrown out on the street and burnt. On the top of this night of horror for all the Jews, came extortionate taxes or the confiscation of all Jewish property.

That night was one more incitement to emigration or flight, and a considerable number of young Jews sought refuge in Denmark in the coming months. Many write in their reports of the relief it was to escape from German soil, and mention briefly a friendly reception, a few with details of it, when for some reason it had made a particular impression. »When we came across the frontier in Padborg, it was as though we had come to a different planet, after what we had been through in Germany.« Padborg appears also in another account »In Padborg I reported to the stationmaster. He took me into his own quarters, called his wife and asked her to make real coffee, buy cakes and whipped cream, and bade me heartily welcome. It is a welcome I can never forget.« Many speak of the search of their persons by the Germans at the frontier, and the contrast in Denmark:

»The Danish policeman bade us welcome with a big smile, and tried to reassure us – I remember that a policeman said 'Now you are free and can work in farming, in safe conditions.' They were so kind, and they offered our two girls white pillows, so that they could lie down and rest during the night's journey.«

Or from Warnemünde:

»We were met already in Warnemünde by a Danish journalist, Merete Bonnesen. It was moving to remember the kindness.« »After Warnemünde on the ferry, which was already Danish ground, a Dane came into the compartment, where we were eight of our group, with the words 'You haven't any currency, have you (each had only 9 German marks). Here's 10 crowns, so that you can celebrate arriving in Denmark.«

It has already been mentioned that the stream to Denmark increased greatly in the weeks and months after the »Crystal Night«, with a last application for a residence permit for a Jewish agricultural trainee on 25 August 1939. Then the travel bureau's possibilities for making any additions to the now 7-year-old immigration of *Hechaluz* trainees came to stop.

A contributing cause was that the British Government, in a state of war, stopped, at least partially, the issue of certificates, and in October 1939, Siggaard had to inform a farmer that in the present situation, the bureau had to stop immigration:

»It is quite impossible to obtain residence permits ... here in Denmark, because Jews' immigration into Palestine has been blocked. The Ministry of Justice informed us here the other day that residence permits for Jewish trainees will not be given before the spring, nor after then, unless the ban on immigration to Palestine is lifted. But much can occur before the spring, so let us see what happens. At the moment, there is nothing to be done.«

The bureau's task was now solely to obtain prolongations of residence permits, and in other ways take case of the hundreds of *Hechaluz* trainees, who on a shorter or longer term was stranded in Denmark.

But to these trainees was added an immigration wave, from the summer 1939, of Jewish children of the ages of 14–16, Their background was quite different from that which had created the *Hechaluz* immigration, and the organisation of their placing in Danish society was also quite different, and we shall return to it later.

Hope or Flight

The violent increase of immigration, especially after the »Crystal Night«, raises the question of the motive behind the emigration. Did it chiefly have its roots in the desire for a happier future under foreign skies, and particularly in Palestine, or was it chiefly a question of flight from an existence which had gradually become unbearable or directly inhuman? Even then, many must have asked themselves whether life would be physically possible in the future. Was it, in such circumstances, the dream or the flight that stood out as the motive.

Of course, no definite reply can be given. Both motives were activizing, and the mixture of motives must obviously have been present, so that an answer must be equivocal. There will be great differences from person to person, and there will be an enormous difference between 1933 and 1939. But with every reservation for the diversity of nuances, there can hardly be any doubt that the early immigrants were, to a greater degree than those from 1938–39, motivated by the dream of Palestine and were more influenced by a search for the new home than the impulse to flight. All through the 30's, the trainees in question, convinced Zionists, were prepared in advance, psychologically, and to some extent physically, for the life of a pioneer, for whom the work on a Danish farm could only appear a desirable preparation for the still harsher toil in a country which needed to be brought under cultivation. Those who passed through the travel bureau's case treatment in the first years were young and younger people who – even before the Nazi regime disclosed its intentions – had decided to turn their backs on the old Jewish view of society, and who, regardless of the cost, were prepared to build up a new future. Many, but of course not all, were determined men and women, for whom Palestine and then Israel was a vision, but a vision hidden behind an unknown mass of conditions and realities. This was a generation in revolt, often against parents.

On the other hand, there was no doubt that the motive of flight exerted more and more pressure, as the years passed, and that for many – probably not least the youngest – it was a predominant motive, if not the predominant motive. A number of letters to the travel bureau from German and Jewish parents speak, not of Palestine, but of escape.

The pupils' attitude in this country reflects this to some extent. During the first six years up to 1938, it is quite exceptional for the contemporary documents to refer to a trainee who has lost heart, or has had difficulties in adjusting to the temporary Danish milieu. The trainees are consistently described as good, clever, eager to learn, and single-minded. With the stream of refugees from 1938, the picture alters somewhat, however, particularly as regards the many children who came to Denmark from 1939. Here, now and then, there is a question of difficulty in adjustment and discouragement, but still only temporarily. As the children grew up and came under the influence of older comrades, often with great qualities of leadership, they too were filled with Zionist visions, and left their flight behind them, with their gaze fixed on the promises of the future.

A contemporary letter, written by a young girl a week after she arrived is an exception

»(here) the farmers were waiting for us already. My master cannot speak a word of German, I can only make myself understood with the help of a dictionary and by gesticulating ... We eat dinner at a large table ... one of them spoke to me in broken German. They have at once garbled my name. After dinner they showed me my bed, and the mistress played chess with me. I cannot play chess, but she is really stupid at it ... in the afternoon I knit some wool, which the mistress has bought for me. The very worst taste ... Altogether I feel wretched.«

Here, undeniably, there was both despondency and acclimatization difficulty, but this attitude would disappear as time passed, and the older trainees took the young one in hand.

The Alijah Immigration

Youth Alijah

The immigration stream in 1939, as already mentioned, was not only a greatly increased immigration of *Hechaluz* trainees. The year would also be marked by an immigration of Jewish children from 14–16 years of age. Here too, according to the plan, it was a question of transit, the idea being that after a shorter or longer stay in Denmark, the children should go on to Palestine. The fact that this was only partially successful was due to the War and the Occupation, which invalidated all the calculations. The planners had chosen that age group, because they considered that young people from 17 upwards already had a natural possibility for reaching Palestine through the *Hechaluz* organisation, and that small children could neither be removed from their homes – however much these were threatened – nor be able to meet the physical and phychological demands of such a sudden move to foreign surroundings and probable hardships.

The horrors of Germany were common to both the *Hechaluz* trainees and the *Alijah* children. They had all undergone misery and most often horror in their home surroundings. And yet there was a noticeable difference between the two groups. The *Hechaluz* trainees were older, they were all convinced Zionists, and many had come to Denmark after preparation in transit camps. The *Alijah* children, in many cases, had been torn up suddenly from their home environment, solely for reasons of safety, and often after the parents' decision that only an immediate departure could save the children's future. The idea of Palestine was vaguer for them than was the case for the *Hechaluz* trainees. They were younger, less mature, and less politically aware, a circumstance that would alter for the great majority of them, during their stay in Denmark.

The idea of an emigration of children, with Palestine as their destination, had arisen in Germany and child emigration was carried out by the organisation *Alijah* – a branch of the Zionist movement. The object of the organisation was to save some children and quite young people from hardship and persecution, and get care and education for them in the

Palestine that was being built up, as a national home for the Jews. The organisation, which was supported by voluntary contributions, acted as a special office under the Jewish Agency, and its work started immediately before the Nazi seizure of power, accelerating thereafter in earnest.

The leader and originator in Germany was a woman from Berlin, Recha Freier, the wife of a Jewish rabbi, and her idea was to rescue German and other Jewish children from want and forced idleness, and instead try to have them brought up in Jewish kibbutzim. The idea was taken up at a Zionist congress in Prague in 1933, and it was decided then to set up an office in Palestine, which was to be responsible for the reception and settlement of persecuted Jews. The management of this office's department for *Alijah* children was entrusted to Henrietta Szold, of whom it was said that she came to know every one of the thousands of children who would soon reach Palestine. In February 1934, the first larger group of 60 children arrived, and the movement quickly swelled. In 1935, about 600 had been taken into kibbutzim agricultural schools and trade schools and at the outbreak of war in 1939, in all c. 5,000 children and quite young boys and girls had been brought by this organisation by many routes to Palestine, whilst c. 15,000 others were sent to various forms of settlement in West European countries, all waiting for the necessary certificates, the numbers of which also here proved quite insufficient. The pressure was particularly intense after the »Crystal Night« in 1938.

As the idea spread, and it became clear that the Nazis' persecution of the country's Jews was not a passing phenomenon, *Alijah* committees were started in a number of countries, and the London committee, and the organisation's London office became especially important for the movement. It was from here that the life-saving certificates must be obtained. The British mandate government's minimum condition for issuing such a certificate was that an economic guarantee should be secured for each child to cover a 2-year's training, estimated at £72 or 1600 crowns in all for each permit. After this 2-years' training it was presumed that the young people could manage on their own. These considerable sums had to be contributed by widespread collections in the countries outside Germany, which undertook the temporary housing of the children until certificates could be obtained.

Melanie Oppenhejm

Up to 1938, Danish participation in this international relief work was very modest. The Jewish tragedy in Germany was public knowledge, but it was difficult to imagine its dimensions and actually perceive a development which for those times must seem incredible. But in the middle of the 1930's, the organisation's initiative also reached Denmark, when Recha Freier contacted Mélanie Oppenhejm, and asked for Danish help. To begin with, it was a question of collecting money, and Mrs. Oppenhejm appealed to the Mosaic Religious Community and the Jewish Denmark's Lodge, which were immediately in agreement and ready to help. To make conditions in Germany more generally known, a Jewish woman, Mrs. Eva Michaelis-Stern, who was working in the »youth-*Alijah*« organisation, came to Denmark. Here, in the Jewish Denmark's Lodge, she described both the desperate situation of the German Jews and the Youth *Alijah*'s work. The first basis was thus created for a later Danish effort.

The appeal to Mélanie Oppenhejm was not fortuitous. She was married to the High Court barrister, Moritz Oppenhejm, who for many years had been Legal Advisor to the German Legation in Copenhagen, a post from which he resigned in 1933, in protest against developments in Germany. As a result of his many years' work, he had a great many contacts, both in Denmark and abroad, and from the beginning of the 1930's, he had already received many appeals from Jewish and other persons in Germany, who wished to leave the country, and in spite of the difficult conditions, he had helped many to go to England and the U.S.A. via Denmark. The work had been extensive as well as time-consuming, and it had required connexions to many sides, both abroad and with Danish authorities, who, largely owing to the economic crisis, were hesitant as regards immigration of foreigners to Denmark, if these came in large numbers.

The Oppenhejm home was thus well informed on the whole situation, in respect of immigration statutes and the possibilities for emigration. When the developments in Germany became catastrophically aggravated in 1938, Mélanie Oppenhejm took the initiative in quite large-scale relief work in connexion with the Youth-*Alijah* organisation. The first move was to find Jewish homes in Copenhagen, willing to receive children, but Mélanie Oppenhejm soon realised that there was no future in this, as there were far too few homes of this kind and, further, they were unable to give the children the training which the Youth-*Alijah* aimed at – a

Melanie Oppenhejm.
(Elfelt fot.)

training which could prepare them for a coming pioneer life in Palestine. The children must be placed in Danish farming homes, as far as possible, and considerable funds must be raised.

Before further initiatives could be taken, however, definite information must be obtained on all the conditions attached to this special emigration, and what the pattern was of the whole internationally constructed organisation. For this reason, Mélanie Oppenhejm wrote, at the beginning of November – only a few days before the »Crystal Night« – to a member of the Youth-*Alijah*'s staff, Mrs. Marta Goldberg, who was in Stockholm at the time, to negotiate with the Swedish authorities – Jewish and others – for a Swedish intake of *Alijah* children. Mélanie Oppenhejm's letter is not extant, but from Marta Goldberg's reply, dated Stockholm 4 November, it is evident that Mélanie Oppenhejm, amongst other things, had expressed uncertainty as to what role the »Women's International Zionist Organisation« (WIZO) played in this cause, and how one should attack a large relief action. Now she received an answer, and the first concrete information. At an annual meeting in London it had been decided that WIZO should support the *Alijah* work, but it was not intended that WIZO should take any independent initiative, which could only confuse matters. The work was in the hands of the special *Alijah* organisation, with offices in Berlin and London, and with committees being formed in a number of West European countries. The best thing would be for Denmark to apply to the London office, the address

Thora Daugaard.
(Det kgl. Bibliotek)

of which was supplied. The letter contained further information on the economic demands for the work, and an indirect hint, as far as possible to work without too much publicity. This latter point had proved useful in Sweden.

On this basis, Mélanie Oppenhejm now went further and appealed to the leaders of the two great women's organisations, the Danish Women's National Council and The Women's League for Peace and Freedom, Mrs. Kirsten Gloerfelt-Tarp and Mrs. Else Zeuthen, as chairman and vice-chairman of the former organisation, and Mrs. Thora Daugaard, chairman of the latter, hereafter called the League. All three were immediately and ardently in favour of the idea, and during November, an effective Danish committee, set up without hesitation or formalities, became a reality.

Immediate Action

The women's first task was to procure the detailed information which could make a reasoned application to the authorities possible, with convincing arguments, and they acted immediately. During the few weeks up to 1 December they obtained reliable particulars on the names and addresses of the *Alijah* offices, which were established in Berlin,

Kirsten Gloerfelt-Tarp.
(Det kgl. Bibliotek)

Vienna and London, and they also obtained information on what was being done in Norway, Sweden, Belgium, Holland and Great Britain to organize the work. By the end of November it was clear that a number of initiatives were being carried on to give help, but also, that the affair was so new that the work in, for example, the Scandinavian countries, was not co-ordinated as Youth-*Alijah* wished. Only in Norway were there six committees, united in a common committee with Odd Nansen as chairman, while in Sweden there were five committees, which were solving the problem »from different points of views«. A report from the headquarters in Brussels for the International Council of Women gave a similar flickering picture of scattered initiatives in Belgium, Great Britain, Holland and Switzerland.

It was therefore evident to the Danish women that relief work must be carried out in close co-operation with Youth-*Alijah*, and a direct proposal on how this could best be achieved was available on 5 December, when Mélanie Oppenhejm passed on to Kirsten Gloerfelt-Tarp the information she had just received from »The British Committee for the Care of Children from Germany«. The information was to the effect that a committee under the chairmanship of Lord Samuel and Lord Selbourne was working to bring at least 50,000 children out of Germany, that the British Government had given permission to bring thousands of children to Great Britain, on condition that these children should not become a burden to the government or seek employment in Great Britain, but that the government otherwise did not demand special formalities as regards visas and passports. The letter reported that 300 children had already reached England, and that a new group was on the way. The first 100 children came from a children's home in Berlin, which had been burned down, and further that children whose fathers were in concentration camps would be accepted first. Then followed the British committee's direct suggestion as to how the work should be arranged. »It is suggested that the best plan is to get the children placed in private homes, and leading persons in towns and villages are asked to form committees immediately, to organise reception of the children, and make themselves responsible for their future, i.e. collect money and send them on, out of the country.« The next day, Mélanie Oppenhejm could follow this up with a statement that she had made contact with the German *Hilfsverein der deutschen Juden*, which had referred her to *Jugend-Alijah*, as the organ which, both in Germany and Great Britain, was responsible for and co-ordinated the work.

While these particulars were being obtained, on 25 November 1938, Kirsten Gloerfelt-Tarp called the chairmen of her 58 affiliated societies or their representatives to a meeting on 2 December, where the one item on the agenda was the question »What can we do to help Jewish children?« Her appeal to come to the meeting was urgent, and read in part, »all emigrant committees etc. organisations are urged to send representatives.« The authorities would now come under pressure.

This had already started, which in itself seems to indicate that full co-ordination was hardly achieved as yet, and that the women felt themselves, with reason, pressed for time. On 26 November, Thora Daugaard, on behalf of the League, sent in an appeal to the Minister of Justice, Steincke, in which she asked for the minister's permission for the League to start working to find places for Jewish children to stay in Denmark. The appeal referred to the earlier experience of placing Jewish agricultural trainees and to the »criminal treatment« of Jews in Germany, and continued:

»We intend to attack the matter in connexion with the Jewish assembly in this country, and will lay particular stress on there being funds available for each child for a ticket for (a destination) abroad after, for example, a year. If England succeeds in establishing a Jewish colony in South Africa, a temporary stay for the children here in Denmark will certainly be of great importance, both materially and spiritually, and we hope that the Minister will give the desired permission . . .«

The letter ended with a rather vague question »In how large a number the Minister will allow us to bring these children in, and how long they may remain here.« It seems that the letter must have been written before Thora Daugaard was fully informed on the plans that the Youth *Alijah* was working with.

Pressure on the Ministry

With this, the siege of the Ministry had begun, and it was followed up with a conversation between the active women and Steincke, on 29 November 1938, and afterwards a more thoroughly prepared application was sent to the Ministry of Justice on 6 December. In this there were more precise demands, a description of the proposed organisation's form, and reference to the attitude of other countries. The application begins:

»In continuation of our conversation with the Minister on 29 November, and in accord with the application of 26 November from The Women's International League for Peace and Freedom . . . we take the liberty to ask the ministry to allow entry permits and temperary residence permit for at least 1000 Jewish children, whom we . . . intend to place in private Danish homes . . . The procurement of exit permits and the decisions as to which children will be considered will take place chiefly through the intermediary of Youth *Alijah*, World Association for the Immigration to Palestine of Jewish Boys and Girls . . . *Hilfsverein der deutschen Juden* . . . Berlin and Vienna . . . and with the co-operation of the Quakers . . .«

After this, the particulars which Mélanie Oppenhejm had received on the British Government's attitude was given almost word for word, and similarly all the particulars were included of relief work in Great Britain, Norway, Sweden and the U.S.A., as well as information on the good chances for the children being able to go on after a stay in Denmark:

»As regards the possibilities for getting permanent residence for the children outside Denmark, we take the liberty of pointing out that Palestine is willing to receive children of the ages 14 to 17 years, when a sum of 1,600 crowns per child is made available, this sum covering a 2 to 3-years' training. Palestine is prepared to receive 2,500 children immediately.«

The letter, which quite clearly summed up all the knowledge available from the hectic activity of the previous weeks, concluded:

»The Danish Women's National Council has prepared collections, in their affiliated societies, to obtain money for expenses connected with the relief work planned. As large funds are needed, we request permission at the same time to carry out public collections in aid of the needy Jewish children.«

The women did not confine themselves to written requests. On 11 December, a deputation led by Kirsten Gloerfelt-Tarp and Thora Daugaard called on Steincke to plead their case verbally. The meeting ended with a negative, as is evident from a letter of 12 December from Kirsten Gloerfelt-Tarp to Melanie Oppenhejm:

»The visit to the Minister of Justice went as sadly as it possibly could. There has been a Cabinet meeting on the matter, and a collective permit will not be given for the children. The only thing they agreed on at the Cabinet meeting was to make an approach to the Oslo States to apply, together, to England to find a place overseas for Jewish refugees, and that Denmark if this was practised, would contribute financially to the implementation of this plan. The only possibility for getting Jewish children here is first 1) that it does not take place in groups, but that there is only a question of individual children, 2) that entry permits to other countries have been secured, so that Denmark shall only be a transit station for quite a short time, probably up to ½ year or 3) that the child or children involved have a close connexion with Denmark, such as family relationship or similar.«

Kirsten Gloerfelt-Tarp recommended that matters of this kind should be canalized through the National Council, and concluded: »I am very sad at the outcome of the case, and at the moment I cannot see any way out.«

This was not the final result in the question, however, and the women were far from giving up. Their pessimism seems only to have lasted for a day or two, to be replaced by undaunted energy. During December, and before Christmas, an appeal was launched by the National Council to all the society's members for help and support for »the relief work for Jewish children«. They were reminded that Danish homes had once opened their doors for Vienna children, and were now urged to make a similar effort »for the crowds of Jewish children who live in Europe today, robbed of their homes and often of their parents«, and two things were requested: promises from homes that could take in a child for a limited period, and contributions for the coming work, which was thus by no means abandoned after the first reaction of the authorities. At the same time, the pressure was maintained, and particularly the pressure on Steincke, who was again visited by both Kirsten Gloerfelt-Tarp and Thora Daugaard, and from now on he was under constant lobbying from the women's organisations.

Before the close of the year, the pressure also gave a preliminary result. At the end of December, after yet another written request to the

Minister of Justice, and after a guarantee of emigration to Palestine from The Jewish Agency for Palestine in London, the National Council was given permission to receive 25 children for temporary residence in Denmark. On 2 January 1939, Kirsten Gloerfelt-Tarp could inform Thora Daugaard of this first result »The Minister of Justice has told me verbally that we may have these 25 children (brought) in. See the guarantee in the enclosed letter from England. The 25 homes can certainly be found through the Jewish Women's Society.« On 9 January, the approval of the Ministry of Justice was given. The conditions were that the children were of the ages of 13 to 16 years, that they had been examined by a doctor, and that they were approved by the Youth *Alijah* in Berlin or Vienna, and that they emigrated to Palestine before they were 17 years old.

The last point was implemented at once. On 18 January, the women in Copenhagen received a letter from the Youth *Alijah* office in London, signed by Eva Michaelis-Stern. She repeated the guarantee for emigration to Palestine and reported that the conditions in question had been sent on to the Berlin office, which would now carry out the selection. At the same time, the London office asked that those in Copenhagen should maintain the pressure on the authorities, to obtain further promises.

The Attitude of the Authorities

It is striking, that the model from the *Hechaluz* immigration was hinted at in the first example of pressure, but also that this model could not be used in the new situation. Here there was no close-knit organisation like *Hechaluz*, which guaranteed certificates in advance, and the international situation had changed drastically between 1932 and 1938. In 1932, Denmark's southerly neighbour was a disarmed Weimar Republic, in 1938 an aggressive dictatorship, which over a period of five years had confronted Europe with one shock after another.

When the appeals to Steincke were delivered, it must have been more obvious to him than to the women, that he could not give an administrative »Yes« or »No«. The affair concerned both the government as a whole, and particularly the Foreign Ministry, and as a collective immigration had been refused at a Cabinet meeting, Steincke asked the Foreign Minister, Peter Munch, to try and obtain the Oslo States' approval of a plan, according to which a collective application should be made to the

British Government to settle the children on British territory or in a British colony, on condition that the expenses for them were covered by the Oslo States. The idea was more humanitarian than Zionistic.

A plan of this kind was also prepared, and sent first to the Swedish and Norwegian Governments for their comments. This »plan to promote Jewish settlements in overseas countries«, after several drafts, received the following text:

»The difficulties which the Jewish refugee question raises at present are so great, not only for the people involved, but also for the countries in which they seek refuge, that in the Danish Government one has under consideration to address a question to the great powers, where there is the possibility for placing Jewish refugees in larger numbers, to what extent it was possible that they can place areas at the disposal of such immigration, in a fairly immediate future, and that one intended to add, that if such possibility exists, there will in Denmark be readiness to recommend the competent authorities that Denmark, depending on a satisfactory participation from other countries, will contribute its co-operation in participation in the payment of the expenses of settlements, etc. proportionally with other countries.«

This was then submitted to the Swedish and Norwegian Governments, with the supplementary question, whether they could give the plan their support, and whether they found it right to address a question to the Dutch, Belgian, Luxembourgeois and Swiss Governments. In addition, the matter was discussed verbally between the Foreign Minister Peter Munch and his Nordic colleagues, the Swede Sandler and the Norwegian Koht. Nothing concrete emerged from this rather vague initiative, simply some good-will in principle, but no collective determination. In both the countries where the question was put, it was pointed out that the problem, to start with, must rest with the great powers, that it was a beautiful idea, but that it must be solved in a broader international forum, etc.

It seems clear that, whilst the women's organisation had their gaze fixed on the Jewish children's need, the Nordic Foreign Ministers had their gaze fixed more on their countries' difficulties in the face of the planned immigration. Both fields of vision were quite understandable, and in accordance with the tasks which the two parties were each confronted with. It is extraordinary, however, that the Zionistic idea was not mentioned in either the plan, or the reply.

Steincke's private viewpoint was well known to the public. On 23 November 1938, he took up the question of emigrants in a radio lecture, which was published a few days later as a double feature article in

»Social-Demokraten«. Here he made it clear what his viewpoint was, as Minister of Justice. In his opening he declared that the problem was not Danish, but international »Our little country is in no circumstances able to give any *substantial* contribution to the solution of the so-called Jewish question, if indeed it *can* be solved.« He then made short shrift, in sarcastic tones, of two myths. One was that »the Ministry of Justice is directed from Berlin, and that my main task is to hand over German refugees who *have* received residence permits, to the German authorities.« This was »nonsense« and »pure fabrication« and Steincke denied the slightest knowledge of German interference. The other myth was that Steincke was described as a »lover of the Jews, who actually collects Jewish refugees and *smuggles* Communist refugees into this country on a large scale«. Here Steincke hit out at the Communist and National Socialist press, which both indulged in »atmospheredelirium«, and the journalists whom he called »fanatics and intellectual dwarfs«. Of himself he declared that »I am not in the habit of loving or hating races, nations or parties«, and he continued later – (I) am neither a Jew hater nor a Jew lover, but even if I was the latter, I would never – especially considering the Jews themselves – be so foolish, by a mass immigration of Jews to this country, to contribute to creating anti-Semitism here.« He was in no doubt that this could happen.

And how did he understand the demand on his post and his person:

»As Danish Minister of Justice, one must at the moment keep ones purely personal feelings in check, in the individual case act as humanely as circumstances allow, but by no means persuade himself or others that Denmark will be able to assume any role of importance in the present European situation, and nor can any normal person expect or believe it.«

After this, Steincke explained how the government actually did try to help with residence and work permits, and he estimated the then number of refugees on 1 October 1938 at 1,262, although this figure did not include those who had entered the country since 1 July 1938. He emphasized that the increase in numbers of refugees in the last years almost exclusively applied to Jews, but »we have nevertheless no more, however, than 900 to 1000 Jewish refugees in Denmark, and neither 20 nor 30,000, as many seem to believe.« He also stressed that it was only a question of giving temporary residence permits with a view to training, or so that the individual involved could wait for an entry permit to a country overseas, and he underlined that it was a question of transit, giving the numbers. In conclusion he regretted that since the possibilities for emigrating to overseas countries were very slight for the moment, he had had to make the demands stricter for temporary residence, and he ended with a cry from the heart: »As the situation has developed lately, it is almost unbearable, even for those who have only to take the administrative responsibility for a stricter, a more and more inhuman treatment of ones fellow-beings, however much it is done in the interests of the country.«

The inhumanity lay outside Denmark's borders. Steincke saw it clearly, but had but few means to counteract it. As Minister of Justice it was his calling to serve the interests of his country. It could hardly be otherwise, than that the Minister had to differentiate between the person and the post. In reality he administered the post in such a way that immigration multiplied, half a year after the two feature articles.

Increased Activity

In the first months of 1939, activity accelerated. Faced with the authorities' caution, a number of the leaders of the women's organisations, at a committee meeting on 20 January, decided upon full publicity for their work, with the object of bringing the greatest imaginable pressure to bear on the ministry and the government, and of bringing the question out into the glare of publicity. Among those present at the meeting was also the editor of »*Kristeligt Dagblad*«, Helweg-Larsen, who agitated for immediate action. Contact was now established with the leaders of Youth-*Alijah* in London, when Marta Goldberg came to Denmark to meet the press on 6 February 1939, and the next day held a lecture on the subject »How can we help the Jewish children in Central Europe?« followed up a little later by a lecture tour in the provinces. At the end of March, one of the leaders of Youth-*Alijah*, Mr. M. Schattner, arrived in Copenhagen, where, in conversations with Else Zeuthen and Thora Daugaard, he could give details of the wishes and possibilities for organisation – details which he confirmed in writing on 11 April in a letter to Thora Daugaard. An important point in this letter was the promise that if a Danish collection did not cover the emigration tax of 1,600 crowns per head, the Youth *Alijah* could make the necessary funds available. In addition, he expressed a wish that the children – if they came – be collected as far as possible in centres, so that during their stay they could be visited by selected travelling teachers. The next day another letter followed, from the London office, with information on the organisation of the work and its progress in Britain, Holland, Sweden, France, Belgium, Switzerland, but with a cry for help for the 50,000 children still in Germany, in dire need of emigration to other countries.

On this background, and under the constant pressure of events, a month-long campaign was now started with meetings, appeals in the press and on the radio, the sale of works of art given by Danish artists, and circulars to Danish farm houses, asking them to take in children. The campaign was conceived on a large scale. It began with the lecture mentioned, by Marta Goldberg, to which were invited a large, selected audience of leading Danish personalities, politicians, scientists and university people, authors, artists, actors, leading businessmen, people from the radio and press, chiefs of organisations and institutions, high school leaders, and naturally a number of leaders from the Mosaic Religious Community, in all 90 well-known personalities. An appeal, which at about the same time went in many thousand copies and was especially reported in the national press, which backed up the cause energetically, contained reasoned recommendations from the Member of Parliament Nina Andersen, Professor Harald Bohr, Chief President J. Bülow, the High School Headmaster C.P.O. Christiansen, Mrs. Henny Forchhammer, the eye specialist Estrid Hein, the Director Karl Lachmann, the Member of Parliament Gerda Mundt, the actor Poul Reumert, the university lecturer Niels S. Søe, the chairman for the Danish Nurses' Council Elizabeth With, and Professor F. Zeuthen.

It should be apparent that a hastily gathered inner circle had in a short time succeeded in mobilizing powerful forces from a wide section of Danish public life. It was decisive that a great many newspapers went in whole-heartedly for the cause, and reported, wrote independent articles and commentaries, and not least made themselves available for a nation-wide collection of funds.

Added to this, although no actual agreement can be traced in the material extant, a kind of division of work developed between the two women's organisations, so that Thora Daugaard, via the League's district chairmen, spread over the whole country, made herself responsible for finding homes for the children, while the National Council took over the largescale collection of funds.

And still the pressure was maintained on the authorities. On 14 April, two requests were sent to the Ministry of Justice, with details of the promises which had been received and were still coming in, for money and homes, and with a repetition of the assurance from the *Alijah* office in London that the necessary funds would be obtained from there, if necessary, and that certificates could be counted upon for each child. To this were added repeated deputation meetings in the Ministry of Justice and the Foreign Ministry, letters to the Prime Minister Stauning and the Minister of Defence Alsing Andersen, who during a period of illness substituted for Steincke, and finally the step was taken to write to 300 Danish families, urging them to write independently, direct to the Ministry of Justice, to exert still more pressure there. The appeal was answered by many, and a shower of more or less well formulated letters landed on the Ministry's tables and in its archives.

Results

All this activity had to give a bonus, and it did. A constantly increasing number of families offered to take Jewish children into their homes, and money in small and large amounts streamed into the National Council's collection. As the year 1939 came to an end, a total collected could be announced of 176,011 crowns – a considerable amount in the terms of the times, even if it did not cover either the emigration expenses for the 1000 children originally applied for, or the emigration expenses for the 320 children who actually came into the country. Here the guarantee from the London office had to supply the difference.

But Danish money was one thing, foreign currency quite another, and on 22 February 1939, Kirsten Gloerfelt-Tarp had asked the National Bank to make a sum in foreign currency up to 300–400,000 crowns available – a strong indication that a still larger sum had been expected from the collection. The Manager of the National Bank, Bramsnæs, was certainly favourably inclined. Two days later, the promise of the bank for foreign currency was received, and thereafter, amounts in foreign currency were drawn on 17 March, 3 May and 10 July, the money being sent to Berlin, London and Palestine.

But the quite decisive result came on 15 July 1939, when Thora Daugaard received a telephone call from the Ministry of Justice with the information that the Ministry had now permitted the entry of 300 children. Mélanie Oppenhejm received the news while on holiday in Skagen:

»Dear Mrs. Oppenhejm, I think I will give you the pleasure of a word or two, for we have now received permission to get 300 children in, in groups of 50. However, the Ministry wants yet another statement from Youth *Alijah* to the effect that the cash for tickets and travelling expenses are there, when the authorities wish to send the children out. I have asked for such a statement from London, and as soon as it arrives we will start getting the first 50 in. We are very pleased with this little victory ... The most important part of it all is that now there is a hope of rescuing 300 of the poor children who suffer so undeservedly. Now comes a great deal of work – in many ways expensive – but we are tackling it with good courage.«

Mélanie Oppenhejm's reply came immediately, with warm thanks for Thora Daugaard's »great energy and the enormous amount of work you have carried out«.

The Ministry's last demand was forwarded at once to the London office, and on 17 July, confirmation was received by telegram:

»HAPPY RECEIVE YOUR NEWS EXTENDED GUARANTEE EN ROUTE.«

A few days later, the guarantee was confirmed by a letter which ended: »The news of the permission for 300 children has been received with enormous pleasure here, and you cannot imagine how much our co-workers have been influenced by this.«

The official written permission from the Ministry of Justice arrived on 25 July. It simply repeated what had been announced by telephone. A copy of the letter was immediately forwarded to Youth-*Alijah* in London.

Urgency

The permits had come at the eleventh hour. Everyone knew that a war might be imminent, and that one must act immediately. From the end of July to September there were shoals of letters and agreements between Copenhagen, Berlin and London. Up to then, it was a case of decisions in principle. Now it was a question of detailed planning with the concrete selection of children, decisions on routes and timing, as well as on cash, luggage, tickets, medical examinations, questionnaires, and the children's geographical placing in the Danish homes offered. In Copenhagen, the helpers started work in optimistic ignorance of the difficulties which must arise in individual cases, when the abstract was to be translated into the concrete, as they started on the verbal assurance from the Ministry of

Justice, before the written approval arrived. On 19 July 1939, Thora Daugaard wrote to Mr. Schattner in London on the details which must of necessity be arranged. She looked forward to receiving the first 50 children in a fortnight's time, and thereafter 50 children each week, until all the 300 were safe in harbour. »I think it is necessary that we act quickly. If war comes, everything is impossible. Let us try to save these 300 souls.« She added that the children were expected in Denmark via Gedser-Warnemünde, for placing on Sjælland, whilst the children for Jylland-Fyn had to come in via Hamburg-Padborg, but that they had to go on to Kolding or Fredericia, because the authorities would not permit them to leave the train at the frontier, as there were too many Nazi-minded people in South Jylland. We have already met this exceptional attitude which the authorities imputed to South Jylland.

In the expectation that the formalities and the practical difficulties would soon be dealt with, a new committee was set up in Copenhagen, consisting of Mélanie Oppenhejm and Thora Daugaard, with two representatives from the Mosaic Religious Community, the director Karl Lachmann and Binjamin Slor, but right from the start, it would prove that far more problems would accumulate than were foreseen. The children neither came at once nor in groups of 50. The immigration would come to drag on for months, and the children would arrive irregularly in groups of different sizes, when opportunities arose, and all the formalities and practical difficulties were dealt with and got out of the way. Before the 320 children were safely across the Danish-German frontier, the war had broken out and the problems had increased correspondingly.

To deal with the practical problems, two representatives from *Jugend-Alijah* in Berlin, Hedwig Eppstein and Kurt Goldmann, came to Copenhagen on 1 August, and a good deal was arranged in consultation with them, but from Copenhagen it was obviously impossible to estimate or understand the great problems which the practical implementation of emigration created for the German organisers, and Thora Daugaard's letters to London in the late summer and autumn reflect both impatience and the character of the problems.

One group of problems was the questionnaires and certificates, which group by group and child by child had to be in order, and a large part of the Danish-English correspondence buzzed around this problem. The certificates came, but the fact that the difficulties must have been greater than appears from the actual documents seems to transpire from a letter written by Mrs. Eva Michaelis-Stern in 1980, 41 years after the events:

»I remember distinctly that we received a request from the Danish Government to supply them with a written guarantee from the British Government to the effect that any Youth Alijah children, who would enter Denmark on a temporary basis would receive certificates for Palestine as soon as the next allocation of entry permits would become available. As we knew from previous experience with regard to other countries, that such guarantees were unobtainable from the British government and as the distribution of certificates was in the hands of the London Youth Alijah office, I choose the only way I could think of and wrote the guarantee on Youth Alijah paper hoping against hope that it would be accepted. We succeeded and I will never forget our gratefulness and relief upon hearing that permission had been given for the waiting groups to enter Denmark.«

In retrospect, the situation is remembered as a once-and-for-all phenomenon. As a matter of fact, there were a number of situations, where an immigration was delayed by problems with the required papers. In Copenhagen the negotiations were met with an impatience approaching desperation, especially when the clouds of war were lowering over Europe. On 26 August, the first group of 50 had not yet arrived, and Thora Daugaard almost lamented to Schattner »We are desperate here because it seems to last so long before we can receive the first 50. Wouldn't you please send us a few lines on the reason . . . Today it seems as if there might be a little less tension in the international affairs. If they would only keep back until we have got the 300 little ones brought up here.« The reply was 77 certificates, and the Berlin office was informed immediately that visas in the passports of the 77 children were not necessary. But now war was imminent. On 30 August 1939, Hedwig Eppstein had to write that for the moment she was prevented from making any arrangements, but at last, in the second week of September, the first 48 children arrived, forerunners of a number of small and large groups.

Another weighty problem was that of money. On 27 July 1939, Thora Daugaard could inform Schattner that the Danish Women's National Council had made 10,000 crowns available, and this brought them part of the way. However, the National Council's collection was earmarked with 1,600 crowns per certificate, and the principal was already allotted to Youth *Alijah* in foreign currency, so that the National Council's funds were limited. As regards the League's obligations, their only duty had been to find foster homes in the hope of assistance, partly from the Mosaic Religious Community and partly from London, and promises had been received from both places. The League itself was generally speaking without funds.

The problem of money must therefore arise, as it was obvious, immediately, that expenses would exceed all the calculations. The children came to Denmark stripped of everything, and promises that their luggage, including bicycles, would be forwarded, in most cases were not kept, and expenses quickly mounted: postage, telegrams, temporary billeting of the children in Copenhagen boarding houses before their final placing in the foster homes, expenses for tickets, clothes, bicycles, doctors' bills and countless types of unforeseen trivial expenses. On 20 September 1939, things had already gone wrong. Thora Daugaard wrote to Eva Michaelis-Stern in London that the Mosaic Religious Community could not shoulder the expenses for more than 150 children, and that the National Council could not run to more than the 10,000 crowns; from then on and until well into 1940, money problems and the need for financial support from the London office were a repeated theme in the Danish-English correspondence. Reassuring answers from Schattner, but often with postponements, were not enough to quieten the anxiety in the League's office, where Thora Daugaard was without funds to cover the daily expenses and a constant stream of small bills from the foster homes. In January 1940, Schattner was informed that if money could not be made available, Thora Daugaard would have to give up getting a last group of 30–40 children to Denmark – »and that is heart-rending«.

Discord

But other problems arose. One of them was touched upon quite briefly by Thora Daugaard in a letter to London of 19 July. A young man from the *Hechaluz* organisation, Bertl Grass, had been in Copenhagen to get orientation on the coming immigration, and *Hechaluz's* interests connected with it, and for the time being Thora Daugaard could say that »we will be glad to use him as our assistant, when the children come«. It was certainly not as assistant that Grass came. He came to prepare Zionist teaching for the children, through visiting teachers and in other ways, and as far as possible to get them collected in districts or centres, so that such teaching could be carried out. The problems connected with this had been lightly touched upon in the earlier correspondence, but Thora Daugaard had not paid attention to this side of things. She stood with her promises from hundreds of homes spread out over the country, and intended to place the children in the homes which she considered best suited, regardless of their geographical placing.

Now the question was put in earnest, and Thora Daugaard had to discover that though the matter had a humanitarian side – the only side that she had hitherto been aware of – there most definitely also were Zionist politics in the picture. On *Hechaluz*'s part, there was some anxiety as to the possibility that the children would settle down too well in secure Danish surroundings, and either never experience or else forget the Zionist cause, which lay behind the whole idea of emigration. The children were the clay, of which the *Hechaluz* movement was to form politically-minded people. Thora Daugaard certainly had not made herself conversant with this Zionist part of the work, and she felt it as an extra burden, on top of all the other difficulties which piled up. On 27 July she mentioned the question in passing, in one of her many letters to Schattner on practical matters:

»Now comes the question of educating the children for Palestine. This is a question we have really not put before us till we were half through the work. If we had been told of it, I am affraid that we should have had to be doubtful. It will be very difficult to get the children centralized, but we will now see what we can do. There will be no lack of good will.«

Schattner's answer of 2 August was reassuring but firm as to the reality:

»I am sure that a way will be found to make it possible to give the children some spiritual and physical preparation for Palestine. In the atmosphere of good will, which so many hundreds of families in Denmark have shown for our cause, this will surely be possible. I hope to hear from you soon telling something about your conversations with our friends.«

The friends were the *Hechaluz* leaders in Copenhagen, with Grass as the motive force. For them there was no doubt. The children were not to come to Denmark solely to reach safety, even if this was the first necessity. They were neither to remain nor to settle down in Denmark. They were Jews under Jewish conditions, and their destination was Palestine. If their attitude was still not marked by the Zionist idea, it was *Hechaluz*'s task to take steps that it should be.

With this, a dispute arose, which had its roots partly in practical conditions, partly in the collision between a Zionist will of iron and a Danish humanitarian attitude. To begin with, the two things were incompatible. On 8 September 1939, Thora Daugaard wrote to Schattner and gave vent to her desperation over the problem. She noted first with pleasure that the first 48 children had now arrived and were placed, and there had been nothing but good reports from the foster-homes, but then came the explosion:

»But dear Mr. Schattner, this has been a terrible mess, and I want to say straight out that several things must be altered, otherwise we must stop the whole work ... Then please do tell Berlin to send certificates to the usual address, Mr. Oppenhejm, Rådhusplads 59, Copenhagen V. They are beginning now to send them to the bureau of the Hechaluz, Nørregade 20. Against this Mrs. Oppenhejm and myself are protesting most energetically. The young people there make a mess of it and we have had a hard time because they have mixed themselves up. They do not belong there, and we don't want them there. If we want their help we shall ask for it, but please understand that the responsibility for this work does not rest with *Hechaluz*, but with us, and if this thing is going to work at all, you will have to tell Berlin that this must be followed ... Mr. Grass is certainly a very fine young fellow, but will you let him know that he cannot do what he has been trying to do, mixing himself up with this work and making a mess of it. Mr. Schattner, I am sure you will agree that it is impossible to have Mr. Grass altering the placement of the children, when we have sent out lists to the police, to the homes, and to the responsible local people. This cannot be done. Mrs. Oppenhejm is sitting here listening to this letter being dictated, and we both sign it, and I hope that you now understand that we are serious, and shall not receive any child who does not conform to what we here have stated.«

There were other problems in the letter, that Berlin had sent children who were orthodox and demanded the Jewish ritual, which was quite impossible to follow, out in the foster-homes, and that Berlin had sent children who were nearly 17 years old, which was the limit for residence permits. Both things should be avoided.

Here too, money matters played a part. On both 2 and 15 January 1940, Thora Daugaard raised the question in letters to London. Relations with the *Hechaluz* office were thus far from harmonious »When all the work in this country has become so expensive, it is mainly the education plan, which is costly. This is altogether a side of the matter which has given us and the foster families a terrible amount of trouble.« And she expressed it still more strongly on 15 January:

»This work has been so terribly difficult on account of the educational side. These young teachers are a trial. They have increased the difficulties enormously. First, they have cost a lot of money for the M.U., and second, they have caused a lot of trouble as regards the connection between the children and the homes. Also the Jewish Women Society.will agree to this now, and before we go on, we must be sure that these young people are under the control of the J.W.S., and that they do not act on their own hands, as they have done hitherto. It is impossible to go on in this way.«

Thora Daugaard had deep understanding for the suffering and the trials to which the Jewish children had been exposed in Germany, and she had been prepared to help to the limits of her capacity and efforts, and often beyond those limits, but the Zionist idea was quite foreign to her. That it also was foreign in many homes goes without saying. It was naturally not foreign to the Danish Jews, but even for them, the Zionist idea was remote, in the sense that they did not themselves think of emigrating. Assimilated as they were in Danish society – often for several generations – their thoughts and attitude in the actual situation were, conceivably enough, nearer the Danish than the Zionist way of thinking. It is perhaps typical that in the religious community's council, there was only one Zionist, Binjamin Slor, and in his daily activities, even he had adjusted himself to a calling in Denmark.

The Children arrive

But long before these troubles arose, a first result had been secured. At an early stage, the Danish Women's National Council, as mentioned, had succeeded in obtaining special permission to receive 25 children, and of these the first 19 arrived in Copenhagen on 19 June 1939, while 6 others followed 15 days later. On the first occasion, there was a festive reception in »the women's building«, with coffee and Danish pastry, considerable press coverage, official speeches and many invited guests from the inner circle which had backed up the National Council's action.

All the ceremony, and especially the photographs and wide press coverage was naturally aimed at the public, with the hope of drawing their attention to the whole affair. A collection was still going on, and enquiries for homes which would receive children. It goes without saying that the journey had been a strain for the children, many of them had been travelling for days, and their feelings must have been a mixture of sorrow after leaving their homes and relief at having escaped safely from Germany.

A large-scale report by the journalist Merete Bonnesen in the newspaper »Politiken« was made up of interviews with the children during the

Smaa jødiske Flygtninge ankommet til København

Midlertidigt Ophold i Danmark et halvt Aars Tid, hvorefter Børnene skal videre til Palæstina

Nogle af de jødiske Gæster fotograferet i Gaar

*D*ER kan næppe i Øjeblikket tænkes større Tragedie end den, de jødiske Emigranter er udsat for. Næsten ligegyldigt, hvorhen de vender sig, er Grænserne spærrede, og overalt nægter man de ulykkelige Mennesker at gaa i Land fra Flygtningeskibene, som ikke véd, hvorhen de skal sejle med deres tragiske Last.

Men i Gaar ankom til København en lille Flok paa nitten tyske, jødiske Børn, som midlertidig har fundet et Fristed i Danmark, indtil de om kort Tid skal videre til Palæstina, hvor der forhaabentlig venter dem en lysere Fremtid end den, de havde Udsigt til i deres eget Land. Flokken bestod af ni Drenge og ti Piger i Alderen fra tretten til femten Aar.

Vi vil gerne hjælpe jer

— *Vi byder jer hjertelig Velkommen til Danmark! sagde Fru Gloerfelt-Tarp i en lille Tale til de tyske Børn. Vi er mange, der ønsker at hjælpe jer, saa godt vi formaar. Vi kan ikke erstatte jeres Far og Mor, men vi ønsker det allerbedste for jer under Opholdet i Danmark, saa I senere, naar I er ankommet til Palæstina, kan tænke tilbage derpaa med Glæde. Det, vi gør for jer, er kun hvad Danmark har gjort for andre Børn i en vanskelig Situation. Jeg vil kun minde om Wienerbørnene, der efter Verdenskrigen havde et midlertidigt Hjem i Danmark.*

Extract of an article in Kristeligt Dagblad, on 20 June 1939.

105

last leg of their journey, as Merete Bonnesen had been in Warnemünde to meet them. Her report tells of the children's anxiety until they were safely past the frontier, but also of the comradeship which had grown up among them during the journey itself.

Immediately after the reception, the children were lodged in a villa near the Arre Lake, made available by the barrister Max Rothenborg. Thus, as an exception, the children were kept together as a group, on the basis of special permission for such »colony placing«, tacitly accepted by Steincke. It was a little later, after temporary billeting in Jewish homes in Copenhagen, that they were dispersed to the foster-homes out in the country, in accordance with the general demand from the police for them to be housed singly.

Merete Bonnesen's report, on crossing the frontier and on the journey, is not without journalistic effect, and, in spite of its humanity, is hardly the best source material on the children's experience of their arrival. It must be left to the imagination, how they really experienced those nerve-racking hours. It is possible, however, to register how two of the children remembered them, 42 years later:

»We were already received in Warnemünde by a Danish journalist, Merete Bonnesen, 'Politiken'. It is moving to remember the kindness. She interviewed us, and there was a report in 'Politiken'. I still have a photograph of the little group of children. It is taken in 'Politiken's' house. Up to September 1939, we were housed in a sort of holiday colony in Ramløse, North Sjælland. The barrister Max Rothenborg generously placed a villa at our disposal. In the grounds there was also a former children's home. He took a personal, active interest in what I experienced as Utopia, to eat ones fill, to feel safe, to bathe and play, etc.«

»We were received in Copenhagen, and it made a fantastic impression on one. Everyone was so kind to us, and we weren't used to that any more in Germany. The town, too, was light and warm after the darkness and cold in Germany. Our group was first placed in North Sjælland, Ramløse Beach, on an old farm, which had been altered for us as a holiday place. We were there for a month.«

It was clearly a relief for the children, that in that way they had been allowed to stay together for a transitional period, before being dispersed to a number of strange homes, and on 12 September, Max Rothenborg wrote to Steincke and thanked him for, as an exception, allowing the 25 children, who »had come on condition that they were placed in private families, to stay in the property I had rented, out at Arresø«. Now things had settled down, and Rothenborg and the National Council had decided that the time had come to distribute the children to the waiting homes.

This form of reception was by no means the norm, as the 300 League children began to arrive. As mentioned, they arrived in groups, sometimes quite small, sometimes a little larger, and those who came in over the Gedser-Warnemünde ferry and so to Copenhagen, were lodged for one night in a Copenhagen boarding house, until, the day after, they were sent direct to the foster-parents who stood ready to receive them on railway stations all over Sjælland. The children who entered via Padborg went direct to the homes in Jylland and on Fyn. At the end of September 1939, 75 children had arrived, while a group of 7 were expected. In December, 265 had come and had been distributed, and the remaining 35 were got across the frontier in the first months of 1940. As the weeks passed in 1940, the urgency escalated more than ever. On 13 February, Thora Daugaard wrote to the State Police and asked for dispensation for two children who were approaching 17, and therefore strictly speaking were too old to fulfill the conditions for emigration before they completed their seventeenth year. But now it was too late for two children from the original lists. They had died in concentration camps, and the two for whom dispensation was asked were also in concentration camps.

»One also expected that they would be killed without being released. If they are released, it is on condition that they leave Germany the same day, and this is presumably the reason for one requesting that two may get through, who also come straight from a concentration camp, in spite of their being a little over the age limit.«

These are Thora Daugaard's words to the Alien Department of the State Police. The »one« in the letter is the *Jugend-Alijah* office in Berlin.

This pressure also succeeded, and on 5 March it could at last be registered that 315 children had come safely to Danmark. A few got through a little later, so that the total was 320, including the 25 for whom the National Council had obtained permission.

The rhythm of immigration was as follows:

1939	3/9	49
	22/9	18
	29/9	7
	5/10	19
	6/10	13
	11/10	25
	24/10	23
	25/10	17
	14/11	25

	23/11	36
	5/12	17
	16/12	1
	17/12	1
	19/12	14
1940	23/1	1
	6/2	9
	1/3	7
	2/3	8

Immigrated in all	290
National Council	25
Total	315

5 children arrived a little later, so that the total number was the 320 mentioned.

Emigration

The final destination for the journey was Palestine. And it was particularly urgent for the children approaching 17 years, which the authorities had fixed as the age limit. No sooner had the children arrived in Denmark, before the work started to get at least the eldest of them out again. After the outbreak of war, a journey through Germany was an impossibility, and the plan was therefore to get some children out through France. In the autumn, a great deal of energy and hard work was devoted to obtaining transit permits from the French authorities for a group of children. Pressure was renewed, and succeeded. On 15 January 1940, the League could write to 50 homes »Today a telegram has come, that the children's transit to Marseilles is assured. Will the homes kindly act according to our last letter. The children are asked to bring their bicycles here. They will then be stored at the Jewish Women's Society for future use.«

The homes had already been instructed on what they should do, when the signal came for departure, and now 50 children collected in Copenhagen with their belongings – maximum 35 kilogrammes – to fly to

København, den 15/1-1940.

Idag er der kommen Telegram om, at Børnenes
Gennemrejse til Marseille er sikret.
Vil Hjemmene saa venligst handle efter den
sidste Skrivelse.

Cykler:De Cykler,der tilhører Børnene,bedes Børnene bringe med herind. De vil da blive oplagret i
" Jødisk Kvindeforening" for fremtidig Brug.- Alle
Regninger paa Cykler,der endnu ikke er betalt,vil
blive det en af de første Dage.

Med venlig Hilsen,

Thora Daugaard

Duplicated note from the League office, January 1940.

Rotterdam, and from there go on by train to Marseilles, and further by ship to Haifa. Everything went according to plan. The children flew off in two aeroplanes and on 29 January they could write a letter to Thora Daugaard, signed by 34 of the emigrants from the ship, on their way to Palestine. The letter was written with great care in Danish, and with almost caligraphic script »Dear Mrs. Daughaart. We would like to permit ourselves to send you our heartiest greetings now from the ship. We hope that in our later life we have the opportunity to show what the stay in Denmark has been for us. We will never forget your self-sacrificing action for us. With hearty thanks for all and a greeting.«

There was still direct contact between Denmark and Palestine. While the children prepared to collect in Copenhagen, Mrs. Ella Melby, who had previously worked with the League, but now had settled in Palestine, wrote a letter to Mrs. Daugaard, dated Haifa 12 January 1940. The letter shone with gratitude, and casts light over the earlier *Hechaluz* work:

»The other day I was sitting outside a pioneer tent, decorated with a little, faded Danish flag, in a far-away, collective colony, which celebrated its 3-years birthday, surrounded by a group of young people who learned agriculture in Denmark. As usual when I visit such young friends, for whom I represent the country they love so much, photograph albums appear with pictures of Danish rustic idylls and the farm inhabitants. I also read letters from the Danish families with whom the young Jews had worked – letters where the contents explain why the young Jews have felt themselves at home in Denmark. Simply and sincerely these farmers, their wives and children write to their foster children in Palestine, whom they still follow faithfully in their thoughts, although they have no idea what a contrast there is between the dangers and privations of pioneer life over here and life on the Danish islands. At the end I was handed a crumpled exercise book, on the pages of which I read of the work which is being done for the huge group, which one has taken up in Denmark recently . . . How strange to see your name in these surroundings and in connexion with this work. In a great leap . . . my thoughts flew back to the time when we prepared the women's constitution protest . . . I have settled here and my greatest riches are my contacts with Jewish youth who have come to this country via Denmark.«

On 30 January, Thora Daugaard could reply with a long letter of thanks:

» . . . I am delighted to know that I now have a Danish connexion in Haifa. We sent off two aeroplanes the other day, with 25 children in each. They have been here for 4½ months and are now to go out via Rotterdam, Marseilles to Palestine. We have now 265 children in the country, and therefore still have 30–40 children to come (our permit was for 300). 16 will come in a few weeks, but when we can expect the rest we do not know, for the Germans are very miserly with exit permits.«

Another letter of thanks from Palestine reached Mrs. Daugaard before the Occupation blocked all postal communication. It came from Henrietta Szold, the Palestine leader of Youth *Alijah*. She wrote on 31 January 1940 and expressed the hope that the League would succeed in getting some more children to Denmark, and then continued

»What has been achieved, in my opinion, is beyond the ordinary words of thanks to which one resorts faute de mieux. What you are doing, and what you have done for the Jewish refugees, at the same time when your hearts and minds are engaged with the refugees from the brave battling north country, fills us with admiration, and no less with hope that you will continue to include our troubles within the circle of your tender care. I wonder whether you can imagine what

110

Palæstina de 29. Januar.

Kære Fru Daughaart!
Vi vil gerne tillade os at sende Dem
vores hjerteligste Hilsener nu paa Skiben.
Vi haaber at vi i vort senere Liv har
Lejlighed at vise, hvad Opholdet i Dan-
mark har været for os.
  Vi vil aldrig glemme Deres opofrende
Værk for os.
        Med hjertelig Tak for alt, og
en Hilsen
                              Deres

Facsimile of a letter to Thora Daugaard from some of the Alijah children who
were brought successfully to Palestine via Rotterdam and Marseilles. But the
Second World War was already in progress, and soon after this it became clear
that all roads were closed.

111

feelings possessed us, when a few days ago we received a cable from our London office in which we were told of the successful transit of our famous forty-nine to Amsterdam and then to Marseilles. That group of forty-nine, which has been on our minds for so many months, has been to us a living illustration of all that I have attempted to say to you regarding your resourcefulness and your action in Denmark towards juvenile refugees. You will understand that I cannot add to what I said any conventioned words of thanks. I leave it to you to read between the lines. Yours very sincerely Henrietta Szold.«

Quota Problems

With this departure, a question of interpretation arose. Had one received permission to take in 300 children in Denmark, or had one received permission to have 300 children in Denmark, and could one therefore now fill up with new immigrants to that figure? Melanie Oppenhejm and the two Jewish members of the committee believed it to be the latter, and their London office used pressure in favour of this interpretation. Thora Daugaard agreed, in effect, with this viewpoint, but found it necessary to make conditions for continuing, if the authorities would accept the favourable interpretation at all. She did this in a letter to Schnattner on 15 January 1940, while the 50 children were being collected in Copenhagen prior to their departure. She raised two questions

»We can of course organise for more homes, there is no doubt about that, but the work must be organised so that it is not felt as a burden on our shoulders in the same way as hitherto. We have pledged ourselves for 300 homes, and we have done the work we shall do. Whether we shall do more depends on:
1) The money question.
2) The agreement of my Board to go on.
3) The agreement of the Jewish Society to fellow up in a more secure way as far as money is concerned.
4) The agreement of our Ministry of Justice to allow further import of Jewish refugee children.
I have spoken with the Police about this question, and they said at once that they could not recommend it.«

This whole question of replacement up to a fixed quota was discussed during the first months of 1940, both with the Danish authorities and between Copenhagen and London, but the discussion remained abstract theory. Before it was concluded, the political realities would overtake all plans for continuation.

In addition, there was another element which from December 1939 was to play a part in the considerations. On 30 November 1939, the so-called »Winter War« broke out between Finland and the Soviet Union, and Danish homes now offered to receive Finnish children who were in need, because of war conditions. Many of the families which had offered to receive a Jewish child, but had not yet been assigned one were now faced with a dilemma. Should they withdraw their offer to a Jewish child, and instead receive a Finnish, or should they maintain their original promise to the League to receive a Jewish child, who might never come.

A number of letters on this question criss-crossed between the homes and the League's headquarters in the weeks from the middle of December 1939 and up to March 1940. The viewpoint in Copenhagen was that children in distress were children in distress, and one could not and would not therefore try to influence the homes. If those in doubt decided to take a Finnish child, they should do so without regard to the League's interests. This reply was so. much the easier to give in that there was actually a considerable surplus of homes to draw upon – if more Jewish children came than were expected. They did not.

Negotiations on this were carried on with the Ministry of Justice right up to the first days of April 1940. A first request from Thora Daugaard was sent in on 4 March:

» . . . we take the liberty of asking that we may always have 300 children within the country's borders, so that the places which are emptied at the children's departure may be taken up again by new immigrating children . . . We are assured from England (Youth *Alijah* in London) that there will be no difficulties with entry to Palestine.«

But in the Ministry there was scepticism, and especially as regards the children. In a fairly long ministerial report on the whole Jewish immigration one can read:

»It is quite obvious that they cannot return to Germany, whether they (still) have their parents there or not. In the event that their parents should have emigrated to another country, there is probably a possibility that the children can emigrate to the country in question. But most probably, the parents' circumstances, at least during the first years, will be so poor that they would not be in a position to receive the children.«

The misgivings as to receiving children were in case they would here become dependent on the Danish homes, that they would go to school, and that they »would thus be adopted into Danish society, and a parting after even one year can be difficult«. Added to this, there was the risk

This picture gives an impression of the Palestine to which the young people came – here it is the old Roman harbour of Caesarea, which later became the kibbutz S'dot Yam.

that parents from Germany would try to follow the children, and such a request would often be difficult to refuse. One should not, therefore, go beyond the existing arrangement with *Hechaluz* for placing agricultural trainees, as here one could stretch the permit for 1 to 2 years.

The consequence of such considerations must be a blank refusal to Thora Daugaard. On 2 April, a note was prepared in the Ministry of Justice with an obviously negative tendency » . . . even if new entry permits are contingent on emigration, it is . . . not without misgivings to grant . . . In addition, experience with agricultural trainees, of whom c. 300 must be considered stranded here, definitely counsels caution.« Further on in the note we read:

»The Ministry of Justice in the present circumstances must feel considerable misgivings at giving permission for the entry of further Jewish children from Germany, and it would in the event have to be a condition that an unconditional promise had been given from official British authorities that those involved would receive entry permits to Palestine before the children reached the age of 17.«

Four days later, it was clear that such a promise could not be obtained. In another note of 6 April 1940 this was laid down with finality »The British passport office here, in answer to a telephoned question, has today given the information that the issue of certificates to Palestine to German Jews

114

is now definitely at an end . . .« and in the margin of the note is added the laconic sentence »It is not so good that we are now stuck with all the 'League children'. This must be an extra minus, not to oblige Mrs. Daugaard.«

One can form ones own opinion on the choice of words. The fact is that the short, unsentimental marginal note hit the bull's eye. Three days later, Denmark was occupied.

The Burden of Occupation

Occupation

The German occupation of Denmark on 9 April 1940 with one blow wiped out all the conditions that had formed the basis for the immigration of both *Hechaluz* trainees and *Alijah* children.

For both groups the Occupation came to mean everything – and nothing! The former is obvious, the latter must be understood in the sense that, to begin with, nothing happened, and that there was nothing to be done, either by the trainees or the children, so that both groups had no alternative but to wait and see – and in that they shared the conditions of the whole Danish nation. For weeks, no one could see the consequences of what had taken place, or have any idea of what could happen.

It seems to have been decisive that both the foster families and the organising leaders at every level did their utmost to give reassurance and combat any tendency to panic. A strange, almost apathetic stillness marked the first weeks of the Occupation, among the Danes as well as among The Jews. The archives are strikingly empty, from the first days of occupation. One letter from Margolinsky to a trainee, written on 9 April, is the only utterance in the dead calm of attitude which sank over the leaders in Copenhagen, under the first impression of the shock: » . . . it is naturally not possible to assess developments, but to judge from the atmosphere, one has the impression here that daily work for all must go on in a normal way.« Similar messages went out in the days that followed, to the homes and trainees. Only time could show what the Occupation would involve, and out in the homes, people remained quiet, chiefly, perhaps, because there was nothing else to do. Mélanie Oppenhejm has expressed herself in a conversation with the simple words, »There was not a single home that failed us.«

One single exception is noticeable, simply as an exception to this statement. On 10 April, a farmer wrote to Margolinsky »Trainee X was among those who yesterday lost their heads, and ran away from here. But instead of his own bicycle he took one belonging to a farm hand working on this farm. I am telling you this, as I do not want to mix the police up in the matter.« Here it is the bicycle more than the panic that is the heart of the problem.

Trainees have reported that in the evening of 9 April and the days following, they gathered to discuss the situation, and that they came to the only conceivable conclusion, that without economic means and without deep contacts in Danish society, they had no choice but to stay in their places and carry on as if nothing had happened. This conclusion was soon confirmed, both from Margolinsky and from the *Hechaluz* offices in Nørregade. Confused plans for flight, or even for the purchase of arms had to be shelved as pure fantasy so everything remained as it was. The League offices and the committee for the *Alijah* children wrote at once to all the foster families and to all the children, that they »must not go beyond the boundaries of their home, must not go to school, and must not meet«. But this instruction soon became impossible to keep. On 8 May 1940, the branch president in Næstved wrote to Thora Daugaard: »It now seems as though the children and the rest of us have settled down after 9 April, and as we have all been ordered to live our daily lives as usual, I would like to ask whether it is not possible that the children can also live as they did before. It is a great inconvenience, both for the children and the homes, that they have to stay at home, and they particularly miss their schooling very much.« The League's leaders approved the idea, and after a few weeks' unrest and uncertainty, the children's lives also settled into their usual course.

In that sense, the Occupation meant nothing.

But of course the Occupation was a catastrophe for the Jews – a »Not again?« The War itself, with the stop for certificates, had been a misfortune for the *Hechaluz* trainees, who after a fairly long stay in Denmark were expecting to emigrate. Now they were stranded, in deep uncertainty about their future fate. Most of the *Alijah* children, on the other hand, had come in after the outbreak of war, and for them the Occupation seemed to nullify their plans. Because of their age, they were also probably more helpless than their older comrades.

On the other hand, although they did not know it, they were in reality little better off than the *Hechaluz* trainees. In London, there was no doubt that the *Alijah* children had landed in a particularly unhappy situation, and on 27 April a telegram was sent from there via Geneva, which was to give the help London could give if help was still possible:

JUGENDALIJAH ZERTIFICATE FUER DAENEMARK SIND EIN-
GETROFFEN STOP BEGINNEE UMGEHEND AUSREISEVOR-
BEREITUNG GENAUES ARZERZEUGNIS NOTWENDIG DRAH-
TET ANZAHL KANDIDATEN TELEGRAMSCHRIFT STAND 312.

With this, the first condition for the children to be able to come out, in
spite of the Occupation, had been provided. The problem was to find a
possible route, and while hectic work with the possible solutions was
going on in Copenhagen, the foster families were told to be ready:

You have naturally all been able to notice recently that work is being done to
get the emigrant children out of the country. It started with the English
mandatory power sending us, unasked, the necessary entry permits for each child
to Palestine. What has given such trouble is to find the way we can send them. To
begin with, one has now stopped at the possibility that they can come out through
Sweden into Russia, and so from there south, either to the right and in over
Turkey and Greece and the last lap by sea to Haifa, or to the left down over
Teheran and in through India and by ship from there south, round Arabia. It is
not decided yet, how it is to be done, but we have in any case just one thing to do –
to hold ourselves ready, to be able to send the children off at a few days' notice.«

Then followed a long series of instructions on medical examinations,
tickets, luggage, bicycles, etc. and a last request to reassure the children
and not promise them anything but keep them close to home »We
urgently request that none of the children must go too far from the
home. It can easily happen that departure can take place in the course of
a few hours.«

The fact that in Copenhagen all possibilities had been explored
appears from Thora Daugaard's letter to the Ministry of Justice on 16
May 1940, in which she asks the ministry to help her to find out, whether
the journey could take place through Germany to Palestine. In the
ministry the idea was considered unbelievable, and it was suggested that
Thora Daugaard must probably herself apply to the German authorities,
but this never took place. On the other hand, another note shows that
from 12 July the Alien Department of the Police, through the managing
clerks Bengt Flagsted and Wilhelm Leifer negotiated with Sweden for
transit visas, before emigration over the Baltic countries and Russia.
Leifer, particularly, was to be a great support in the stubborn work,
which was now approaching, to get at least some of the children out.

The Long Journey

It was Mélanie Oppenhejm and Leifer, who for many of long months after occupation were to take the lead in the tough work of getting hold of the necessary visas, permits and practical possibilities, to get some of the children, in spite of the Occupation, safely to their destination in Palestine. Both she and Thora Daugaard felt a special responsibility for the children's fate, and did what was in their power to save what could be saved.

A number of interviews were undertaken with Danish, German, Swedish, and Russian authorities, and in the first of several journeys to Stockholm, Mélanie Oppenhejm tried to open a path which on 9 April seemed to have been closed. She was greatly helped in her efforts by Wilhelm Leifer, who both then and later used his service contacts with the German police to promote Danish and, in this instance, also Jewish interests. As adjutant to the Chief of the State Police, Thune Jacobsen, and from 1 November 1940 as Chief of the Visa Office, Leifer was in a key position, and actually able to obtain visas for emigration for all the young Jews who might have the chance of going on, and he also obtained visas for the leaders of the work, who needed to come to Sweden for negotiations. As regards visas for transit through Russia, Mélanie Oppenhejm received the support of the Soviet Russian Minister in Stockholm, Madame Kollontai, and later in the summer, the future looked brighter for the *Alijah* children.

The original hope had been to get all the children brought out via Sweden, and on 7 August, Mélanie Oppenhejm could apply to the Foreign Ministry to obtain support for a planned mass departure. She could then show that certificates had been given by the British for all the remaining 270 children, and that after a series of negotiations, transit visas had been secured from Swedish, Russian and Syrian authorities. The German passport office in Copenhagen had given a verbal promise of exit permits from Denmark, a promise which, according to Leifer's description, was quite easy to obtain, so long as the Germans were met with sufficiently frontal demands for co-operation. Mélanie Oppenhejm, referring to all this, asked the Foreign Ministry to intervene with the Turkish authorities in Ankara, to obtain transit visas for all 270 children, adding that this would not contain any risk for the Turkish authorities, as the Danish State Police, to be on the safe side, had promised return visas for a period of three months, here too with Leifer's help. The problem was therefore the Turkish permission, and the fact that the British certificates had a time limit, so that emigration should take place as soon as possible.

The Ministry reacted immediately with a telegram to the Danish legation in Ankara, giving all the details of the formalities which were already in order, and adding that the journey through Turkey could, if necessary, be made in a sealed coach. In spite of this, hesitation in Turkey became the bottleneck in the plans. In the first place, the Danish legation in Ankara had to reply with the information that similar requests from other countries had been refused, up to then, and that the affair would be dealt with at a Cabinet meeting. The background was elaborated in a report from the Danish Chargé d'Affaires in Ankara, Paul Friis, on 12 August. The Turkish Government was sceptical, because a large number of Jewish refugees, although they had had valid papers, had been stranded in Turkey, with no possibilities either for going on or being received by those who had sent them. Late in the autumn, Friis reported on his repeated efforts to get Turkish approval, and as late as in November, the Danish Foreign Ministry in Copenhagen was considering persuading the German authorities in Copenhagen to exert pressure on Turkey to allow this emigration. But just then, Leifer could report that a Turkish promise had at last arrived, and the approach to the German authorities was dropped.

The next block was that the Russian »Intourist«, which was to be responsible for the lap through Russia, would only approve the transit of groups of 45. The way thus lay open for a first group, and temporarily shut for all the others. On 5 December 1940, this first group left. It consisted of the oldest of the children, who were now or were approaching 17 years. On 3 December, the Foreign Ministry instructed the Danish Legation in Moscow to afford every possible assistance to the children and their *Hechaluz* teacher, Elchanan Jizchaki during the journey, »if necessary by agreement and in co-operation with the German Embassy«.

Mélanie Oppenhejm and Elchanan Jizchaki, who had both been in Stockholm in November to prepare the first part of the journey, accompanied the children to Stockholm, after which the latter took over the leadership of the tour, which went through Finland and Russia to Odessa, and from there by ship to Istanbul. In all, 44 children reached their final destination by this route, and one more journey by the same route was successfully arranged for 4 March 1941, this time with 42 children. After this, 184 children were left in Denmark. It was they who, with c. 350 *Hechaluz* trainees were to experience the Occupation most acutely and personally.

120

A group of Alijah children, colected on Odense railway station before departure for Palestine, in 1940 or 1941.

A Travel Memoir

It is possible to follow the last emigration group right to their destination. An *Alijah* boy, who in March 1941 was nearly 18 years old, reports:

»In Copenhagen we were gathered (c. 40 young people from the whole country) at Ny Kongensgade 6 (the community's centre). We were not allowed to go out, as the Germans were not to notice anything. A day or two later, the long journey began. We came to the Free Harbour and went on board an ice-breaker, accompanied by Mrs. Oppenhejm, who had made all the arrangements for our stay in Denmark. The Germans checked our passports, very confused. On the ferry the mood was good, and we felt that we were again sailing towards freedom. When we reached Malmø, we were given a meal by the Swedish-Jewish community, at the station restaurant, and we left Malmø already on the 22.00 train for Stockholm. The community had arranged an evening for us, and I remember, amongst others, a lecturer who spoke about the long, long country we would travel through from Stockholm to Haparanda.

»It took two days and 2 nights to the Finnish frontier, Tornio. In Stockholm, 5 *chawerim* joined us, and we were 42 from Denmark. The one from Stockholm was to be a sort of leader, as it was very uncertain whether we would get the transit visa in Turkey – we should know at the frontier. We got a very fine comradeship on the journey, although most of us did not know each other ... At the Finnish-Russian frontier there was a very strict check, and a Russian guide from

»Intourist« took over the group and accompanied us until we went on board the ship in Odessa. From Tornio via Helsinki to Leningrad, the journey on the Russian railway was in short jerks. In Leningrad we were housed at a tourist hotel, where only diplomats stayed. We spent about 1½ days at this fine hotel, with masses of luxury, good food, tours in the city, cinema, etc., and so we were well prepared to journey on. From Leningrad we travelled for 2 days and 2 nights through Russia to Odessa. The train was very long and actually completely shut. One could see where one was. After half a day in Odessa, which was a very pleasant city, we went on board a ferry . . . The ship touched at Varna (Bulgaria) and we saw Germans for the last time, on the quay. The Turkish visa proved to be in order, and we came to Istanbul.

»In Istanbul we sailed from the European to the Asiatic, through the Bosporus, which was a fantastic sight, which I can still remember and see before me. We were billeted in a very nice hotel, where we stayed for 3–4 days, saw something of the town and walked in the neighbourhood. It was very beautiful. We passed through Turkey in a train which stopped at all the stations, to Beirut in Syria. In Beirut we spent the night, and drove the next day in a bus to Haifa. At the Syrian-Palestinian frontier we were received by a lady, who told a brother and sister from our group that their parents were alive. They had been rescued from the ship 'Patria', which sank in Haifa harbour, where several people died. The British would have sent the ship back to Cyprus.

»In Palestine we were sent to two different kibbutzes . . .«

A year and a half later, our narrator took part in the battle of El-Alamein as a volunteer in the British Army. His war memoirs from four years as a soldier are limited to a mention of the »great offensive which led to the invasion of Sicily, etc.«.

Shut in

Departure during the Occupation had to be a rare exception for the young Jews who were still in Denmark in April 1940. The hammer had fallen for the *Hechaluz* group as early as September 1939, with the news that Great Britain, at least for the time being, had stopped all issue of certificates. Their chances for slipping out were therefore minimum. For the *Alijah* group a similar situation arose in the first weeks after occupation. The telegram with the information of the blanket certificates, with a time limit, did not arrive until the end of April, and the children, homes and leaders had to face the fact that the children would have to stay in the homes for an indefinite time, perhaps for years. There was some hope for this group after the telegram, but it was only a flickering hope, as one can see from a letter from January 1941 from Thora Daugaard to one of the district chairmen, who had a fairly large group of children in her care:

»Then I had better tell you at once that there is a possibility now that the children will not get away. As a matter of fact, no more than we had expected, but when we received a definite message from Sweden, we had to act in accordance with it. We have not given up hope yet, and it may well be that it is like the last time, and that everything works out at the last moment. This work had become frightfully difficult for all of us, and it is naturally in a way worst for the children, who are treated like 'dumb postal packets'. It is no wonder, if they become worried.«

But how worried were the children and the trainees in fact? The remark quoted is one of the few references to any special unrest in connexion with the Occupation. A letter to the League's headquarters on 10 April 1940 is quite exceptional in its expression of anxiety:

»In the country's new situation, we are far from pleased at having responsibility for him. Kalundborg is flooded with German soldiers, and there is, after all, the possibility that we may have to have them quartered on us – and if the boy is exposed to chicanery, it will be almost impossible for either the children or us not to react – and what then? . . . but we do not think we can very well fail the boy . . . because he has no one else to lean on.«

The letter concludes with a question as to whether there is a more reassuring home available for him, but the boy remained where he was.

The trainees' reports on their time in Denmark say practically nothing about the psychological effects of the Occupation. The occupation phenomenon is avoided in the accounts, even in quite detailed accounts. The archives contain scores of letters from April 1940 and they all deal with day-to-day problems, after 9 April as before that date: that so-and-so must find a new place, and one suggests farm X in Y town; that the trainee must »make do« with the pocket money agreed; that the 3.20 crowns for the doctor's bill sent in will come, all right; that the work clothes will be sent from the Jewish Women's Society's clothes centre; or that one is trying to find money for a second-hand bicycle, if the trainee cannot borrow one any longer. All-in-all trivial letters, where one could have expected panic-stricken letters.

And yet, the Occupation had come as a shock for the Jewish immigrants, as it had for the whole population. Perhaps the lack of statements generally reflect a fatalistic attitude, which was not unlike that in the Danish homes, where people lived in a kind of paralysis at what could not be otherwise – a situation which must simply be registered. Perhaps it was not without an effect, that the pupils, younger as older, children as well as mature young men and women, were all staying in the country-side, where the Occupation was not immediately noticeable. And finally, it can perhaps serve as an explanation that the pupils, like the population, continued their daily lives with a »wait-and-see« attitude. Who could know, in April 1940, whether the attacks on Denmark and Norway were not a last desperate military action on the part of the Germans, and whether the whole action could fail, and be the beginning of the end of the Nazi adventurer policy. At least it was impossible in those days to imagine what the Occupation meant, and how long it would last. A posterity, which knows what happened, can find it difficult to force itself to imagine what was thought and hoped in April 1940. The immediate catastrophe could perhaps imply a coming freedom. The Great Powers in the West had still not moved.

But even if it is extremely little that the documents and reports are able to tell about the stranded Jews' reactions to the Occupation, they make it possible to decide their number. In April 1940, Margolinsky prepared a carefully kept list of names of the *Hechaluz* trainees, who still had not obtained certificates and emigration, and who now were staying for an indeterminate time and with an unknown future before them in Denmark. The list covered 379 trainees in all, giving date and place of birth, and to these, after the departure of 50 *Alijah* children in January 1940, 270 persons must be added from the *Alijah* group. After this, the total number was 649 Jewish immigrants from the two groups mentioned, to which there is another small number of Jewish refugees outside these groups who are not covered in this book. The numbers were reduced for the *Alijah* group after the departure of the 86 children via Sweden, and in the first week after occupation, it had been possible to get a similar journey arranged through Sweden – Russia – Turkey for about 10 *Hechaluz* trainees, mostly students of gymnastics, and also a very few managed to reach Sweden and then were helped to get to Palestine by the Mosaic Religious Community in Stockholm. But for the great majority all the roads were blocked.

In October 1941, Margolinsky had not quite lost hope of getting at least a few more of the Jewish immigrants out. A number had relations in various overseas countries, and both they and Margolinsky pressed to obtain money and travelling permits with their help, but on the whole these attempts stranded after difficult and copious correspondence. In

October 1941, Margolinsky made a further count, in connexion with an approach to the Ministry of Justice, and the number was then »363 persons, who are employed as agricultural and domestic science trainees and the like, in office work and as teachers for the so-called 'League'.« The office work meant, in this context, engagement at the *Hechaluz* office in Nørregade 20. To these must be added the remaining 184 »League« children, after which the total of permanently stranded persons who had to live through the Occupation up to October 1943, was 547.

Changes in Administration

The outbreak of war and occupation seven months later brought administrative changes. From September 1939 the almost daily letters from the Agricultural Travel Bureau to the State Police, with applications for residence and work permits for »German subject« X for engagement as unpaid agricultural trainee with farmer Y, stopped abruptly. When the certificates stopped, all immigration of *Hechaluz* trainees stopped. Generally speaking, the War terminated the bureau's exchange programmes and as far as Germany was concerned, the stop was total. It was soon quiet in the bureau, and notes to the State Police were confined to information on changes of workplaces, until this activity, too, ebbed away, and support and supervision with the trainees passed into other hands. In the autumn 1939, the bureau made an energetic effort to obtain places in farming homes, when trainees for some reason wished or were forced to change their places, but gradually this work of the bureau with the Jewish agricultural trainees came to an end.

At the end of August 1940, Siggaard made a long report to the State Police on the work of »exchange« of Jewish agricultural trainees, as it had taken form since the beginning of the 30's and on the conditions, according to which the work had been organised, as described above. He then concluded:

»For the present, these conditions cannot be kept, because entry permits to Palestine for the Jewish trainees residing in this country are refused on the English side. Prolongation of these trainees' residence permits must therefore be carried out, until normal conditions return, but the bureau will consider it best that the conditions as unpaid trainees be maintained in the case of the Jewish trainees. This gives the fewest difficulties for the Administration and the best conditions for the Jewish trainees. Nor will it be possible to find paid places for these, towards the coming winter.«

The key words here were that prolongation must necessarily be carried out, and that Siggaard definitely believed that the principle of unpaid work should be maintained. The former, with the prevailing anti-Jewish terror in Germany, was obvious, but the latter, both in 1940 and in the years following, involved increasing problems. Siggaard found it most expedient to avoid using the expression »wages« and to keep to the idea of training. This would ease relations with the authorities and trades unions. On the longer term, this obstinate insistence on »pocket money« as the only, and casual pay, could not but give rise to difficulties. The 19-year-old trainee from an immigration in 1938, was 22 years old in 1941. He was no longer a »trainee« but a fully trained farm worker, yes, even a farm foreman, and the principle must seem unjust and unreasonable both for him and for an understanding farmer. Vis-à-vis the authorities the word »pocket money« could be maintained, but the word had to be interpreted with some elasticity, if understandable tensions were not to arise.

The principle of unpaid manpower did crumble, little by little with every imaginable variation from district to district and from farm to farm. What is certain is that agreed wages meant, in every case, police intervention, a ban on an agreement otherwise in order, and with that, the loss of a desirable place. However, the longer their stay in Denmark lasted, the more impossible it was to avoid either a demand for wages, or possibly money under the counter; and at every change of situation, which always had to be reported to the police, it was important that the fiction that it was a question of training and unpaid work be maintained. The problem eased, as the Occupation brought with it increasing demands for manpower, and unemployment disappeared, but both trainees and their employers had to take care not to disclose the real situation.

Some idea of the changing wage situation can be gained through one of the circulars from the *Hechaluz* office for the information of the leading, and trusted trainees out in the districts. It is a question of a circular from 21 April 1942, where the wages are accounted for to the Holbæk centre. This consisted at that time of 12 members, who were then described as paid as follows:

1. 75 cr. – without laundry.
2. 25 cr. a month + 550 cr.
3. 30 cr. a month + requirements up to 600 cr.
4. 60 cr. a month (without laundry. Nursery garden.)
5. 30 cr. a month + 375 cr. without laundry.
6. According to amount of work (c. 100 cr. – without laundry)
7. At present in hospital.
8. c. 40 cr. + current overtime money at a good rate.
9. At least 125 cr. + laundry and sickness insurance.
10. At least 125 cr. + laundry and sickness insurance.
11. 700 cr. – without laundry.
12. 50 cr. a month.

It is not clear whether, for trainees 1, 6, 9 and 10, it is a question of monthly payments, but the individual agreements seem clear. A single concluding remark on the last-named trainee seems to indicate, however, that in Copenhagen one operated with wages up to 600 crowns per half year, as the reasonable minimum. The trainees' wages were fixed at 300 crowns for the half year up to November, and the circular mentions that »the pupil will not change his place, even though in our opinion he receives too little payment. Otherwise he is very pleased with his place.« It was out of wages like these that the trainees were urged to and agreed to pay their »masser« to the common fund. A circular from January 1942 establishes that the contributions for December 1941 have been better than previously, as they amounted to 650 crowns. Such a little glimpse into a local situation does naturally not allow for more general conclusions than the one in question, that the blanket expression »unpaid« was not quite maintained, and that the expression »pocket money« could be interpreted and was, although the trainees' economic situation was Spartan.

When the Agricultural Travel Bureau lost touch with the trainees, the work of obtaining prolongation permits, new places and supervision of the trainees' conditions passed from the bureau over to the »Secretariat for the Jewish Agricultural Trainees«, in theory the earlier Slor-Margolinsky committee, in practice Margolinsky, who dealt with the day-to-day work alone. The designation »committee« was changed to »secretariat«, as the occupying power did not allow the activity of the existing emigrant offices to continue. Margolinsky's secretariat now took over all the functions which had previously been covered by the travel bureau. These included liaison with the State Police, some of the work of finding places and arranging the changes for the trainees, and together with Slor, liaison with the Mosaic Religious Community, particularly in connexion with the community's financing of a great deal of the work, which after the Occupation had to be completely dependent on contributions of Danish money. In addition there was the quite personal contact with trainees, the homes and centres with guidance and activity, congratulations and encouragement. Margolinsky himself describes this transfer with the words:

»Our work (continued) quite undisturbed under the German Occupation and no obstacles have been put in the way of the Secretariat for the Jewish agricultural trainees at all. The official Danish authorities had, as hitherto, full confidence in the leaders and had sufficient experience that they were able to uphold law and order in the young people's ranks.«

The short statement can give an impression of a more streamlined form in the secretariat than there seems to be backing for in its myriads of documents. The authorities probably had confidence in the secretariat, but its dispositions were constantly supervised in detail. If the rules were not strictly kept, observations and refusals came in.

Margolinsky did not let the contact with the Agricultural Travel Bureau slip altogether. Even in June 1941, Siggaard gave Margolinsky valuable advice, partly verbally, partly in writing. On 16 June 1941, Siggaard refers, in a letter to Margolinsky, to a verbal conversation and summarizes his sober advice:

» . . . the Agricultural Travel Bureau . . . suggests that as far as possible one should avoid mentioning, on applications to the State Police, that there are agreements that pocket money should be a fixed amount. In addition, one must suggest that the secretariat, after the trainees have arrived, should avoid writing to the places of work stating that the trainees must have so and so many days' holidays. In the same way, the demands that the trainees shall have their clothes washed at the places are harmful. There are notifications that the trainees who receive good gifts at their places shall pay part of the gifts to a pool from which the less clever shall have a contribution. Such an arrangement is probably not a good idea . . . as it is practised at present . . . The complaints about the places must be investigated a little more thoroughly, so that only the good places are used, and that the poor trainees get a pep talk, so that they are prepared to become skillful agricultural trainees. That is after all why they came to this country.«

The well-meaning advice rings a little of pedantry, but Siggaard knew from long experience where the shoe could pinch, and evidently based his advice both on experience from the 1930's and on information from the police. Both formally and actually, there was a good deal in his advice. It was the categorical condition for Margolinsky's work of obtaining places and permits, that there was never a question of agreed wages or other agreed conditions, and that the trainees never replaced Danish manpower, or more realistically, that this did not let itself be proved. When the police believed that this took place refusals were received in a running stream, and new places had to be found; and a great many warnings had to be sent to trainees and homes, that there must be no official, fixed agreements. Avoidances were another matter, and they took place in large numbers. Margolinsky asserts that the trainees' conditions of work were changed, with the years, so that in 1943, most of them had obtained the same wage level as Danish farm workers.

In this many-stringed administration as Slor's nearest helper, Margolinsky came to work in close co-operation with the *Hechaluz* office, often in such a way that the two offices' work came to overlap each other. In principle the division of work was that Margolinsky looked after the actual administrative work, as well as a copious, wide-spread correspondence, for example in an attempt now and then to arrange a slender contact between certain trainees and relations in Germany, or relations in far-away countries. The possibilities for contact with German relations disappeared altogether during 1941, whilst right up to 1943, the establishment of contact with relations overseas was attempted, with a view to obtaining money and visas for possible emigration. These attempts practically always stranded on endless administrative difficulties, particularly because communication by Red Cross letters and telegrams was so extremely difficult that the provision of visas, travel possibilities and transfer of money inevitably ran into a wall of bureaucratic difficulties.

Side by side with this always chaotic administration , there was the *Hechaluz* office which, with the Occupation, received an almost impossible task. The office was staffed with the trainees' chosen representatives, and its principal duty was to keep the trainees together during training and work for their final departure at the end of that training. And now there were no possibilities for departure. For an indefinite period, the office was shut in with a vision, which up to 1939 had been compatible with practical work and concrete solutions, but which now had to fade into uncertainty. In this situation, it became the office's duty to take care of the ideological and educational side of the time of waiting. It had to keep first the *Hechaluz* group, and soon also the *Alijah* group to the Zionist idea, and as far as circumstances allowed, deepen the trainees' knowledge of the special subjects, which could serve to prepare the pupils for what was now only an uncertain prospect of life in Palestine – for this idea, in spite of the hopeless indications, they never allowed to fall. This was done through the establishment of the visiting teacher system, through the continual despatch of informative circulars to the districts, and through energetic attempts, as often as possible, to arrange seminars or other forms of meetings, with as many trainees as it could be possible to collect, in the circumstances. As occasion arose, the leaders from Nørregade 20 travelled out into the country in a tenacious attempt to build up and maintain a fellowship in spite of all external circumstances. When overlapping occurred between this office's function and Margolinsky's administration, it was partly due to the fact that Margolinsky, of necessity and by conviction, kept himself thoroughly informed on the activities in Nørregade 20, and partly because the *Hechaluz* office often interfered in the work of finding places, and particularly better suited places, for their trainees out in the country. It was almost a matter of course that the trainees normally turned to the *Hechaluz* office, when things did not turn out as they wished. There was always an enormous amount of help and support to be found from »Margo«, but the office in Nørregade was after all their »own« office, which at least in the eyes of the trainees was responsible for the *Hechaluz* group's well-being and development, even though the competence of the office had never been established, and had to be more than vague.

When trainees for some reason had not been able to find a suitable situation, a possibility for extra training, or something of the kind, they often appealed to their »own« office, which then, with or without Margolinsky's help, had to try to clear a path for them. One example can illustrate the situation. In a circular of 28 October 1941 from the *Hechaluz* office to all the trainees, there is an urgent appeal to find a place locally for a married couple, for whom it had not been possible to find places. The circular adds that funds did not allow for having them unemployed in Copenhagen for a longer period. It was often the trainees that found suitable places, and it was up to Margolinsky to get the necessary approval granted. There are countless examples of this overlapping work. It was Margolinsky who normally kept the trainees informed on the rules which had to be strictly kept, when places were changed, as they so often were. But this did not prevent the *Hechaluz* office in a circular of 14 April 1942 from backing this up by impressing the regulations on the trainees with an order that they keep strictly to the authorities' demand, and a warning that the latter were very particular.

Normally, finding places posed no great difficulties, but now and then it could be hard especially for married couples. It proved particularly difficult in the autumn 1940, where both farmers and trainees were uncertain as to the possible complications in the situation. Margolinsky then turned to Siggaard, and asked him to help, which he readily did, and at the same time, Margolinsky sent out a circular to all the trainees with a request for them to find work places locally. He explained that, because of the sudden immigration in the last 1½ years before the Occupation, it had been impossible to find suitable places, and asked them to obtain offers, preferably on farms of 50–120 acres land, and of course preferably »suitable« places, that is, places which were not too isolated. There was great joy when a good place was found. »At last we have succeeded in finding a place for Leopold. I can assure you, dear Margo, it is extremely difficult to find anything now, and certainly not when it is a condition that there must be other employees. He has been running from pillar to post, but if they can get a work permit, everyone must be pleased.« The »they« in the letter was the farmer, who had to have the approval of the police. »Honoured Mr. Margolinsky! Wonders will never cease! The new place in the case of my wife and myself is with the farmer X. I have informed the police of the move.« Both examples are from the autumn 1940, and in both instances it was a question of married couples, who at least wanted to work near each other. Later the problem became much easier to solve.

It is impossible to draw a definite borderline between the two offices' sphere of activity. They supplemented each other without marking out the limits. In many cases Margolinsky followed the individual trainee's situation, gave guidance, instructions, and encouragement, or obtained permits, sent congratulations, etc. In his care for them he often crossed into *Hechaluz*'s territory, while the latter sometimes took administrative decisions. This little Jewish enclave had to live a day at a time, without definite, fixed rules as to who had the authority for this or that.

The Consequences of the Occupation

The Occupation had naturally to have immeasurable consequences. The first consequence was that already mentioned, that the whole future became uncertain. This was a consequence which hit trainees, children, homes, leaders and authorities. All decisions, all activities and all permits had been based on the definite condition that there was a question of a purely temporary arrangement, a training or case with a time limit, followed by a continuation of emigration to Palestine. Now it all lay in ruins, and no one could foresee how long the postponement would last, or what conditions the Occupation would bring. All that was clear, after the German military triumphs in 1940 and 1941, was that there was a question of years and not of months, and that the possibilities for rescue must lie hidden in an incalculable, but in every sense faraway future – if there ever was a rescue.

The problem here was not acute nor particularly urgent for the farming families which had Jewish agricultural trainees in their service. The fields had to be cultivated at all events, and whether this was to be done by Danish or Jewish manpower must be of secondary importance to most farmers, even if many farming families felt with the trainees, and tried as far as they could to share their anxiety about their hopeless prospects. It was different for the families which had *Alijah* children in their care. They had volunteered for a temporary task, and they had a more care-oriented attitude to the work than was the case at the *Hechaluz* trainees' places of work. These homes were now encumbered with an extra burden. The reason for this is obvious. It was one thing for a family to take care of a child in need for a limited period, and shoulder the duties of a foster-home for a time. It was quite another matter, in spite of all the good-will, if months were to pass, or years, before the fostering could come to an end. And it was yet a third matter, when it became quite uncertain whether it ever would come to an end, and if so in what circumstances. Perhaps the expression »Jewish child«, as it had been used in the appeals to the foster-families, was somewhat misleading, and had suggested false associations when it was used in 1939. It had contained an appeal to feelings which did not quite fit in with the realities which time would bring. Many of the children were in fact 16 years old when they arrived. When they stayed – and had to stay – until October 1943, the 15-year-old had become 19, and the problems of clothes, education, and physical and intellectual development had to accumulate.

The conditions of occupation did not make things any easier. The families had volunteered in peacetime, and on the basis of peacetime conditions, but first the War and then the Occupation created conditions which could not have been foreseen. The position was drastically altered by insecurity, situations of lack, and tension, which increased in all the homes where not only material but moral responsibilities were felt. The arrangements became out of date, without the foster-parents having any influence as regards the underlying and determining factors. It probably helped matters that the children were in the country, where conditions brought about by the Occupation, such as rationing and the black-out, and later the curfew, etc., were not felt so acutely as in the towns, and where the occupying troops' green uniforms seldom showed themselves, if ever. But even in the most peaceful village, the shadow of the Occupation lay over daily life and thinking.

The material difficulties were only the lesser side of it. Even trivial everyday problems became extremely relevant for the one who has an acute, momentary need, and children and families were to struggle with many trivial problems. Clothes, shoes, bicycles and petty requirements had to be procured, at a time when their provision was difficult, and the letters from the *Alijah* homes to the League's office were full of questions and trivial problems. A promise had been given, when the *Alijah* children arrived, that luggage and bicycles would be sent after them, but in countless instances, the promise was not fulfilled, and the child could have been robbed of everything but the clothes he or she stood up in. Working clothes, winter clothes and rubber boots were not luxury articles, when there was work to be done in the fields or stables, in all kinds of weather; and a bicycle supplied the child's only means of access to education and to meetings with comrades. None of this was easily obtained, and trivial problems of this kind gave the League office an inordinate amount of worry and trouble. Much of it was solved by the fosterparents, but they were far from always able, practically or financially, to find solutions. To help with the problem of clothes, the Jewish Women's Society set up a clothes centre, which received and distributed second-hand clothes and shoes, and a similar centre was started by Mrs. Ulla Blatt, the wife of the Aarhus professor. The stream of requests gave a great deal of worry, and bicycles and bicycle tyres constituted a problem of their own, as for the Danish population.

Obtaining clothes, bicycles and other necessities was also an economic question, and there were never enough, when things became worn out or growth demanded new sizes. Some vanity may have played a role, even though the times were not exactly fashionminded. In February 1941, the League office had to write to the district chairmen about both clothes and bicycles – mostly clothes. The office, after careful negotiations with the clothes centre, had to instruct the district chairmen:

»that for the future, account must *only* be taken of the clothes questionnaires which are sent *here to headquarters;* that no account will be taken of any clothes questionnaires which are not signed by the foster-parents and recommended by the district chairman. There are now so *few clothes* and so *little money* to dispose of, the homes and district chairman are asked, from all sides, that the children do not make too great demands . . . *There is no money for more.*«

The last sentence was heavily underlined, twice. An enquiry was added to the instructions, after the bicycles from the children who had left Denmark in December, which had not been sent in. From the 44 homes only 3 cycles had been returned, and the office asked the district chairmen to arrange for the rest to be sent immediately.

The League's work depended upon the members' modest subscriptions and occasional contributions. Since no publicity was possible, this meant poverty for an office which was strained to the utmost and constantly undermanned, with voluntary workers alone.

But when deliveries did come from Copenhagen, there was great joy. When a national meeting was held in the early summer 1941, small contributions were made, unasked, and when 50 crowns from these were sent to one of the district chairmen, thanks were prompt:

»I have used them for a raincoat and underclothes. How I wish that these unknown givers could see Hertha's grateful face. This girl has never been lucky and had no proper clothes. She had practically no clothes, when she came to Denmark, some of her comrades have helped her and given her some nice things from their clothes. She needed a raincoat badly, so now I took this opportunity, and bought one for her. Will you give . . . the children's thanks . . . and thank the givers for the money, which has been well used. They are all happy that Hertha acquired a raincoat.«

Hardships of this kind were, of course, trivialities in the whole context, but as long as the triviality existed for an individual, it was far from being felt as a triviality. First and last, however, it was the gloom of the War and the year-long, restless time of waiting, as well as the »children's« growing independence which was bound to create difficulties. Motherly care for the 15-year-old, who in 1942 was now 18, was neither enough nor desired. As »the children« from 1939 grew up, it was actually undesirable.

There are great changes, at all events, between a letter from September 1939 and a circular from January 1941. In September 1939 the *Hechaluz* leader Jizchaki can write to Thora Daugaard that, as arranged, he has been in Aarhus to receive a group of children whom he had undertaken to accompany to the foster-homes on Mors. The journey had gone well, and the foster-parents had turned out to meet them on the quay in Nykøbing Mors.

134

»We have placed the children on Mors, following your permission for it. At my visit I found all the children, without exception, satisfied and happy. They have no words to describe the love, kindness and care which the farmers have met them with. The farmers, too, are very satisfied with the children, so everything seems to be working towards a harmonious life in fellowship.«

Jizchaki mentions language difficulties, but adds that this will right itself, with time, and he says that certain ritual problems have also been arranged with great understanding on the part of the farmers. The letter breathes optimism, and hints at an idyllic beginning. In contrast with this, there is a circular from the League headquarters to all the children on Fyn in January 1941. Here, to put it mildly, there is no idyll. The letter is at the same time stern, and – in motherly tones – admonishing. It contains a strict order to the children under no circumstances to leave their homes and collect in groups, on the excuse of the necessity of school attendance. They must not take long bicycle rides on the main road, they must not telephone, and if they receive a different message from a visiting teacher, this message is not to be obeyed. They must in all circumstances stay at their homes. The circular was prompted by a large number of worried letters from a number of families, who felt that the children – who were no longer children – were slipping away from their homes, partly because of their understandable urge for mutual comradeship and for being with the visiting teachers of the districts. The families then felt their responsibilities, which became more and more difficult to live up to. Individual letters from Thora Daugaard to individual families are couched in the same worried tone. Here, a single example from June 1941:

»The work with these poor maltreated Jewish children must, after all, be regarded in the first place as a deed of mercy. There is one thing which complicates matters. The boy must *learn* something, but may not be given 'wages' and may not take the place of a paid worker. Next: the boy must go to school and be allowed to meet his fellow-Jews if the occasion arises, but in the *present* circumstances they must not bicycle too much on the roads, and especially not in flocks. It is not at all easy, either for the homes, the children, or us.«

There were many reasons for local anxiety: the children's age, maturity and ever-increasing urge for independence; the influence of the visiting teachers and comrades in a Zionist direction, which could seem quite incomprehensible for many foster-families, and also the conditions of occupation, which created an extraordinary sense of insecurity. What could not happen to »the child« on the often long rides to the day's meeting-place, and how late did he come home from the constant meetings with equals or teachers? On top of the worries which are familiar to all parents, for the children's well-being, there were the special worries which the black-out and unsafe roads produced, if in no other way, then in the imagination of worried foster-parents, who at intervals complained to Thora Daugaard, and later also to Margolinsky. There were naturally big differences between the homes, and there was an enormous difference between 1939 and 1943. In by far the most instances, matters were cleared up in the homes or in discussion with district chairmen, and the general satisfaction seldom reached headquarters in Copenhagen. But if problems arose in a district, they were posted upwards in the system, and could then take on glaring proportions, quite out of balance with the realities of the affair, as in a letter in January 1943 from a district chairman to Margolinsky, where, regarding the local *Alijah* group, it reads:

» . . . similarly they cast their dissatisfaction over us, and we have no responsibility at all for the forms under which the Ministry of Justice have given them their residence permits in this country. God give that peace may soon come, so that the impatient young people can travel to their desired destination. In the hope that you, with your authority, will be able to persuade the family (the visiting teacher) to leave . . . and also ask the family . . . from keeping the young people until late at night. There are constant complaints about them – they know it quite well – but they want absolutely to revolt, and we are all quite dumbfounded at the shameless way in which they continue to behave . . .«

This indignant outburst from a lady, who for four years had devoted unbounded time and all her energies to helping the children to get a quiet, secure existence, can only be understood if one takes the date into consideration. The children from 1939 had become young rebels, at a time when the Government's admonitions on law and order probably worked in a pacifistic home, but was increasingly waved aside by a population in growing illegalisation. And in that climate, young Jews, more than all others, must feel themselves drawn to whatever approached conspiracy, and if possible participation in a dawning resistance. If it was only a question of reading and distributing illegal news sheets it was bad enough. Margolinsky's reply gently and patiently smoothed over what he must have considered a storm in a teacup.

This was in 1943, when problems could be approaching breaking-point, but anxiety already arose in 1940 about the special occupation conditions and the risk they could contain for the *Alijah* children, as when a district chairman from Sjælland writes in to Thora Daugaard in connexion with two boys wanting to travel to Thy, to visit a comrade. A question as to whether this was advisable received the following reply:

»Yes, if they have the money for the journey, there should not be any objection on our part. The trouble is, whether they might meet surprises, crossing the Great Belt which is still under the foreigners' control. Not that I believe that this should be any obstacle, but still, I will make that reservation by pointing out the difficulty which is certainly present.«

Yes, the Occupation left its mark. Its conditions created difficulties for foster-parents, district chairmen and leaders, and they were difficulties piled on the top of far greater difficulties – passage of time, developments and nervous tension – which the long internment created.

Security Zones

The first months of occupation passed without having concrete consequences for the immigrant trainees and children. But in November 1940, North and West Jylland were declared »security zones« by the German Army, and with that, immigrants, families and leaders were faced with new problems.

On 23 November, Thora Daugaard wrote to the district chairmen in Thisted and Holstebro: »So the hammer has fallen. The children in North and West Jylland – on the German Army's orders – have to be moved. We have written to the district chairmen involved, and you will perhaps get in touch with them, if you think it necessary.«

The practical problems in connexion with the moves fell to the leaders in Copenhagen; the trainees, children and foster-families had to share the psychological problems. Many of the trainees had settled down well, and for all those involved the order meant a new break in an already disturbed existence, quite apart from the fact that it was a warning of the German authorities' watchfulness over the Jewish emigrants. So they were neither hidden nor forgotten. In addition, the order came after both the travel bureau and Margolinsky, as well as the League's leaders, had carried out a number of moves, and had just set up some centres in the area. Now came new moves, but with them also a chance to close ranks around the districts and in areas which were still »free«. In practice it turned out that there were enough farming families who were willing to receive trainees or children, and most of the moves went smoothly, although only two days' notice had been given, and although no fewer than 65 of the League children, alone, were involved.

Six months later, however, more difficulties arose. In June 1941, the German »security zone« was extended again, to include mid-Jylland and Bornholm, and again moves had to take place. This time there was slightly longer notice, and the Occupation had now lasted so long that German orders did not give the same effect of a crack of the whip as in 1940. But marching orders did come, and hit, among others, a number of agricultural trainees on Bornholm, and a fairly large group of League children, who had just settled down with their visiting teacher in the Østbirk district north-west of Horsens. Here the move was announced in a number of letters from Thora Daugaard to the visiting teacher, the local district chairman and the district chairman in Vejle, who were asked to find foster-homes as soon as possible in the Vejle-Kolding area. The local district chairman received the final instructions on 20 June 1941 on moving 30 children, and a little glimpse of the League office's difficulties:

»It is quite out of the question to move the children to Sjælland and Fyn. They are so overburdened, that it simply cannot be done, until the most acute need arises. There could sooner be a question of Lolland/Falster, but for the time being there is after all, a refuge in Jylland, to which the journey is not all too expensive, and these 30 children can remain with their visiting teacher, which I consider very necessary. If we have to bring them to Sjælland and Fyn the group will be split up and none of us want that.«

The refuge was the Vejle-Kolding area, where the district chairman on 19 June was asked to obtain places, since no one might be placed south of the Kongeå, as South Jylland was also a closed area. The problem was not solved with that, however. For one reason, because the German order was so vague that for several days, people were in doubt as to where the actual northern border of the »refuge« went, and added to this, the Foreign Ministry and the police announced in the middle of the move that they considered it unwise to move the children to the Vejle area, »as it is expected that the children would have to move again before long«. In a letter of 19 June, to one of the families in the Vejle area that had volunteered a foster-home, Thora Daugaard mentioned her difficulties: »Now that the security zone has been extended in Jylland, we must move 30 children from where they are, just north of Horsens down south of Vejle, or where we can find room for them. It is not easy, but we have had slightly longer notice this time than last, when 65 had to be moved in two days.« On 10 July, the visiting teacher had to be informed that the children could not be settled in the Vejle area, but had to go to Fyn and Sjælland; this was then changed and some of the children were temporarily collected in the Vejle district.

The problem was not only to find homes in the district, limited as it had become – still more limited in that the police did not allow the children and trainees to be placed in the Copenhagen county, where there was a great deal of unemployment in 1941 – but also in that the League's office could not accept every offer of foster-homes, when the principle of keeping the children together in districts was to be maintained. And both the *Hechaluz* office and Margolinsky insisted on this, at first to Thora Daugaard's dismay. But she had promised good will, and in spite of all the trials she lived up to her promise, although, in the first weeks of the immigration, her quite understandable irritation slipped out, as it did in a letter in September 1939 to the district chairman on Mors:

»In the committee, I must now be allowed to say, the general impression was – and this applies also to the Jews on the committee – that what was the principal task was to get the children out to freedom and peace, and straighten them out a little, both mentally and physically. I do not know of one single Jew in the Mosaic Religious Community, who places such enormous emphasis on this teaching. It is principally the young Zionists who have come up here as agricultural trainees, who are so zealous in this respect, and perhaps one cannot complain at it. It is good, when we can help them, but it gets more and more difficult to centralize all these many children.«

Here the distance between the *Hechaluz* trainees and the resident Danish Jews is more than hinted at. The latter supported the former, but the former went their own way.

The order in June also had consequences for the quite large number of trainees staying on Bornholm. Long before the German order came, Margolinsky had had considerable misgivings about too much concentration on Bornholm. On 27 October 1939, when the League was preparing to receive a new group of *Alijah* children, he wrote to Thora Daugaard and expressed his doubts as to the advisability of placing children on the distant island of Bornholm, where many families had volunteered homes:

»This *could* perhaps have unfortunate consequences... You may perhaps know that we have some young people over there, some fishers, some farmers. Because of the situation mentioned, a number of these young people have felt themselves rather isolated from the rest of the world, and if the present situation continues or perhaps becomes more acute, communication with the rest of the country may become even more difficult, I am afraid that this circumstance can have a psychologically unfortunate effect on the children, whose psychological constitution is sometimes rather unstable.«

Now the situation had become more acute, and the result was that a start was made on moving a number of persons to Sjælland – a process which had actually been going on from the spring 1941 – and the idea of expanding the group of fishermen had to be shelved. This small group had shrunken to three men. After a time of practice, they had been allowed to train at Rønne Navigation School and in 1941 had just finished a one-year term there, financed by the Mosaic Religious Community, and were now ready to resume fishing. The order on the security zone seemed to preclude this. A large number of plans were discussed, back and forth, on transferring them to Reersø, Kerteminde or Marstal. The plans for this were proposed by the trainees themselves, after fishing in Tejn, where they had come into contact with fishermen from this area of the Great Belt, which was not a closed area, and where the fishermen had shown themselves prepared to receive them. The plans for this were not realised, however, and perhaps the control with the Bornholm area was not particularly effective. At all events, the three fishermen remained on the island, and this was later to have consequences not only for them, but also for others.

Districts

If the problem had been purely humanitarian, its solution would have been easier. But the problem was not purely humanitarian, and not at all for the *Hechaluz* group. The young pupils had not come to Denmark to find refuge, but to prepare themselves for their pioneer existence, and in the eyes of the *Hechaluz* leaders and many of the pupils, there was a danger that an enforced, long stay could tempt the least Zionist-oriented to take root in Danish soil, seek advanced education here, and distance themselves from the movement and its fellowship.

It was no easy task to hold the group together and the trainees to the original, primary idea of emigration, which was pushed out into a distant future by the Occupation, and could perhaps never be put into practice. The task fell to the trainees' leaders, the *Maskirut*, who administered the *Hechaluz* office in Copenhagen, and another elected body, the board of leaders of *Merkas*, together a trusted and varying inner circle. This latter group had to be largely chosen *ad hoc*, from the best qualified and most committed, since a formal election was excluded because of the actual dispersal of the trainees and the impossibility of bringing all the trainees together at the same time. The movement was democratic by conviction and in theory, but the little Jewish *Hechaluz* enclave had to live dispersed, in Danish society, without a constitution, rules, or the possibility of administering other than unwritten laws.

If the task had been difficult throughout the 1930's, it was actually impossible, when the War and the Occupation created an enormous blockage in the work. Up to 1939, all trainees had been able to live in the knowledge that sooner or later they would obtain the certificates which meant emigration to their final goal. A certificate could arrive with a few days' warning. But from 1939, emigration became not only a distant aim, which faded in misty ideology. Perhaps it would be unthinkable for years, and what would the future bring? Should the individual trainee think about adjusting his plans, on account of the new, unformed realities? And what plans were thinkable at all?

In this situation, untiring work was needed, if the movement was to be held together, and the leaders shrank from no efforts, even in the new, desperate situation, to bring the movement through the maelstrom years of occupation. The means used were partly stubborn work, as far as possible to collect the trainees in groups, where they could maintain and deepen their solidarity, partly by regular visits to the groups by delegates from the headquarters in Copenhagen, for conversations, debates and discussions of practical and ideological questions, and also the issue of circulars to the members of *Merkas*, interlarded with letters and articles from the *Merkas* members and others, where practical, organisational and ideological information and viewpoints were set forth. Now and then there were also letters from the leaders of the *Hechaluz* movement in Sweden, and up to 1940, single letters from Palestine. The contents of the circulars could thus be spread throughout the groups for further debate and orientation. None of this was new. The same thing had happened in the 1930's. But within the confines of the Occupation, and in a situation, the consequences of which had become insuperable, and where all plans and debates had to be hypothetical, the work became more important than ever. Who, in 1941, could know that the end of

Alijah youth from the Faaborg district, gathered in Horne on South Fyn.

their stay in Denmark would come two years later, and that the Occupation would come to an end in four years' time? Could it last ten years, could it become permanent? It needed faith as well as will to keep up ones courage, but there was no lack of either in the *Hechaluz* office.

In a circular from the *Hechaluz* office in 1939, to all newly arrived trainees, a great deal of information was given on working conditions, formalities, equipment with clothes and shoes, money questions, free time and travel, etc. In a special section the necessary cultural work was dealt with, in the circumstances as they were:

»As you know we have no placing here in kibbutzes, only placing in centres that is, within a circumference of some kilometres, 10 to 20 trainees are placed in various places. One meets several times a week, in most cases in our own rooms, but also in the homes of farmers, clergymen, etc. There are only special cultural advisers or visiting teachers in very few of the centres. So each centre is left to its own resources. Delegates from the office visit the centres at regular intervals, about once a fortnight. In the summer, particularly, meetings are held of neighbouring centres.«

In this way, building on the available material, every effort was made to cement the movement together, and when the immigration of *Alijah* children took place, it was their hope and intention, also to convert this group to Zionism. After this, the work began as soon as the children came

142

Alijah youth from the Odense district, gathered for a meeting in Dømmestrup.

to Denmark, and as we have seen, its first and decisive condition was to collect the children in groups, a solution which could only be used after a while, and always only partially, as it was always a question of interpretation whether a home was so near the middle of a district that it could reasonably be considered as belonging to it. It could make a difference, here, whether it was summer or winter, fair weather or snowstorm. An appeal must also be made to the foster-parents' understanding for a cause which they often did not understand. And here distance and the state of the roads played a part. Not all the families liked to see their foster-children go out on long tours to distant teaching centres, often in bad weather, and the fonder the foster-parents were of the child and felt responsible for him or her, the more they must dislike it.

And where were the centres, then? It is not possible to answer the question, as the group and the centre was started, dissolved, newly created or moved, and its locality therefore changed, right from the first immigration, with the moves caused by outside circumstances. »I lived/worked in the period from April 1939 to October 1943, on 6 different farms in all,« is not an exceptional remark in the accounts. On the contrary, it is typical. They all changed their places of residence, from a farm to a different farm, to an agricultural school, to yet another farm and in a new district. But in the circulars from the *Hechaluz* office to the

143

members of the *Merkas* there is normally a list of the centres existing at that moment. A list from 6 February 1942 can give a reasonably average picture. Here one operated with centres in ... Faaborg, Fredensborg, Frederikssund, Holbæk, Haslev, Gelsted, Odense, Ringe and also with the centre in Copenhagen, which included the *Hechaluz* office personnel. At this point, as already mentioned, the centres were concentrated on Fyn-Sjælland. If one goes back to 1939–40, and the time before the security zones were set up, one finds centres in Jylland and on Bornholm, on a line with other localities with centres on the islands. Here the place names appear of, Aalborg, Silkeborg, Skanderborg, Aarhus, Fredericia, Kolding and Bornholm, and on the islands, new place names such as Faxe, Roskilde and Fuglebjerg. The words »centre« or »district« need further explanation. The place names mentioned are mostly names of towns, although the trainees lived in the country. There is a question, therefore, of an approximate locality, and nothing more.

Crisis and Criticism

It should be obvious that the long confinement under the Occupation was bound to undermine the many efforts to maintain the trainees' solidarity. Purely physical conditions such as the limited possibilities for travel, lack of money, and the fact that they were bound by the working rhythm of their service played their part, and there is an evident stubbornness in the leaders' unremitting struggle to keep the movement together. This became more and more difficult as the prospects of emigration faded. This distant possibility must naturally be dominant in the thoughts of all of them, and long after the occupation had taken place, the *Hechaluz* leaders had still not quite given up the idea of a theoretical chance. As described earlier, in the first weeks of occupation, a few trainees had escaped through Sweden, and in March 1941, many still clung to the hope of emigration. In a circular from the *Hechaluz* office, of 13 March 1941, a weak hope still fluttered:

»You have read that last week a second transport of *Jugendalijah* took place. With this, 5 *chawerim* have also crossed to Sweden. When other groups can leave is not clear at the moment. The political situation on the travel route is stable, it is true, but at any moment, a change can, naturally, take place.«

The circular then explains that 350 certificates have been granted for Palestine, which run out on 31 March, and if they have not been used by then, they will be redistributed. The possibility that Scandinavia will then receive a quota is mentioned, in connexion with the Jews in the Balcans, who now are exposed to the same difficulties as the Jews in Denmark. But even at best, one must reckon with a possible completion of emigration taking a long time.

There was no completion! No one left the country after March 1941, and in May, the leaders faced up to the reality, in a circular to members of the *Merkas* group. The circular deals with the problem that a number of trainees were separating themselves from the movement, and gives several reasons for this development: the pupils wish to be free of the payments to their common pool, *»Masser«*, their wish to get special training, and so leave their circles, and many of the trainees wish to attach themselves to comrades who are particularly close to them, which also contributes to breaking up the established circles. This negative development is then discussed:

»The explanation is quite simple. So long as our movement gave trainees the prospect of emigration, one was often ready to submit to decisions which, for the individual, meant the limitation of personal wishes. Today, this element is no longer present, and the consequent reaction is clearly seen ... In addition, Copenhagen's help with regard to finances was previously of the greatest importance. Now this picture has changed, as the trainee gets by far the largest part of his oncome from his place of work.«

There was naturally no question of actual resignation from a fellowship which had no binding form. It was rather a matter of passive defection, which did not always come to the knowledge of the leaders, and which could only be registered indirectly, by the trainee's absence from gatherings, or when he gave no sign of life for some time, but went his own way. But it did happen that a trainee gave direct expression to his disappointment and frustration at the movement's stifling impotence, and wrongly transferred his bitterness to the Copenhagen leaders. In March 1942, a trainee wrote sarcastically to Margolinsky from Børkop High School, on the lack of support received from the leaders in Copenhagen. He withdrew, as regards continuing agricultural training, declaring himself unsuited to this work, and then continued:

»Now you can count up all the reproaches you have ready ... yes, why have you come to Denmark, or:, I ought to be happy to be free in this country – in comparison to many many other Jews, etc. etc. I've heard that several times, and I understand it, too – but the natural way for us human beings is to go forward, to go up – and if one has spent 7 years with something called *Hachscharah* and has waited and waited and been disappointed and disappointed, again and again, well, then it's no wonder that some fine day one wakes up from his ecstacy . . . As far as *Hechaluz* is concerned, I just have a sympathetic smile, when I think of them! It is a shame that more and more leave *Hechaluz*, won't they soon have to stop the work for lack of 'manpower'.«

Margolinsky's answer was caustic. He stated briefly that he had, as requested, put the trainee's papers in order, and concluded: »I should be glad if in future you would refrain from all too many immature and clownish remarks in your letters to me, as I can assure you that even without your stupidities, our work gives cause for many serious anxieties.«

Margolinsky's letters were nearly always helpful and understanding, and in close co-operation with the *Hechaluz* office, he tried as far as he could, to open the way for the hundreds out in the country. But when, as here, he and the other leaders in Copenhagen met reproaches, wrongly addressed, he could give as good as he got. And here it certainly was the wrong address. It was a clear illustration, however, that the powerlessness inherent in the situation could lead to the trainees' desertion.

Since the leaders had had to put the hope of an imminent emigration behind them, and all expectations must therefore be dashed, a reaction was perhaps understandable. If *Hechaluz* could not help, who could? Each trainee must be tempted to look for other solutions. One cannot measure misgivings in numbers, and yet the *Hechaluz* office tried to make an estimate of the numbers, in a circular of February 1942. The result was depressing. In the words of the circular:

»We still have 281 *chawerim* today, whom we can describe as *chawerim* attached to *Hechaluz*, that is, all the men and women trainees who have neither declared their resignation because of emigration abroad or for other reasons, or have been directly excluded from *Merkas*. Of these 281 *chawerim*, 120 are in centres and 161 *chawerim* are outside the centres . . . This large number of *chawerim* outside the centres will surprise everyone, also those who actually are very well informed on our movement.«

The statement continues with an analysis of who contributes financial support (*Masser*) to the movement, and notes that all those who live in centres do this – as a matter of course – while contributions have only come in from 44 of those who live outside the centres. The writers then make a retrospective analysis of the whole organisational form, as it has developed, and state: »The organisation, which covers all the agricultural trainees in the country and is responsible for them, is the Secretariat for Jewish Agricultural Trainees,« but at the *Hechaluz* office they note that this has only found its present form after quite a long period of development, and the form must be discussed: »We can no longer be interested in being a movement which includes all the trainees, but we must try to carry out our work in the circles of trainees who today still consider themselves as belonging to us.«

This discouraging stocktaking led, during March/April 1942, to a reorganisation and tightening up of the *Hechaluz* work. In a circular to the members of *Merkas* of 13 March, seven clearly defined points were set out, fixing the conditions on which trainees could rank as members of the movement:

1. The will to go to Palestine.
2. The duty of physical work.
3. The duty to live in a centre fellowship, unless there are reasons (against it) recognized by *Merkas*.
4. The duty to learn Hebrew.
5. The duty of each trainee to submit, in a centre, to social equalization among the trainees of the fellowship.
6. The duty to pay *Masser*.
7. The duty to take part in the cultural work as laid down by the *Hechaluz* movement.

Trainees who fulfilled these obligations, after having distanced themselves from the movement, if approved by *Merkas*, could be reinstated and would in that case receive a membership card. A new circular followed on 30 April 1942, in which trainees were asked to work to expand the existing centres and start new, so that as many as possible of the trainees outside the centres had the opportunity of joining the movement, particularly married couples with children, who found it difficult to join or manage to live in the centres:

»Many trainees, especially married couples with children, would like to join the centres, if they were given the possibility for it. We must once and for all realise how essential it would be to bring in these very trainees, so that, above all else, their children do not lose all their connexions, in completely non-Jewish surroundings. We already have children who are in danger of becoming totally danicized'.«

Danicization! That was the real danger, in the eyes of the firebrands of the Zionist movement in Denmark. The problem arose and was intensified, the longer residence here lasted, and that was something on which the *Hechaluz* leaders, however keen, could have no influence.

The appeals and the increased strictness gave results. In October 1942, in a new circular – which this time did not only go to the members of *Merkas*, but as far as possible to all the trainees – the writers could register that the movement now numbered 285 trainees, of whom 30 were orthodox Jews living in colonies in North Sjælland. 88 trainees no longer belonged to the movement, and of them 33 had actually been excluded. But there were still only 152 trainees in centres. These centres were and continued to be a project and a hope, which was never quite fulfilled. The numbers tell us, incidentally, that a number of *Alijah* children had now joined the movement.

As things were, with dispersed residence and constant moves, it must be impossible to establish a real trainee democracy. The election of leaders – and this applied to both *Merkas* and *Maskirut* – had necessarily to be somewhat haphazard, and electors and elected belonged to an inner circle, who, according to the circumstances, could take part in the meetings collected at intervals, with the participation of those trainees who were able to come and who were not prevented from taking part because of their work or their geographical situation – and this was as a rule the majority of the trainees. Some inbreeding among the leaders was bound to manifest itself, and this could give rise to criticism, bordering on revolt. In May 1941, one of the trainees sent out a circular on his own initiative, »*Chawer spricht zu Chawer*«, to all the trainees whose addresses he could get hold of. Here he violently attacked the »office leaders« in Copenhagen, who in his opinion were out of touch with the realities of the working trainees out in the country, and who laid far too much emphasis on theory. He accused the leaders in harsh terms of paternalism and underhand arrangements which in his opinion prevailed in the group of leaders:

»So we believe that 'the powers that be' in our *Hachscharah* have always been an affair for a small group of people, who also constantly and on their own evaluation, expand, contract and reorganise. Certain external circumstances in Copenhagen, on which we are completely dependent, have simply favoured this line even more.«

His argumentation proceeded to the basic question, as to how one could establish a really democratic election of leaders, with decisions put to all the trainees in and outside the centres. Here there was a question of the formation of a wing within the movement, with an appeal to write and enroll.

The circular caused a hot, temperamental debate in other circulars to the *Merkas* members, but the fact was probably that the idea of wider influence was not practicable. The situation was too hopeless for that. The strict leadership was partly determined by that situation, and very likely, the only possibility. In spite of all the talk of centres, the trainees dispersed during the constant moves from one place of work to another, or from a place of work to a training school, now here, now there. It was a question of emigrants wandering through a foreign land, where circumstances had put a stop to all their plans, and had made it an open question, what their rights and their duties were, and who was responsible for them and had duties to them, or who could act on their behalf. In November 1941, they lost their German citizenship on a unilateral German decision, and if one probes into the question of who actually was competent to act on their behalf, the secretariat, the *Hechaluz* leaders, the Danish or German authorities, their places of work, the local police, etc., one soon finds out that there is no answer. Dependent and outlawed, they had to live from month to month with the circumstances as they were, and without being able to claim rights or fix binding rules for their internal organisation. It was in this situation, that Slor, the *Hechaluz* leader, and Margolinsky's secretariat had to try to intervene with regulations and leadership, and struggle for an authority which never was or could be legally and formally established. Those who would act, acted, and so had to hope that persons and authorities would approve decisions and initiatives.

Seminars

Ever since the creation of »*Kibbuz-Alijah-Dänemark*« in 1933, one of the main tasks of the *Hechaluz* office had been to care for the spiritual needs of the trainees, and make sure that they became ideologically prepared for life in Palestine. On the existing material, ones thoughts can follow it back to a circular with trainee contributions from October 1935, sent out by the *Hechaluz* office. In this the writers emphasize that the office »will and must refuse exclusively to serve as an organisational organ for the transfer of people from dispersal in exile to Palestine. Trainees who regard the organisational tasks as the centre for its tasks basically misunderstand these tasks.« It is developed further that it is a main task for the office to prepare the coming immigrants for life in Palestine, and that this demands precise knowledge of the conditions which will meet them, after an immigration which can be delayed. This preparation did not only apply to the agricultural training, but also to a comprehensive theoretical and political education, expressed, for example, in these words from a representative of the Jewish trades organisation:

»The *Alijah* serves to realise our aim, the concentration of the Jewish masses in Palestine, in the creation of an actual Jewish home, including: The solution of the Jewish question. The quantitative solution will only become positive, if it is connected with the qualitative. A large number of immigrants will be of no value, if these simply transfer the abnormal business pyramid from their exile to Palestine. Palestine will only be the home for the Jewish masses, if a strong, resident, agriculturally-oriented work of colonisation can arise, and if, connected with this, the basis can be found for a healthy social structure and a progressive Jewish culture.«

It was ideas of this kind, which in the 1930's had led the *Hechaluz* office to devote much time and great efforts to the work of training, and particularly the special Jewish cultural work. One of the means to this was to hold seminars, when time, money and circumstances allowed. In the 1930's, such seminars could receive impulses from outside, in the form of visiting lecturers, for example from Palestine, but after the Occupation it was necessary to manage with their own and local talent. The seminars came as an addition to the regular cultural work out in the centres, with or without visits from the leaders in Copenhagen, and they were important as forums for general debates on ideological and practical questions. Obviously, everyone could not take part, but as large a participation as possible was aimed at.

A description of the many seminars which were held, during the Occupation, does not come within the framework of this book, but to illustrate the form, subjects and course of such a seminar, a particularly important and long seminar will be mentioned, which was held at the International High School in Helsingør, from 20.12.1939 to 7.1.1940, in all 17 days. This seminar was especially important, because the possibility became evident that the *Hechaluz* trainees' stay in Denmark might be a long one; that the *Hechaluz* group might become quite isolated; and because at this seminar it was possible to go through the educational programme, which was just beginning, for the *Alijah* children who were

150

Members of the Hechaluz movement, collected for a seminar in 1941.

arriving. The seminar numbered 37 participants from the centres, 8 from among the *Hechaluz* leaders in Copenhagen, and 9 chosen visiting teachers. In addition, there were a few lecturers, 2 from abroad and 4 or 5 from Denmark.

The time table was long, with meetings and discussions from 9 a.m. to late at night, and the list of subjects shows that the plan must been long: Hebrew, Hebrew literature, the history of Palestine, the conditions of the population, young people's problems, young people's psychology and the question of upbringing, Jewish literature and Jewish history, Zionist history, excavations in Babylon, Jewish economy and sociology, agriculture and the co-operative movement in Denmark, and the Danish peasant classes in the 18th century. Also a number of discussions on topical subjects, and the preparation of the visiting teachers' coming educational programme. The seminar, lying on the borderline between a normal and abnormal situation, was both longer, broader and better attended than later seminars, which had to be completed in a shorter time, with fewer participants and narrower frameworks of subjects.

In addition to technically oriented seminars, there were a great many more informal meetings and gatherings, whenever and wherever these could be arranged. In the midst of Danish surroundings, which could be very friendly, but also often extremely monotonous, the trainees often had a restless need to meet companions in adversity, and in spite of all the differences, with the same background for their time in Denmark.

A Zionist Task

With the immigration of the *Alijah* children, a formidable task presented itself to the leaders of the *Hechaluz* group in Denmark: to inform the many children, with very different backgrounds, and in widely different momentary situations, on the deeper reasons for their present position, and the distant life which the Zionist movement offered them for a possible solution of their future existence. The children must be given a hope in the future and an aim for it, and it must be explained to them why they were now in temporary exile in Denmark, what duties they had in this foreign country, with its foreign customs, and the duty they had, as Jews, to hold fast to their Jewish identity. They had to be given the vision of a Jewish future in a Jewish society, in Palestine, in the longer term perhaps a Jewish state. Regardless of how good and well-meaning their foster-parents might be, they were quite unable fundamentally to understand the children's Jewish background, or build a bridge across the cultural gulf which might separate them from the children.

Whilst the *Hechaluz* trainees, who had come to Denmark during the 1930's, were convinced Zionists, and had often prepared their agricultural training in Denmark with shorter or longer terms in Jewish preliminary camps in Germany behind them, many of the *Alijah* children were unprotected and bewildered at their impressions of calamity and sudden flight, and they had the most acute need of guidance, explanation and, not least, the spiritual support which could restore their self-confidence and a minimum of faith in the future. For the moment they could breathe again in peaceful surroundings and reliable material circumstances. But they were children in puberty, and, robbed of all but a temporary abode they were a prey to thoughts and feelings which must be wildly diffused and confused. Who were they? Where did they stand? What could the future bring? Was the break with the past irreparable? For the leaders of *Hechaluz* there was no doubt. The children must not be left to themselves, and to a random Danish farming home. They must be initiated into and learn to understand and live with the Zionist movement's ideology. Only in this way could they be lifted out of the spiritual rootlessness, which must be their momentary fate, after a childhood in catastrophe and sorrow, parting with home, family, country and language, and with an abrupt transplantation to surroundings and a life which must be fundamentally foreign and bewildering.

The leaders of *Hechaluz* took up this task immediately.

In a circular from November 1939, the leaders in Copenhagen turned to the *Alijah* children, who were now arriving in Denmark, and gave them a detailed explanation of the situation in which they had stranded, and of the way in which they should meet the difficulties which they now faced. The children had personally experienced much at first hand, but how much had they comprehended of all that had overtaken them and their homes? The authors of the circular, Bertl Grass and Heinz Reinach, first gave a description of the catastrophe, which had now struck the Jews in large parts of central Europe, and which surpassed, in cruelty and organisation, all that Jewish society had been exposed to, even during the worst Jewish persecutions down the centuries. Now the disaster was explained, without their being spared the facts. What was now taking place had knocked the bottom out of any idea of assimilation of Jewish society in the countries where they lived, and in the attempts to assimilate, Jewry had lost its consciousness of a shared task and, unprepared for the tragedy, had been split into groups, torn from each other. In the face of the rootlessness, there was only the Zionist idea:

»The national Jewish movement has never indulged in the illusion that the assimilation of Jewry would be a solution to the Jewish problem in the long run. Zionism has foreseen, long before the catastrophe, that an adjustment of the Jews in the countries where they live, is not possible and has already at an early stage pointed to the omens of this«.

It only remained to act, and to act meant to rebuild the Jewish nation in its own country, Palestine. Every effort and every sacrifice to achieve this would be a milestone on the way to the final goal: national independence. The circular therefore urged the *Alijah* children to be aware of their real situation, and to express this in letters and articles for coming circulars, which should not only contain »beautiful, happy accounts of groups and experiences, but also must deal with questions and problems«.

A fairly long account followed of the circumstances in which the whole *Alijah* immigration to Denmark had been made possible, with thanks to Kirsten Gloerfelt-Tarp, Thora Daugaard and Mélanie Oppenhejm, and the circulars continued with an exhortation to learn what there was to be learned in Denmark, to understand Danish conditions and the Danish mentality, and to submit to the Danish conditions without, however, ever forgetting what their final purpose was, with their time in Denmark: to prepare a life as a working citizen in Palestine. The circular indicated what was demanded, under three points:

»1) To learn physical work and achieve an inner relationship to their work. 2) To get to know the geography, history, art and language of Palestine. For only in that way can we live as fully worthy members of our country. 3) To live and work in fellowship with our comrades. For with the life in our new homes we connect the idea of a just social life.«

Inserted here and there in the circular, the great difficulties which awaited the *Alijah* children were mentioned, and towards the end of it, this was again emphasized:

»In Palestine we shall not only be workers, but also Jews. Bearers of a Jewish culture. Just to achieve the most essential condition – to master the language – many efforts are required. Unfortunately we no longer have the possibilities which existed in the town. The number of hours during which we can work are few, the way to the homes often long and difficult. There will be many needs which it will only be possible to balance up through our strength of will.«

The circular, here mentioned in brief, was long and detailed. However, a short resumé of some parts of it must be sufficient to show that the leaders of *Hechaluz* did not intend to abandon the *Alijah* children in Danish surroundings and under Danish influences, but that they were certain of their mission: to convert the children into convinced Zionists. The circular was only a first step on the way. The selection of visiting teachers for the *Alijah* children was the decisive means to a massive Zionistic influence, which was both to give the children a foundation, and to promote what was for the *Hechaluz* group a sacred cause.

Visiting Teachers

Placing the trainees of the *Hechaluz* group in centres, which was attempted with varying success, was also carried out, as has been mentioned, in the case of the *Alijah* children. With the backing which the cause had received, there were in fact enough homes for the League to build on, but the task suddenly became a quite different and more complicated one, when homes had to be found which were more or less concentrated in a definite district. Some examples from the autumn 1939 can illustrate that the desire for this was a demand, and that the demand took the League's leaders somewhat by surprise. In a letter of 6 September to a farmer in the district north of Struer, Thora Daugaard had to ask for an immediate move: »Yesterday a young girl arrived ... who is the Jewish child, you so kindly offered to take into your home, and we thank you for your kindness.« There follows a fairly long explanation of the children's schooling and the demand involved for them to be collected in districts:

»It is therefore necessary that the children are centralized as much as possible. We had started, when all this rained down upon us, but we had not paid sufficient attention to the fact that Barslev lies so far from the little centre of emigrant children, which we have set up on Mors. Our chairman up there has telephoned to draw our attention to this, and we ask you to let the young man, who is coming down to you tomorrow, take the girl with him up to Mors, where we have found a good home for her. Please rest assured that we are very loath to make these changes, but as things are, we are obliged to, and we count on your understanding in this work of mercy. If it is possible to make a centre of 10–12 in your neighbourhood, may we count on your willingness again to take a child into your home.«

The creation of a centre on Mors was being hurriedly prepared, but a letter written a fortnight later to the district chairman on Mors seems to imply that the centralization was only middling:

»It may be correct, as you write, that the distances are great, but then the children must be collected in two different groups, and the visiting teachers must go to them. It is a quite frightful black eye we have received at the last moment, that we have to centralize the children, and I am very sorry to burden the foster-parents with getting the children to the visiting teachers. It was not at all the idea from the start. Will you say to (the visiting teacher) that we shall do our best, but that in no circumstances will we permit that a child be moved from a home where a letter has been sent that a child is coming. We had to move two homes in another district, and we will not do that again.«

An attempt in December 1939, to establish a centre based on the Vrå district had to be abandoned, and a number of districts were only considered if a centre chairman could collect several more or less neighbouring homes, as can be seen from a letter of 2 November to the centre chairman in Vejle:

» ... as we only have two homes at the moment, your own and one more in this district, it is very difficult for us only to send these two children up there, because, as we wrote to you the last time, the children should preferably be collected in centres, and have some teaching from a visiting teacher. We understand from your letter, however, that there is a possibility for you to be able to get more homes in the district, and we shall be glad if you will send us the enclosed forms, filled in. As soon as a sufficient number is established, you will get some children over there, there must preferably be half a score.«

When the »security zone« came at the end of 1940, the Vejle centre became a reality. Similar problems arose elsewhere, and the office work one senses behind the letters quoted, was at the limit of what the modest League office could manage.

But as with the efforts to create centres of *Hechaluz* trainees, here too, the formation of centres was not a single phenomenon. Departures, the establishment of »security zones« and many practical considerations, including the children's own desire to move to new districts so as to be near friends, and perhaps relations, was bound to lead to the break-up of centres and actual regrouping, so that here too it is impossible to carry out a definite analysis of the localities of the centres. In the period 1939–40 it can be stated that there were centres in Thy, Mors, Østbirk, Assens, Odense, Nyborg, Faaborg, Sorø, Skelskør, Kalundborg, Hillerød, Karise/Tappernøje, Sakskøbing, Lyngby, – the town names standing for the area, not the town. But only a year later, the situation had changed, as for example most of the centres in Jylland had to be dissolved and the children increasingly concentrated on the islands, except for Bornholm.

The original and principal reason why the *Alijah* leaders in London, with the support of the *Hechaluz* leaders in Copenhagen, had insisted on the demand for the creation of centres, was that the children, particularly in this special situation, needed both general and special education. The former was due to the fact that the situation in Germany had often not allowed a normal schooling. The anti-Jewish laws and the anti-Jewish measures had precluded a reasonable education in the normal school subjects. This should, and must, be corrected. But added to this, since the children's only hopes for the future lay in Palestine, this demanded an introduction to Zionist subjects, and Zionist thinking. Education in Danish schools was out of the question, for reasons of language alone, and also the Danish curriculum must be irrelevant for the Jewish children. This, therefore, was the task of the so-called visiting teachers, chosen by the *Hechaluz* office from among the *Hechaluz* group's best qualified members, often a little older, with previous teaching experience. They were to fill this vacuum, and the teaching was normally arranged with two weekly school days in improvised premises, often changed. The children then had to come in from the district, often with a very long way to school, often at times which could be inconvenient for the foster-homes' daily rhythm.

The expression »visiting teacher« could apply in the first phase, where there really was a question of the teacher leaving his home to visit the homes and schoolrooms in the district, but soon the teachers settled in the districts and came to play an important part, not only as teachers, but also in many cases as advisors for the children and as intermediaries between them, the homes and the leaders of the League. It was typical of the whole situation that the competence of the visiting teachers could never be established, just as the competence could never be established of any other authority or person behind this whole arrangement. This could in itself give occasion for tension between foster-parents and teachers, and between the teachers and the leaders of the League. And for the very reason that the whole immigration arrangement was based upon loose agreements and particularly upon conditions which had broken down, at a time which was already difficult and strained, conflicts could arise, which no one had the formal authority to smoothe out. Much depended upon the teacher's personality and his attitude to the foster-homes, always so different from each other. Most of the friction was smoothed out amicably, but now and then things reached boiling point, and then the problems out in the districts were referred, by the foster-parents or the teacher, up to the leaders of the League, to Margolinsky or to the *Hechaluz* personnel, who then had to mediate, without actually having any other means but admonition and persuasion, or possibly rearrangement of districts or teachers.

The Teaching Plan

The teachers were placed in a difficult position. It was not until the turn of the year 1939–40, that a definite plan for teaching was fixed, and up to then, the teachers had to improvise and decide their own plans for teaching. Apart from this, there was always a lack of teaching material, and rooms must be sought where they could be found. The teachers' financial position was extremely poor, and must be so; and, as mentioned, it was always an open question, what authority they had, for example, to intervene in a child's personal affairs, if they judged these to be undesirable for him or her. It was also difficult for them to demand constant participation in the teaching, and both distance and the weather could easily cause absences.

A glimpse into the function of these special schools is possible, from a talk to the foster-parents, held in November 1940 by the visiting teacher in the Østbirk centre, and then circulated to the homes. Here a short explanation is given of the background and form of the visiting teacher's school.

The teacher began by reminding his hearers that a year had now passed, since the children had come to the homes, and he spoke of the difficulties they had had to overcome, before, as now, the children had settled down. The object of his talk was to give them an orientation on »the schoolwork which robs you of the foster-children regularly for a time every week«. He mentioned the Danish High Schools, as schools which would bring up the pupils to be valuable citizens, and continued:

»Our school occupies ... a special position, and to make this really comprehensible, I should like ... to illustrate the Jewish youth's spiritual point of view. The milieu from which all these young people come is doubly closed. Closed as regards the Christian world surrounding them in their previous fatherland, and this on its side for everything spiritual which may be moving the rest of the free world, owing to the political situation. Only in this way can the prevailing ideology bite fast into every brain.

»From a technical point of view, these young people are poorly equipped for Denmark. Knowledge of their own mother tongue, stylistically and grammatically ... is possessed only by a few. Arithmetic and other elementary subjects must not be mentioned here. The Jewish schools in Germany have done everything possible, inspite of all the difficulties, to give their youth what it needs for its hard road through life ... You will then see that already here lay a considerable task for a teacher, filling in crucial holes and correcting distorted ideas. The latter must be particularly emphasized in this place. One does not live in a country whose propaganda machine daily roars in ones ears, without oneself being influenced by it as regards the ideology mentioned above.

»Now came the young people's upbringing with its vast complex of challenges. The teacher then faces the question of how he could make use of the few weekly hours most usefully. It was clear that a number of important subjects must be dropped, and thus it happened that it was not possible to find time for such a justified demand as lessons in Danish, especially as we all believed that their stay here in Denmark was for a limited time.«

The teacher then went over to a description of the special subjects:

»The greatest weight lies naturally in acquiring a knowledge of the rather difficult language ... With Hebrew, the position is such that this language, which has not the slightest relation to the Germanic, cannot be learned from the surrounding (people) . . . Group education in Palestine, and the great mass of recently arriving emigrants, leads to inhibitions in the use of the language – inhibitions which we try already here to conquer. When we demand . . . more of the young people than simply to be immigrants in the Jewish country, knowledge of Hebrew is so much the more important in that it constitutes the actual key to public life and culture . . . as far as the Jewish section of the population is concerned, it is in Hebrew alone that the will of the people is made known . . . education for Zionism constitutes the other part of our efforts at upbringing. This movement of renaissance in the Jewish people we owe to the activity of hitherto slumbering forces in a nation, for the recapture of the old fatherland in spirit and in deed. The Jewish youth living in this country represents a number of the assistants. Steadfastness in their will, particularly in a time when a whole people's consciousness has become uncertain, is the most important task. Beliefs, which were deeply rooted yesterday, yield to the storm today, and the Jew, who has no solid foothold anywhere, is torn away even more with the stream.

»Our efforts are thus directed at giving the young person a fast hold. All that in one way or another falls into his actual sphere of life is taken into consideration. From a historic point of view, the Jewish problem is illustrated on all sides, cultural, racial, economic, political, etc., and everywhere it is shown that only the return to the land of our fathers can bring a normalisation of conditions for living.

Here we come to the second section of our educational programme, which can perhaps be covered by sociology in other countries, and yet is so fundamentally different, since the constituents of our state are for the most part voluntary. Our government organs, the Zionist Congress, the Jewish Agency, the workers' organisation in the country (Palestine), whatever contributes to building it up, but particularly the national funds, are only organisations on a voluntary basis. Submitting to our organisations' discipline demands high personal morality. No government stands behind us with its statutes. This 'submission' demands the degree of recognition that we try to give our Jewish youth: It is not only what 'the outsiders' try to interpret as *idealismus*. *Idealismus* springs from feelings alone. Possession of this is what characterizes *all* conscious youth: Nevertheless, feelings disappear, if they are not borne up by the clearest recognition and will.

»Consider now, from all this, our school, and you will easily be able to admit that here an education is cultivated for a society, a school which, with the special aims which must be achieved, demands a different consideration from that which we usually take of schools. The pupils' relations with each other is more sincere than usual, and the teacher needs not only to represent a pedagogical authority. Add, then, that the teacher and pupils stand under the same yoke of a common heavy fate, and then you will understand how close the step is to intimate comradeship: This comradeship binds age and sex. It shall not be left unsaid that we are well aware of the danger which can arise from such a relationship: Here I am thinking of the often mentioned isolation of the young people among themselves, and in general of the evident and hidden rocks in the whole work. Here comes the teacher's sideline, which is to mediate between the homes and the young people.

»A common fate – under this sign, the union took place. A common life – that shall be the future. Denmark had its place as the country of preparation to this union, which will find its continuation in collective training in Palestine.

»Even though I cannot describe the teachers' activity exhaustively, I think at least that I have given you an outline of a work, the meaning of which consists of creating forces for the rebuilding of a national society in a country, which means the whole of hope for a nation fighting for naked life. You especially, who have regarded the strengthening of your nation as the most important aim of your home policy for the last six months. You will understand this appeal to support our efforts, also in the future.«

It can be left to conjecture, how much the Jylland farmers understood of this circulated speech. One thing is certain: »the children« from 1939 continued to grow older and more mature, and under the influence of their teachers and comrades, they formed an ever more independent attitude, which had to separate them from the Danish milieu in which they lived. The families who did not understand or even sense this, and clung fast to the point of view of mercy from 1939, often had problems, when the »foster-child« went his or her own way.

A maturing Process

It is not possible to establish how many of the *Alijah* children were more or less consciously Zionistically determined, when they came to Denmark. All the *Hechaluz* trainees were on their way to Palestine, whilst the children were fleeing from Germany. Without much doubt, they must all have heard of Zionism, but many of them, when they arrived, were still such children that they can hardly have made realistic decisions, and in several instances it was their parents who had taken the decisions. One account will be quoted as certainly covering many:

»The War had been going on for a month, when I said good-bye for the last time to my father. It was in the evening of 3 October 1939, on the railway station at Münster. My mother was to accompany me to Berlin, where the transport to Denmark was to collect. Only through my parents' persistent efforts was it possible to get me included among the small number of children who were successfully saved (and brought) to Denmark.«

160

We know the small number: 19 children – with arrival at Copenhagen in the afternoon of 5 October. There are two expressions which are burnt into ones thoughts: »last time« and »transport«. It *was* the last time, and it *was* a transport. Let the expressions stand as the monuments to infamy they are.

But if it is not possible to establish how many of the children were Zionistically determined when they arrived, it is possible to establish that they practically all became Zionistic quite soon after their arrival. Any other idea would of course be impossible. Separated for all the future from home and country, and only supplied with a temporary life full of risks, there was only one possibility for these children to look forward to: a future in »Erez Israel« – the Jewish land, Israel, or as it politically was still called in 1939–40: Palestine. The Zionist attitude had to announce itself by reason of the situation, alone, but added to this was the visiting teacher's help to give the children a foundation, a hope and a meaning with their future. The visiting teachers had received the task from the *Maskirut*, of giving the children a dream to live with, and that task was fully completed through the teachers' persistent influence over the children in their most receptive age.

The teaching plan from those years gives us the possibility of glimpsing the explosive development the children were rushed into, when they had been robbed of everything but the dream of a better future. The teaching plan included pupils' assignments, and a collection of assignments from a single district has been preserved. They are written in the winter 1940–41, and extracts from them speak for themselves. Let the maturing children speak. No one knew better than they, what was reality and what was dream. The assignments all have a title, though one cannot see whether it is the teacher who had formulated the assignment, or whether the title is the pupil's own:

External duty – internal reply: »I grew up in Vienna, and was the youngest child, and therefore I am very spoilt. The day went without worries, for my parents kept all the daily worries from me. School, sport and outings and a little in a youth home, that was all . . . All this has suddenly become quite different here in Denmark. The principal thing is that now there are no parents with me, who lovingly look after me. They are somewhere or other on a ship, in a country, I do not know. All that I have are my foster-parents. My free life is gone, and I am left to strangers' whims. I have a definite day's work and work's division, which I mostly cannot keep, yes there is always more work than I can foresee for the coming day. Now there is no chance of running away from the work. One has to keep at it until one has finished, also when one is burning to get away. But it is very good, for what would have become of me otherwise? Still cling to my parents? No! Before, I saw it as a goal to find myself a job ... Now I have a real goal which no one can take from me or throw down. I know that Erez Israel is not easy, and that this is only a preparation.«

The pupil then describes how all free time quickly goes in intellectual work, for example the study of Hebrew:

»From day to day my experience continues to get richer. The work now goes much more easily and quickly. I am glad I can work. Often it is bad, and I long for my parents. But then it comes over me again. I cannot imagine anything else.«

Objectivity – demands to ourselves: »When we said good-bye to our parents, we had an idea that even though we had now left all the hard (part) behind us, all would still not be pure joy and bliss ... We got to know people and they us, and it all lost the charm of novelty, and we felt ourselves faced with reality. Forced by the impressions from the grey everyday, we forgot all the noble feelings, that for our hosts had helped to bring us to a better fate, and based our judgement only on the trivialities of daily life. We began to scold our surroundings, foster-parents, work. Every other word was: Denmark is terrible – oh, if only I was in Erez Israel ... But now I have got to where (I can see) that our attitude was completely wrong. Why not try to see the bright side of things. Everything has good and bad sides. Denmark is difficult for us young people, it stands fast. Much in our lives is not understood by our foster-parents, or it is misunderstood ... but we want to be *chawerim*, don't we? And to be *chawerim* means that one can bear what is heavy. How could we expect to bear what is heavy in Erez Israel, when without just a bit of self-respect we indulge in an indifferent or sad mood ...And we must not forget it. Here we are children, who have no material worries. In Erez Israel we shall, even if it is in a fellowship, have worries about the daily bread. It is a difficult and long way to Erez, and here the difficulties really begin. Let us imagine that we came direct to Erez Israel. We should then have arrived completely unprepared, without being able to work, with no idea of what the everyday could mean. We would all have been deeply disappointed ... When one has reached this point, Denmark is no longer so 'terrible'. Clearly I would be fearfully happy if I could go soon, but as long as it lasts, it is a question of our not being irritated about what is unpleasant, but looking for the beautiful in everyday things and being glad of it. For it is easy to find, if one does not, because of prejudice, shut ones eyes to it.«

Thoughts on the Work. »Erez, when one hears this word, one believes that it flows with milk and honey. But no, that can only happen if one does something and helps to build up. In Erez, land workers are needed, and I am happy that I found my *Hachscharah* in a country suited to that. I do not know how long I shall stay in Denmark, but as long as I have to, I will try and learn much from Danish agriculture. In Vienna there were houses, streets, noise and dust for me, but nature? I did not see all the beauty. And it is just that, that I can look at in this country. Have I ever thought about how much sweat and toil lies behind the

162

production of food? Now that I know that a cow must be milked, and that I can help in this, how lovely it is when I drink a glass of milk, to be able to say: 'This is my work' . . . But I will also prepare myself for Erez with intellectual work, and for that, the evenings give me the right opportunity. I often think, what have I contributed today? How were my first efforts? How slowly I started on a thing, then. It all goes at a higher tempo now, after much practice and endurance, and I believe that in Erez I will be able to work like a grown man.«

Schoolmaster Denmark: »Here with my foster-parents I have found a real home, and have been treated as a son of the house. And even now, when I can hardly expect to emigrate (*Alijah*), it will be hard for me to go away from here. What I can do, I have learned here, and it is quite a bit. Denmark is a good school for all of us. And the knowledge we have gained here we will be able to value in Erez Israel.

Intermediate Station: »So long as we are in Denmark, we face the problem of uniting our ideas with the ideas of those around us . . . I know very well that it would be much easier for me in my place, if I joined up with my hosts rather more, but I am perhaps too Jewish in my upbringing for that, and for me it is more important to maintain my Jewish character. This does not mean that I do not prize the people around me. On the contrary, I respect them very much, and I could wish that we in Erez could contribute just as much in agriculture as these Danish farmers . . . Our training here gives every one of us something, for we learn something new and important every day. No one will later regret this time.«

Jewish and Danish Mentality: »There is such an enormous difference between the Danes, who are an agricultural nation – and us, who some day will be one. We can in most cases show the Danes respect and understanding. We are in (undecipherable) movement, while the Danes walk in paths they are used to – now in bad times, perhaps with more feeling of solidarity, but otherwise simply carry on their usual life . . . we have left the non-physical professions, to become farmers. We therefore seek a new beginning in everything. We refuse the old social forms and have therefore become formless. Formlessness is a condition for later, new forms. But here, where so very much weight is given to forms, people do not understand us. In many ways we have to try to be like the Danes, and this applies mostly to the work. But it does not only apply to the work, but also to this uniform calm, which the Danes have in them. We are all as overflowing as water, for which the sluices have been opened. One must hope that all this sparkling water will one day join in a wider, peaceful stream, which flows fruitfully to our country.«

Assimilation or Understanding? »I have already been a year in Denmark, and quite often discover how much I join in everything that was so foreign at first. Still, I do not always feel at all at home, but am only attached to the work and the whole farm. I have a good understanding with the other farmers in the village, and I am very glad of this. A little while ago it was harvest, which ended with a harvest feast. Again a big problem: 'Should I go?' And if so, should I dance? In the village where I live, solidarity between the individual farmers is very strong . . . I have not hesitated a moment about whether I should go, and this would also be a matter of course for my foster-parents. For is not such solidarity also in our interest? I find it unreasonable, to say from the start: 'I refuse this or that', without there being a real reason for it. Just as we demand that people meet us with understanding, so it is, the other way round.«

Can our false Attitude to Work be improved? »We have come here to Denmark, conscious of having to work. But even though we were prepared for all this, yet we are disappointed by so many people. We thought that people's way of thinking was just like in our circle. We were wrong about that. We thought that we would be entrusted with all the work, and that when the work was finished, we would be free, and could do as we liked. There too we were wrong. We saw that the farmers do not understand us in any way. They neither understand us nor acknowledge our ideals – nor do they understand us as people. All this has considerable influence on our attitude to work ... This attitude to work is wrong, but here in Denmark one cannot change so quickly. I am sure that in Erez Israel I shall work as much as I can, but here I will prefer a meeting with my comrades to work. How can one improve this situation? The best, but perhaps also the hardest, would be to improve ones relations with ones foster-parents, as we must make an effort to arouse understanding for our aims. I think that if we could move about more freely, enjoyment and pleasure in our work would become much greater.«

My Attitude to Work: »Often I had no desire to work. I would not accept the methods here. Nothing was right, nothing good enough – but it has changed fundamentally. Today I try to take on all the work there is. Often I am not allowed to, but I try to, again and again. I have already learned much, and the more I learn, the greater my pleasure in the work becomes ... I hope that as regards work, Denmark has had the same effect on many as on me. For when we go to work with pleasure, we have the best conditions for learning – and what each of us knows is to the advantage of our final goal – Erez Israel.«

More Initiative: »A problem which often meets us, and which one must not underestimate. A little example can perhaps best explain what I mean. A *chawer* works on a farm in Denmark. His foster-parents treat him well, from their point of view. He is just sitting at evening coffee, when the telephone rings. It is the visiting teacher, who says that the *chawer* in question is to come to lessons tomorrow. But this must be definite, as all the other *chawerim* are coming. The *chawer* tells his farmer. 'No, that is quite impossible. Tomorrow we have our neighbour's birthday, and we are all invited to coffee. He will certainly be offended if you stay away' The *chawer* protests – the foster-father insists that tomorrow he cannot go to school. What is the *chawer* to do in such a case? It is a question that we meet countless times. Is he to give up the lessons, which take place once a week and constitute the only link with the *chawer* world? Or is he to risk the farmer going around with a sour face for days? No definite answer can actually be given ... The individual *chawer* must know, on his own, what he has to do in the given situation ... (he) should in my opinion insist on going to the lessons, and then accept that the farmer may be a bit angry. With time, the farmer will realise how intensely we are attached to the school, and knowledge, and how much it means to us, and then he will also approve our spending our evenings learning. This will be more likely to contribute to mutual understanding.«

Many small Things create something great: »What did we think of the Danes, at the start. I do not think there were any of us who were satisfied with everything . . . (one) works from morning till night, and yet in a certain way are foster-children. Even though I fly from morning till night, I am still grateful to 'the old ones'. How have I learned to endure? In Denmark. From whom have I learned to keep house with little? From the Danes. Who has had the patience to look after us, teach us to plough and all the practical work? The Danes. We cannot be grateful enough for what we learn, for better farmers than the Danes are not to be found . . . I could list thousands of little things, which we cannot thank them enough for. I have never and I never will regret that I was in Denmark, and I hope that in Erez Israel we shall be able to prove what we have learned.«

We and the Danes: »There are none of us who have not noticed the difference between us and the Danes . . . Let us consider our contemporary Danes, in the environment here. Since they were quite small, they have been brought up to work, and are not used to anything else . . . He already takes the place of a farm hand . . . We, who were brought up to anything but physical work, and did not begin until a relatively late age, are often underestimated by them, perhaps often without a cause . . . In addition, also, we belong to a completely different culture and sphere of interest from his, and we have quite a different idea of the future. So we regard the life which we desire as the best, and at the same time, we believe we have also found a cause through which we can feel superior . . . We Jews, who after 2000 years of dispersal and assimilation have just begun to form a nation, must at all events devote all our energies to succeeding in achieving this difficult aim in this difficult time. We must learn and learn again. The Danes, who have always constituted a national community, do not have to learn it to such an extent, as maintaining their cause does not demand so much strength as the actual capture and the fight. We must always keep this in mind.«

Children – Homes – District Chairmen – League

As the League children grew up and matured, the division between them and the *Hechaluz* trainees faded to some extent. First of all, they acquired the same aims and found themselves in exactly the same situation, and after a year or two, many of the League children also gained experience and work on a line with the agricultural trainees, even though they were still considered »foster-children«, at least in many of the original foster-homes. The difference – for there still was a difference – lay, for example, in the fact that the League children were under a different organisation from that of the *Hechaluz* trainees. The latter had their »channel of command« to the *Hechaluz* office, Margolinsky's secretariat, and further up to the State Police and other authorities, whilst the League children's relations with the authorities came under the home – the district chairman – the League office – the League, etc. If there were difficulties in a home or a district, if a child had to move, or was ill and had to go to hospital, some necessities had to be bought, a bill paid; if some permit had to be obtained, or a special arrangement made, – and this constantly occurred – it was the foster-parents and the leaders of the League in Copenhagen, who had to take the matter up and put the thousands of cases in order. This took place in a whirlwind of letters, at meetings with district chairmen, and through many visits of the League ladies out in the centres. Problems mounted daily, from the trivial to the heart-rending, and in the final count it was the voluntary women, who looked after the office in Copenhagen, without secretarial help, who had to take matters in hand and solve the problems as well as possible. Usually it was Thora Daugaard and Mélanie Oppenhejm who took up the problems, but often it could be Else Zeuthen and Mrs. Fanny Arnskov, who took over, particularly during some of Thora Daugaard's periods of illness.

Regardless of the fact that »the children« had grown out of the original fostering, this still continued, partly in the sense that most of the children felt themselves attached to the families and *vice versa*, and partly in the sense that the foster-families, the district chairmen and the League office maintained the idea of responsibility for the children's fate, and were thereby screwed into the roles of guardians and authorities for »the children«, roles which the latter were far from always ready to recognize, even when relations with the homes were the best imaginable. The longer the time of waiting lasted, and the more independent and mature »the children« became, the more artificial was the fiction that they were under different conditions and ties from those of the *Hechaluz* trainees. They could then, with more or less harshness, demand to be set free from all guardianship.

When the constantly overburdened League office met even small irregularities, or when the district chairmen or foster-families met actions on the part of »the children«, which they either did not understand or for some reason disapproved of, explosive protests lurked just beneath the surface of daily life. The foster-parents, the district chairmen or the League office could meet not only Jewish sensitivity, but also a sensitivity,

As Vice-Chairman of the League, Fanny Arn-skov played an important role in the League's daily work. During the action against the Jews in October 1943, she was arrested during a German raid on a church loft in Gilleleje, but set free a few days later. She then took over the running of the office and the organisation of the League's parcels to Theresienstadt.

which was quite understandably intensified by a situation which was strained to the utmost. A little spark could then set temperaments ablaze. In January 1941, a situation of this kind blew up on Fyn, when some colliding circumstances made the League office send out a circular emphasizing the generally applicable rules that »the children« must obey the decisions of the foster-parents, as it was they, and not the visiting teachers or others, who had authority. There was a slight tone of command in sentences such as that »the children« should »keep *to* . . . the homes and keep *our* orders properly«. The background was that a girl had left her place without permission for a week, for a holiday with friends, without informing either the foster-parents or the district chairman – certainly thoughtlessness which could not but cause much unnecessary anxiety. Unluckily, the police came to the home that very day, to give the girl her passport, and had to make a note that, against all the rules, she was not to be found. With or without reason, the leaders had the impression that the local visiting teacher was aware of the situation, and it was demanded that he be dismissed – a decision which was actually a matter for the *Hechaluz* leaders. Added to all this, a quite large group of League children on Fyn had arranged a meeting in Odense, on their own initiative, and this had given rise to anxiety in a number of homes, and fear that rather large Jewish gathering could attract undesirable attention.

All this turned out to be trivialities, due to thoughtlessness, and perhaps also to a lack of understanding of the seriousness of the situation, but it was the background for a letter from the League in a sharply admonishing tone, which showed some nervousness, reasonably enough, and contained bans on leaving the homes, holding meetings, and staying away from the homes after nightfall, etc.

The writers received as good as they got, and the reply disclosed the gulf which now could easily appear, between the increasingly grown-up League »children« and their guardians out in the homes as well as in Copenhagen. Scores of League children wrote, day in day out, to »Dear Mrs. Daugaard« with pleas for assistance in one way or another, and received the patient help she could give; but when a group of 15 League children gathered on 10 January 1941, to compose a letter of protest and sign it, she had suddenly become »Much honoured Mrs. Daugaard«.

»Various events in recent times have led us to (write) this letter, which must clarify the situation once and for all. In advance we will request that you do not regard this as a letter from 'naughty children', as such an attitude will be an unforgivable mistake. It will be a mistake of the same sort, to relate this and other actions from our side as influenced, or even ordered, by our 'visiting teacher'. We suppose that you in the last 1½ years which *Jugendalijah* has lasted in Denmark, have already learned so much about the structure of our organisation, and about the character of our work, that you do not believe this of us. We are aware that you and the League bear a certain responsibility for us, and up to now we have also tried to respect this, but for the future this is impossible.«

The letter then went over to a protest full of strong feelings and against all interference in the League children's internal affairs, the holding of meetings, appointment of teachers, etc. »We believe we can ourselves decide what is necessary for our work« and

»we believe that those prople who must serve as our models, and to whom therefore we stand in a quite special relationship, those, only we ourselves can choose. A general ban on 'school' will only lead to still greater resistance from our side, as we under no circumstances can or will give it up. Thirdly and lastly, we hereby protest officially against our private correspondence being read by outsiders, and being used as 'evidence' against our visiting teacher. We ask you respectfully as to your attitude, but add that we will not give up any of our aspirations, as these constitute the minimum of what is needful. We hope that you will work up the necessary understanding of our work, and that we can again achieve a fruitful co-operation. Then we can leave here one day in real gratitude and look back on Denmark as the most beautiful time and that most rich in results in our preparation for Palestine – and this must be both your and our desire.«

When the League office replied a few days later by insisting on the instructions and, in particular, impressing it upon the »children« that they were most strictly forbidden to »collect for something you call 'school', but where your teacher is not present«, and apart from that, repeated the earlier warnings, there came a sharp reply again, to »Much honoured Mrs. Daugaard«:

» ... The result of your letter is that you have aroused incredible anxiety in the homes, without, however, being able to frighten us. You do not seriously believe that we will allow ourselves to be influenced on account of vague suppositions about our private life. Our working hours correspond to a Danish farm hand's, so that our free time begins after the black-out. In addition, we will ... once more stress that we do not intend to co-operate with any other teacher than our own organisation's ... We much regret that we cannot take your demands into consideration, as with knowledge of previous episodes and actions, we cannot believe the reasons you give.«

»Our own organisation«! As this group saw it, their organisation was no longer the League, but *Hechaluz*. It was *Hechaluz* leaders who chose the visiting teachers. That it was the League personnel who carried out daily deeds to help and support the League children, and it was with them that the authorities were in contact, the group, in their indignation, had no feeling for, and their remarks, to put it mildly, were out of touch with the facts.

If this broadside did not evidence much maturity, and if it was marked by profound ignorance of the practical realities of the time, it was, however, the expression of a radical feeling of independence, and if the signatories were still in the rebellious age of puberty, they were nevertheless no longer helpless foster-children, who angled after the work of mercy which the League and the many foster-families were supposed to stand for.

The affair was soon straightened out, and feelings calmed down again, but the harsh exchange of words bears witness to the development which was going on in the League children's camp, away from the first months' thanks for safety and on to a marked Zionist attitude. Normally, this development did not lead to abuse, but the fact that there was a clear and unavoidable tendency must be clear to all the initiated, whether children, foster-families or leaders. The situation was exposed with much calmness and maturity in December 1942, in a letter from a group of 8 League children to Mélanie Oppenhejm, with copies to Else Zeuthen and Karl Lachmann, as well as Margolinsky, although he had nothing to do,

169

directly, with the League children. Two years had now passed, and the foster-home conditions had become still more unreasonable. Now the group grasped the nettle:

»For some time now, efforts have been made among us, within the limits of the possibilities in this country, so far as possible to manage our own lives. Representatives have been chosen who should occupy themselves with the concrete possibilities for making ourselves independent. Our efforts aim at promoting the development of *chawerim*, who were children and were treated as children, into independent people.«

The signatories then explained how the League children, practically and theoretically, had sought and still sought to train themselves to become fully effective workers, who could live from their work. They did not omit to express gratitude for the help which had been given to the visiting teacher schools. In continuation, the group now felt itself ready to take charge of carrying out advanced education, with help from a neighbouring teacher. and then turned to what was the main subject of the letter:

»We know quite well that we have given the League difficulties in their work. We therefore belive that it has become necessary to find a solution which meets the interests of both parties. The best solution would be if we were attached as an independent group to *Hechaluz*, with the same rights as it has.«

The group finally asked for a meeting on the proposal, with the participation of a representative for the visiting teachers and for *Hechaluz*.

No organisational alteration in principle of the League children's situation was ever made, and right up to 1943, the League did not drop its care or responsibilities for the children it had brought to Denmark in 1939–40. But athwart all organisational theory, developments had to lead to the League children in practice gradually coming to share the conditions and fate of the *Hechaluz* trainees, so that although there was no formalized integration or fusion, it could be difficult to differentiate between the two groups, which shared a common fate.

Right from the start, the League leaders had felt the visiting teacher system to be a burden. It gave difficulties, both during the first placing and with the later moves, and also when the children asked, for some reason, to be moved to new districts, with other comrades and teachers. They also found the arrangement expensive, and even though it was the Mosaic Religious Community which financed most of it, they compared its expenses with the sparse means which the League could scrape together. The visiting teachers, and behind them the *Hechaluz* leaders, intruded as a foreign element in an arrangement which was conceived as purely humanitarian. Some of the foster-families could also show their dislike of the system, and made no secret of it in their letters to the League office, even if the complaints were seldom particularly concrete, and usually only hint that the children were drawn away from the foster-homes, and that the arrangement created disturbance. Now and then, the drawbacks with the system were clearly explained, for example in a typical letter from a farmer who, in February 1941, stated his view of the matter to Thora Daugaard:

» ... Personally, I regard placing the children in 'centres' with accompanying teaching as a great mistake. But the League has probably no responsibility for this, since as far as I understand, it was a condition for their being brought to Denmark that 'the children' should learn farming and Hebrew, and this was of course difficult in any other way. When I believe the dispersed housing was better, it is for two reasons. Partly because then they were referred to the home, when difficulties arose for the children, instead of to teachers, comrades or district chairmen. Many conflicts arise for that reason, and the easy and constant association with their comrades give rise to assessment and criticism of conditions in the homes, and of the work, that can only have a harmful effect on co-operation between the homes and 'the children'. The differences and the deficiencies in the different homes and places of work are always numerous and obvious, and compared with the often very well-to-do homes 'the children' come from, there can be much unnecessary and sterile criticism, which was avoided with dispersed housing, without attendance at the schools.«

The farmer developed the problem that theoretical education easily became primary for »the children«, and that under the influence of the visiting teachers, they could easily come to idealise life and work in Palestine, and that the teaching

»glorifies the work to such an extent, that it turns the pioneers into completely new and better people, and 'the conquest of work' into such an event, that it seems plausible to young, unstable souls, who under the influence of this, perhaps not untrue, but one-sided and 'coloured' description, have made their choice and therefore would like to be called idealists. But this idealism can only be fulfilled in Palestine.«

He adds, somewhat sarcastically, that the »conquest of work« could very well begin here and now. He also declares himself to be quite satisfied with his own »child«, whom he now considers trained in what his farm can contribute. He would therefore like to obtain more advanced training for him, but this is held back for the very demand for centres and theoretical education.

This sober and realistic description finds its mark as regards two things, which in the homes could create dislike of the visiting teacher system. But there were various other causes. One of them was to be found in the loving families, who wished to cosset the »child«, who in the course of his or her stay was growing up, and anxiously saw the »child« leave the farm once or twice a week – often in bad weather – to take long bicycle rides far from the home, and then perhaps return filled with strange and foreign, perhaps rebellious ideas. It could also happen that the »child« returned home with unpleasant comparisons. The families were far from having equal material circumstances to offer the »children«, or from being able to understand and follow their development. On the practical level, the »child's« attendance at the school could upset the rhythm of the home completely, and lastly it should not be forgotten that the very families which were attached to the Women's League for Peace and Freedom would normally be prepared to support the Danish Government's exhortation for law and order, which was to cover everyone – an exhortation which was often challenged by a Zionist-minded young man or woman, at a time when the Danish population was breaking away from the Government, and minds were changing. It was not only Hebrew that was spoken in the visiting teacher schools. The more time passed, the greater became the possibility of clashes of opinion.

In many homes, there were of course no serious problems, and many foster-families tried honestly to understand »the children's« thirst for knowledge and particularly for comradeship, and even in homes where the importance of their education was not quite understood, much good-will was shown as regards the schoolwork and the inconvenience it could cause. In quite a long letter to Else Zeuthen in August 1941, one of the district chairmen reports on her efforts to find rooms for classes, and lodging for the visiting teacher, as well as the loan of modest furniture for him, and concludes rather resignedly: »It is a very expensive affair, with these schools, but all that the children enjoy is the 'comradeship' with each other on school days.« The district chairman in question had nearly 50 »children« in her care, and put her livingroom at their disposal for three years, keeping it as an always open meeting-place for the League children who felt the need to meet, get advice, discuss or relieve their feelings of sorrow or happiness. But this was only one of the ventilators. The other was the schoolroom.

All in all, the visiting teacher system was to complicate a situation that was already confused, and misunderstandings often arose, for example when the League or district chairman gave one order, and the teacher quite a different order. Misunderstandings became unavoidable, when several people made arrangements at the same time and on the same question, and when an opinion in one place collided violently with those in another place, and foster-families and teacher could often talk over each others heads. If that happened, first one and then another family could consign the teaching to limbo. Without doubt, in many farming homes, it played a role that the schooling drew the »children« away from the daily farmwork.

»The children« had a different view. For them, comradeship and association with the teacher were the bright moments of their existence. In all the accounts given by previous *Alijah* children, this is repeated again and again, when so much else is forgotten or omitted. A few examples are as typical as many others:

»From 15–18, a very important period in a youngster's life, I drank in Danish culture, literature and language . . . As far as I was concerned, I (had) received no education. Only what we got from the youth leaders once a week, and more specialized in Jewish and Zionist subjects.«

»One formed small groups, living in a vicinity of about 5 kilometres, and twice a week were taught by a member of the Zionist organisation.«

»There was no really marked psychological understanding for our situation, at least not for those of us who lived in the country . . . I had contact with 'the others from home' the whole time . . . as well as from the twice a week when we went to school, we met in the evening, had sometimes meetings and gatherings during a week-end, and once in a while, in the summer, some summer camps of a week's duration. To a very great extent, that was what one lived for.«

»We had the coldest winters in the memory of man, but still walked 16 kilometres a couple of times a week, just to be with 'our own'. We met to go to school, where a visiting teacher taught us in subjects which were important for our later life in Israel. Amongst other things, we learned Hebrew.«

»I regularly met my comrades, partly for ordinary togetherness, partly for regular teaching from our visiting teacher. The teaching was intended as partial compensation for our interrupted schooling in Germany, and as preparation for emigration to Palestine.«

»As others have certainly reported, we had a weekly meeting (teaching day) of our group in the Sorø area, and this took place in the Judge's house, when the

Judge's wife (a member of the Peace League) received us with coffee and cakes. Our youth leader taught in orientation on Israel, and language, and several other subjects such as information on Denmark and topical information from abroad ... In Denmark I always had contact with comrades from the *Hechaluz* organisation.«

»We met once a week in Sanderum, that is, all the children in the vicinity of Odense. There we studied Hebrew one day a week, English, Jewish history and various other subjects. We were also in contact with children from other centres, such as Nyborg. We spent some week-ends and holidays together.«

»Gradually, as time passed, we felt that time was crumbling away from us. We wanted to get an education in one direction or another ... Psychological problems could not be avoided, some suffered from home-sickness in the first period ... But these things we 'repaired' ourselves ... with the help of comradeship and solidarity. Without this, there would probably have been some who went under.«

Another decisive element is also remembered: the misunderstandings and the ill-feeling that could arise between »children« and foster-parents, and between »children« and the League leaders. They all arose from lack of shared understanding of the unsolvable problems which all the parties faced, and which sprang partly from the unforeseen length of their stay, partly from the disparity between the »League ladies« humanitarian aims and the »children's« growing self-awareness. One reason which contributed considerably to this was that the Danish authorities, regardless of age, increased physical strength and increasing experience, did not permit the »children« to be given agricultural trainee status, but insisted that they had come as foster-children, and remained foster-children, excluded in principle from regular work, paid on the lines of what was now the case for *Hechaluz* trainees. The demand for this did not make things easier for the League office, and its decisions could be difficult for the »children« to understand. This, too, appears in the accounts:

»There are so many aspects to this problem. Could one have expected greater understanding for our problems from the League? I do not know, they were in a difficult situation, on the one side they had us with all our desires, on the other side the »foster-homes« with their expectations. When the Germans invaded, the situation did not exactly become easier.«

»This could unfortunately not be carried out, so we came into opposition against the 'League ladies', who were after all responsible for us. A number of restrictions were laid on us, which we found it difficult to accept. Those responsible had forgotten that in those years we had become grown-up people.«

»Because of various moves of our comrades from North Sjælland, after a year's stay in Gørløse I became the only *Alijah*-youth youngster in the district. I then carried on a considerable correspondence with the comrades in South Sjælland,

and expressed my strong desire to move to them. My foster-parents were told of it and were offended that I wished to leave them, as they looked on it as a matter of 'honour' that I stayed with them ... and as a punishment I was moved to a centre in Kalundborg. So 'one' could allow me to move, but not to Næstved, where I wanted to come. The League's district chairman ... had a big warm heart, and when I had got to know her, I plucked up courage and asked if I could move to my comrades in Næstved. Of course I could.«

The correspondence in this affair is extant, and contains the explanation that the leaders of the League were just then under the pressure of two circumstances: that the Næstved centre was overcrowded and the police had demanded as few moves as possible, preferably none. The date was 23 June 1941, the day after the German invasion of the Soviet Union. Nevertheless one can understand the writer's memory of being disregarded and exposed to injustice.

But the fundamental problem was that as the League children grew up and matured, they must feel the League families' well-meaning care and the League's leaders' just as well-meaning authority as an intolerable guardianship. It did not help matters, that the individual »child«, with his or her private, vital problem, could not have any idea that the always under-manned League office was bombarded, day in and day out, with letters from children, foster-parents, district chairmen, authorities, institutions, organisations, hospitals, firms, well-meaning private persons, etc., or that the office always had countless restrictions hanging over their heads, and therefore only a limited scope for their decisions. That the leaders' estimates were now and then incorrect was probably unavoidable. But a »No,« from the League office could be felt as a bitter blow, out in the districts, for out there it could seem a simple thing to arrange things with a »Yes«. And if a »No« came, because the rules or circumstances, or perhaps simply overwork did not allow for a »Yes«, the »No« was felt as an injustice by those who knew nothing, either of the rules or the circumstances. The letters of thanks to »the ladies in Copenhagen« were many and sincere, but when disappointments came, sorrow went deep and could leave scars. Then neither patient letters nor – occasionally – a rebuke or explanation could help.

It was best, when matters were arranged out in the districts, and in the accounts and contemporary letters, much gratitude was expressed to the district chairmen – »Aunt Anna«, »Aunt Selma«, »Aunt Gerna« and many other »aunts«, who worked unceasingly to smooth the path of the young people. That it nevertheless went wrong as often as it did must be attributed mainly to the situation.

It must not be forgotten that all help to refugees involved a double problem: on the one hand, the refugees' understandable anxiety, rootlessness, and sometimes irritability; on the other hand, the hospitable families' just as understandable expectations of some form of gratitude and adjustment, and disappointment if this was altogether lacking, or even changed to the opposite.

»Der neue Weg«

The *Hechaluz* group. The *Alijah* group. The expressions are used, amongst other things, to summarize the position. But within each group there were naturally important differences, and particularly because here there was a question of large groups, which only counted as groups simply for organisational reasons. There were subordinate groups, fractions, cliques, individualistic and contrary opinions. The group size was never constant, and the position was constantly changing because of geographical situation, and the influences of the times and surroundings.

As time passed, the difference between the two groups decreased. This must of necessity occur, but it also occurred because the *Hechaluz* leaders in Copenhagen, the *Maskirut* office, deliberately worked to promote such a development. In a lengthy correspondence between the *Maskirut* leader Bertl Grass and the visiting teacher Ernst Laske, extant for the period April 1941 to July 1942, a number of problems are discussed, connected with the conditions in the centres, the visiting teachers' circumstances, relations with district leaders and foster-families, as well as the internal problems within the *Hechaluz* organisation. Here Grass repeatedly took up the complicated problem of the *Alijah* children's position and their possible, and desired, integration into the *Hechaluz* organisation, including their participation in the decisions on the make-up of the trainees' *Merkas* assembly. The attitude of the leaders in Copenhagen is illustrated, for example, in a letter of 11 May 1941 to Ernst Laske:

»*Participation of Jugendalijah.* I am at all events in favour of their taking part in some way or other. Your objection as regards their lack of insight is justified, so we must discover some form or other. But one cannot for all eternity treat them as children, and must in some way let them take part. This, in my opinion, has nothing to do with the question of legi- or illegitimacy, and I do not remember that this has been put forward in this connexion. I suggest that *Jugendalijah*, this time, in view of the lack of insight, should be represented by the visiting teachers,

Bertl Grass grew up in a strict orthodox Jewish home in Frankfurt. After 1933, he broke with his orthodox view of life, became a Zionist and socialist, based in Hechaluz. In 1939 he came to Denmark and was given the principal task of leading the Zionist education of the Jewish agricultural trainees.

and that the centres, where this is possible, also send delegates without the right to vote.«

Grass's remark on legitimacy must be understood in the sense that membership of *Hechaluz* demanded the head organisation's approval, and in the circumstances, this could not be obtained.

It was not altogether easy for the *Maskirut* leaders to insist on and carry through this line. They met some scepticism and opposition in both the districts and some of the homes, where there was anxiety at letting »the children« go, and difficulty in understanding the necessity for them to take part in the larger meetings and gatherings, to which the more independent *Hechaluz* trainees were admitted, and which must be a matter of course for those of the *Alijah* group, who felt themselves more and more attached to the older trainees, and their ideology and stand-point. Nor were the League leaders enthusiastic about the idea. When the question of »the children's« possible transfer to *Hechaluz* had been raised, out in the districts, and two district chairmen had poured out their forebodings about the disturbance which agitation on this could cause, Else Zeuthen, on 6 January 1943, sent a letter to five district chairmen, which reflected the leaders' scepticism regarding the idea: »With respect to the question of the children's transfer to *Hechaluz*, we are of the opinion that the situation for many reasons is so difficult, that their position is *most secure* with us. A meeting between us on the question will perhaps be necessary in the near future.«

It made matters no easier that it was difficult to explain the *Hechaluz* idea to the foster-parents and indeed to maintain its realistic possibilities, as things were. The foster-families could offer temporary security, and anything else could appear pure fantasy. A planned holiday meeting for a number of *Alijah* children in the summer 1941 had therefore to be called off. The political situation at that moment was unfavourable to the plan, and the committee for the *Alijah* children, who felt responsible for »the children«, and formally was so, turned against an initiative which seemed to contain a quite unnecessary element of risk. The attitude of the committee, strongly supported by its representatives from the Danish Mosaic Religious Community, was that Jews in Denmark – Danish as well as those in transit – were best served by keeping quiet as far as possible. That was also the Government's signal, and direct instructions. But nevertheless, time and circumstances led to the artificial division between two groups, which were only divided by age and organisation, being gradually eroded.

Under the pressure of this situation, in which the young people in both groups found themselves, constant discussion took place on conditions and possibilities, and uppermost in everyone's thoughts, naturally lay the chances, inspite of all the barriers, of achieving what had become the aim of nearly all of them: emigration to Palestine. And yet! Here too there were exceptions. Their lengthy stay, the influence of Danish families and schools, and particularly the fact that emigration could only become a reality years thence or never, had to lead to some of the young people considering that a permanent life in Denmark could perhaps be a solution. For the visiting teachers it became not only a duty to convert the trainees to Zionism, but also to hold on to those who might be wavering as to this final, and, for the teachers and their leaders, indisputable goal.

Opposed to this tendency, through all the ups and downs, the firm will of the majority was sustained, inspite of the impossibility of blazing a trail to the promised land, or at least maintaining the dream and so the will to reach the goal. In 1941–42, everything spoke against it being possible to realise the dream. Most of Europe was occupied by the Germans, and every road was thus closed, and the mandatory power, Great Britain, had everything but the issue of certificates on her mind – and their issue would in any case have been useless, since the possibility for using them was precisely nil. Grass could still, in April 1941, cling to a faint hope, in a letter to Ernst Laske, but the hope was overshadowed by pessimism:

»On the possibility for an approaching *Alijah* for the next group we know nothing. On the contrary, we are at the moment very pessimistic, first because of the general political situation, and secondly we have received the news from Sweden that all certificates become definitely invalid during April, and new ones must be distributed. It is of course possible that Denmark gets certificates again, but it is doubtful whether we are given a corresponding number.«

This last hope of emigration by legal means was crushed, with the German invasion of the Soviet Union in June 1941. After that, all the Sounds seemed to be closed.

As far as the host country, Denmark, was concerned, it was occupied. Both the Danish authorities and the Danish Jewish community cherished the illusion that the Danish Jews, and with them also the young immigrants from the two organisations, would be protected, inspite of the Occupation, from German persecution – so long as a Danish government, and from 29 August 1943 a Danish administration still had dealings with the occupying power. As a consequence of this reasoning, all appeals to the Jewish inhabitants of Denmark, both the Danish and the immigrating, were to the effect that they should heave to, and keep quiet. Every disturbance and every action, which could attract the attention of the occupying power to the Jewish presence in Denmark, was regarded as dangerous – and not without reason. Between the authorities and the Danish Jewish community there was complete agreement on the correctness and necessity of an absolutely passive attitude.

In the period up to 22 June 1941, when the expression »resistance« at most lurked in the consciousness of a very few in the Danish nation, and when a journey via Russia was still a faint possibility, the order for a passive attitude posed no problems for the young Jews. No other alternatives existed. But during the next two years, they were to experience a dawning change of spirit in the population, and particularly among Danes of their own age. They experienced the national stir which passed through the country, the appearance of an illegal Press, the start of sabotage, and in the summer 1943, the great national strikes, which bore witness to a growing protest against the Government's instructions on law and order.

It is clear that these signs could not but influence the young Jews, and that this whole development was followed and discussed during their meetings. Theoretically, the possibility must emerge that they could find a place in the illegal activity. There is no doubt that many of them would have been more than willing to take part in resistance against the occupying power. But the idea had to remain theory. It was in the towns, that the early resistance groups grew up, and the trainees lived in the country. But what was more decisive was that participation in resistance work was contingent on a water-tight security and an intimate knowledge of each other, which could never be extended to foreigners. Physically and linguistically, the young Jews had to accept the role recommended or ordered, of passive onlookers at a development which both deeply touched them, and at the same time avoided them. Passivity and caution were not only the Government's instructions. They were a prayer and an order from the foster-families, the leaders of the organisations, and the Jewish community in Denmark.

But in the *Hechaluz* group, a subsection was forming, which did not share this view. This group, whose initiator and informal leader was Bertl Grass, was not prepared to wait passively for the fulfilment of the dream. When all legal ways were closed, the illegal ways must be taken into use, and the group therefore began a long series of experiments, the object of which was to find and develop an illegal route to Palestine. The author, Uri Yaari, in his book »Confrontation«, has described how Grass conceived the idea that on a particular type of railway truck, one could crawl in under the truck and lie on the iron construction between the wheels, supplied with food, drink and the necessary stamina. When he had discovered this, deadly dangerous experiments began.

The word »experiment« must be stressed. It was not a question of an individual trying his luck to get to the Near East in that way. It was a question of finding out by experiment, whether the method was feasible for the whole group, or at least parts of it. The members of the group went to work, therefore, methodically. Uri Yaari gives an account of his first journey Copenhagen-Helsingør, his preparation and, literally speaking, his training on longer stretches, also including finding out whether the frontier could be passed, and whether the journey through Germany could take place unnoticed – not a risky adventure for an individual, but methodical experiments for the benefit of the whole group. He describes a journey of this kind to Hamburg, and after a short wait, on to Maastricht in Holland and back to Fredericia. On yet one more tour he reached Munich and could perhaps have gone on, but also this time returned to Denmark. »The agreement was that we must come back and report,« he writes.

It was this agreement which was to be fatal to Grass himself. The idea was that Yaari should go on a longer journey, but his interest in the railway sidings was observed, and Grass decided to test the further possibilities himself. He started from Nyborg, and, with changes in Germany, came as far as Sophia in Bulgaria, quite near the Turkish frontier – a neutral country with good *Hechaluz* contacts. There – on the threshold to freedom with great possibilities for getting through to Palestine – he turned back. The group's discipline passed this test, also. In Copenhagen his comrades waited for him in vain. Yaari registers the tragedy, in his terse, reserved style, devoid of any expression of great emotion: »But when Bertl had reached Bulgaria, he turned back. He had to. We had agreed on it. And that was his death. On his way home, he was discovered by a zealous railwayman in Hamburg, and ended his days in the concentration camp, Auschwitz.«

Yaari and the friends in Copenhagen did not receive news of what had happened until years later, when one of the group, who also landed in Auschwitz but survived, could tell about their comrades' death in the German camp. In ignorance of Grass's fate, the group went to work, preparing and testing a new, desperate attempt, related in detail as regards planning, in the book mentioned, by Uri Yaari:

»Heinz worked on a farm. About 2 kilometres from the farm there was a machine factory, and Heinz had made friends with one of the workers. He loved talking about the factory. And he told him also that the factory was still exporting. Inspite of the War. Amongst other places, to Turkey. If only one could be one of those machines and be taken to Turkey. Direct. We talked a lot about this direct transport from Denmark to Turkey ... Gradually the plan took form. It must be in the truck itself and not underneath it. It was both safer and pleasanter ... We found how it all went. The large machines were packed in cases 2 metres high. The railway trucks were led in on the factory ground. Then the cases were loaded on to the trucks. They were then taken to the frontier, where they were examined by the Customs and sealed with lead seals. What we had to do was really quite simple. Get into the truck and hide ourselves so well that the Customs men did not find us. And the end station was Turkey. The first two who were to travel were Alfred and Yehuda. We were only waiting for Heinz's message about when the next load to Turkey was to go. And then we had to hurry. There were two trucks on the ramp. We soon found the right one. So we thought. The equipment was also in order. Tools to open the cases and install themselves in them. Masses of food. Masses of beer and water.«

The attempt ended in disaster. It was not the right truck. It turned out that the goods were not to go to Turkey, but to Switzerland, and that the truck was delayed in a siding for days, until the two refugees, burning with thirst, had to give up and finally – not knowing that they were at the

Swiss frontier – had to reveal themselves, were turned over to the Gestapo, and so to deportation to Auschwitz. Only Alfred survived. His account from 1980 is laconic:

»In February 1943, I took a friend, Yehuda, to Høng, where we smuggled ourselves on board a goods train. We hid in a packing case, which contained a machine, intended for Switzerland. After travelling for about two weeks through Germany, we were caught in Singen (near the Swiss frontier) and transported to Auschwitz. When the Russians came closer, the Germans evacuated us, and after the notorious 'death march' those of us who survived reached the concentration camp Buchenwald. We were more dead than alive, ill, and famished, and we could hardly move. In some way or other I found out that there were Danish prisoners in the camp, and I succeeded in speaking to them, and telling them my story. They gave us food, which I shared with my friend, and after two weeks, we had recovered a little, and first of all had gained new hope of being able to survive the War. One evening I was fetched out to a transport to a labour camp, and as my friend was in another barrack, I could not get him with me. I never heard from him again and must take it that he perished. In April 1945, I was liberated by Allied troops in South Germany, and in May I hitch-hiked to Hamburg, tried first to get back to Denmark, but then I met some members of the Jewish Brigade, who sent me via Belgium and France on an illegal ship to Israel.«

After a month or two, the group in Denmark heard through the Danish police about the tragedy. Nevertheless, a new attempt was made, which would cost the lives of three more comrades. This time, the truck went to Turkey, but the three refugees did not get further than Warnemünde. The Germans had now been warned of the possibility of these machine cases being used for illegal transport. At Warnemünde they broke the seals, and Heinz, Ella and Ruth never returned. Again the group heard of the tragedy through their connexion with the Danish police, and had now to cancel this route, at least. Uri Yaari tells in his account from 1980 of the actual dissolution of the group:

»After the arrest of the 3 passengers in the Høng truck, Heinz Reinach, Ella Reinach and Ruth Mokry, the group, which at that point numbered 50 members, held a big meeting in Sønderskov near Sorø. After discussing the situation and the failure of the attempts, it was decided to give the members freedom of choice. This was, broadly speaking, between flight to Sweden and joining the Danish resistance movement.«

Uri Yaari chose the latter, and was to take active part in sabotage work in Odense, until he too was arrested and landed in a German concentration camp.

But the group never succeeded in finding the »new way« to Palestine.

Flight from Bornholm

It was to be flight to Sweden, that would be the salvation of the Danish Jews, and it was to be a little group of *Hechaluz* trainees who would show the way. It was the three Jewish fishermen on Bornholm who, with the local fishermen, laid the plan and organised its practical execution, but it was the group centred on »Der neue Weg« that were behind its realisation.

One of the Jews from the inner circle of this group, Heinz Mosse, fathered the original plan, which was for a group, via Bornholm, to get to Christiansø and here smuggle themselves on board one of the Swedish fishing boats, which even during the War touched at Christiansø. Mosse discussed the plan with both Slor and Margolinsky, and mentions in his account that, as far as it went, they agreed with his underlying belief that the Germans, sooner or later, must be expected to resort to force against the Danish Jews, and that these could be compelled to look for some way of getting out of the country. They believed, however, that one should wait before putting all such plans into action, because the very attempt at flight could help to draw German attention to Jewish presence in Denmark – a belief which the Danish Jews shared with the leaders of the Mosaic Religious Community. Hitherto, the Government had been able to protect the Jews against attack, and it was the Jewish hope that they could continue to do so. But Mosse was not to be deflected. He put the planning in the hands of the three Jewish fishermen on Bornholm, who were familiar with local conditions, and they decided on a simulated theft of a fishing boat at Tejn, and together with local helpers made various preparations. The date was fixed for the eve of 1 April, which because of the new moon was a dark night, the necessary amounts of fuel were procured, and information obtained about the local harbour and coast guards.

Late in the evening of 31 March, nine Jews went on board the little cutter the owner of which had agreed, and later, by way of an alibi, raised a demand for damages against Margolinsky, on the grounds of lost earnings. A week or two later, he fetched his cutter back from Sweden. The boat was towed out with ropes to the harbour entrance, where the sail was set, and the cutter glided silently to sea, until half an hour later, the motor was started. The idea was that at least they would have a start, should their departure be discovered. Everything went according to plan, and the night's events will be described here with a report which Heinz Mosse wrote in Sweden on 2 April, and which he sent to the

Hechaluz leaders in London, where the report was sent on to a number of British authorities, the Foreign Office, the Political Intelligence Department, the Ministry of Economic Warfare, etc.

The report reads:

»I am able to give you the good news that a group of 9 comrades have arrived in Sweden from Denmark. It consists of 3 fishermen, who have been on Bornholm the whole time, Erich Marx, Helmuth Julius and Werner Bamberger, also Seew Pergamenter, who has been working in the secretariat of Youth-*Alijah*, Herbert and Paula Schönewald, Secretaries in the *Hechaluz* office, Norbert Kammermann, Manfred Sachs and Heinz Mosse. As you will probably be able to see from this list, this undertaking was made possible by the help of our 3 fishermen. As you will no doubt be interested in hearing the details of this voyage, I will give you a short report on it. It is not because there was any immediate necessity to leave Denmark, but we had recently come to the conclusion that it would be right to bring the comrades over who had the courage and will for it, to Sweden. This is naturally no easy matter, as the German authorities have forbidden any form of emigration, and both the Danish coast guards – who are stationed at all, even the smallest, points – and the German navy keep a sharp look-out, and as all who are caught are liable to punishment, if not the death sentence, then a long prison sentence in Denmark. Our journey was prepared in detail by our fisher comrades, and the plan was to steal a fishing cutter from the harbour in Tejn on Bornholm, bring the comrades on board during the night, set sail to come out of the harbour, and after half an hour, when we were far enough from land, start the motor and set course for Simrishamm in Sweden. Now that it is all finished successfully, it can be said that it really was a splendid effort on the part of our fishermen, and it has once more shown how important training in this particular field has been for us, and the training's justification will not only be shown in this special instance. During the night that the voyage lasted, the wind force was 11, so no Danish fisherman had so much as attempted such a trip, and of course the risk of discovery was so much the less. After a 6 hours' sail, we anchored up in the harbour of Simrishamm, where two of our fishermen slipped through the military barricade and established contact with *Hechaluz* in Hässleholm. We were arrested, of course, but were released the same day, after the local *Hechaluz*'s intervention, and we are now in Hässleholm, where we are awaiting Swedish work permits.«

The successful flight gave rise to considerable anxiety in Jewish circles in Denmark, just as the attempts at flight by the »Der neue Weg« group had given rise to anxiety in the inner circle who had heard of the plans and attempts. The Germans had naturally got wind of what had happened, and through the Under Secretary in the Ministry of Justice, Eivind Larsen and the Public Prosecutor Helge Hoff of the Public Prosecutors

Department, let the Mosaic Religious Community know that any repetition of such an attempt at flight could have the most serious consequences for the Jews in Denmark, and Margolinsky reacted by sending out a serious appeal to all the *chawerim* in Denmark – *Hechaluz* trainees as well as *Alijah* children – to keep from similar attempts in the future. The appeal stressed that the situation of the members of the two groups was not essentially different from that of the country's other citizens in general and the Jewish citizens in particular; and that any action which could attract German attention to the Jews in Denmark could make a serious situation even more acute.

For Margolinsky to send out such a general appeal was an obvious duty for his secretariat, but that he regarded an illegal solution as wrong and uncalled-for, even in 1943, appears from a private letter he wrote on 15 April to a doctor Blume in Svinninge, who had for the past two years opened his home for regular gatherings of the Jewish agricultural trainees, and with whom Margolinsky had built up a grateful, confidential relationship, in a constant exchange of letters. His words in this private letter were:

»I also enclose a couple of copies of an article which I have written in these days. The reason for this is amongst others that some of our young people have had the idea of going to Sweden, and have thus exposed their comrades here, and wider circles in the religious community, to various forms of unpleasantness, which *can have extremely serious consequences,* if anything of the kind should be repeated. As concerns the contents of my article, it is kept in general terms, but I count on you, Doctor Blume, perhaps to find an opportunity to comment on it, when you are with the young people. As you can certainly understand, it cannot be tolerated that our folk travel illegally out of the country, or try to. For the time being, four of our *chawerim* are in prison after unsuccessful attempts to get away, and there have been no sensible grounds whatever for the attempts at flight. On the other hand, it must be feared, as I say, that repetitions will have very serious consequences, not only for *Hechaluz,* but also for many others.«

The Danish Jewish problem was not solved in April 1943, and no one could foresee that it could have a more or less happy solution through illegal efforts so that Margolinsky had to consider both the hundreds in the *Hachscharah,* and the thousands in the Danish Jewish community.

The description of the Bornholm flight should not end with the mention of this single flight. After its success, and particularly with the arrival of the three »Bornholm fishermen«, the idea arose in the Swedish *Hechaluz* organisation (started on the initiative of Binjamin Slor's brother-in-law, the Army Doctor Emil Glück) of procuring a boat with which, with the three »Bornholm fishermen« as crew, to come to the help of the comrades in the Danish *Hachscharah*.

The first problem was that of money. As luck would have it, one of the leaders of the Jewish London office, »The Council of German Jewry«, S. Adler-Rudel, was in Sweden at that particular moment, to negotiate with the Swedish authorities, and he showed immediate interest and promised help to find the needed funds, just as, from the 1930's, he had given economic help to the agricultural trainees in Denmark. A fund was started with gifts, and at the end of the summer 1943, enough money had been collected for the three »Bornholm fishermen« to look around for a suitable boat. On 8 September, a contract of purchase was signed, for a cutter, which under the name of »Julius« was put at the disposal of the Swedish *Hechaluz* organisation, with Marx, Julius and Bamberger as crew. The idea was that with this boat they should try and help as many of their comrades to Sweden as it might prove possible. Under cover of fishing, they tried to get in touch with Margolinsky on the Danish coast during September, but did not make contact, partly because his office had been moved, on grounds of security, in those turbulent weeks. The original idea with the boat, to rescue comrades and bring them to Sweden, came to nothing. On the other hand, the boat gave excellent service, when it was chartered for escape transport by the Danish-Swedish Refugee Service in Malmø, started and led by the editor Leif Hendil. In the period up to the middle of December, »Julius« would transport in all 370 refugees across the Sound, but here it was not a question of *Hechaluz* or *Alijah* especially, but of anyone who needed to escape.

So a Jewish trail to freedom had been blazed, and »Julius« was only one of many tools, even if at first it was the most important and the most deeply engaged.

A Jew looks at Denmark

In his report to the *Hechaluz* leaders in London, Heinz Mosse did not confine himself to a description of the flight from Bornholm, but took the opportunity, which his freedom in Sweden gave him, to give a concentrated report on what he called the Jews' position in Denmark, although his account dealt mainly with the situation and atmosphere in the *Hechaluz* and *Alijah* groups. The report reached London on 18 April, and gave first the Hechaluz leaders and then the British authorities a glimpse into the actual situation in Denmark, as it was regarded by one of the leaders of the *Hechaluz* organisation there. With a few exceptions of minor relevance, the report is quoted here as a contemporary expression, by the leaders of *Hechaluz* and *Maskirut* in Copenhagen, of their estimate of the situation in the spring 1943. To start with, Mosse mentioned the attempts to set up centres and carry out cultural and political education there, and he continued:

»*Hechaluz* has both internally and externally achieved a fairly free status, but it must also be pointed out that the working conditions for the comrades out in the country are very limited. Even today, after 5 years in Denmark, our comrades are only regarded as agricultural trainees and can officially only earn 25 crowns – and they are not allowed to replace Danish workers on a farm. These conditions are naturally impossible for our work, and we have therefore always been forced to ask the farmers to give false information to the police, so that we have been able to get better conditions. We have naturally made efforts to improve our official status, but unfortunately only with very, very meagre results, as there is un-employment now among the Danish workers, and because we, in Denmark's present situation, have preferred to continue in the old way, and altogether avoid attracting attention from a different side to these conditions. In spite of this, it has been possible, even in these conditions, to build up a *Hachscharah*, which is generally speaking independent, and which can manage with its own earnings, and only social cases may receive support from the Jewish Religious Community. It is important to point out that the official status described above has a very depressing effect on every single comrade. It is true that most of the comrades have good places, but all depends, to a greater or lesser extent, on the farmers' sense of justice and propriety. For people with really first-class working capacities these conditions make for dissatisfaction after a time. *Hechaluz* naturally tries to get the best possible conditions, in the situation, sending a number of comrades to schools or courses, and others to agricultural research work, etc., but in all this we are very much limited by all sorts of official rules. Fortunately, the local authorities themselves acknowledge how meaningless many of the rules are, and they often shut both eyes, but of course they cannot act directly against their instructions. A particularly difficult problem arises in this connexion, for comrades who, for reasons of health, are not able to go on working on the land, as they cannot obtain work permits for any other work, and are forced to rely on the religious community for help. Even trained artisans – and there are c.50 of them among the comrades – have never, during their stay, had the opportunity of working in the trade they have learned, and as these trades are mostly of special interest for our future, this situation is naturally particularly depressing for our movement.

Co-operation with the gentlemen you know, Slor and Margolinsky, has been altogether good the whole time. There has been agreement on all questions, and the problems which arose after the Germans' occupation, particularly in the financial area, were solved satisfactorily with their help. However strange it may sound, inspite of the lack of Joint money (American Joint Distribution Committee, for example) and an annual budget of 100,000 crowns, there were never financial difficulties, thanks to Slor's position in the Jewish community in Copenhagen. Even for the very considerable cultural expenses, the necessary funds have always been available, either from the comrades themselves or from the community. In spite of their attitude, this constituted a very great burden for the Jewish community ... The financing of the cultural work was made possible with about equal amounts from the *Hachscharah* and the community, and on an average, 2,200 crowns were made available per month ... A *Hachscharah* library has been started, which today contains 2,000 volumes, and we were lucky enough, in the Royal Library, to find a Jewish department, collected by the well-known Professor Simonsen – previously Chief Rabbi in Copenhagen – which today is probably the largest Jewish library in Europe. It also includes all the new Hebrew books up to the year 1940.«

Mosse then mentions activity in cultural and political work, subjects, study circles, etc., and continues:

»The last meeting was a continuation of the previous discussion on the Jewish people's amoral life, with a talk by Bertl Grass, in which he pointed out how impossible and inconsistent our attitude was as Zionists and pioneers, as long as we waited passively, and quietly remained here in Denmark and in all the other countries of the world. He formed a group of men, altogether good comrades, I must say, who are intensely occupied with the possibilities for *Alijah* (emigration) ... You can imagine that the disappearance of the Council, the invalidation of our certificates for Denmark, the endless wait for *Alijah*, the comrades' poor status, etc. must make the comrades, particularly the younger ones, receptive to the idea that in the end one must do something. Bertl's answer to this was to the effect that the various possibilities for illegal *Alijah* must be investigated. It soon became evident that the most active of the comrades seized upon this idea – people who belonged to the core of the movement, including Heinz Reinach, who naturally had always been one of Bertl's best friends. For a long time, the Secretariat believed that all these problems existed in the ideological sphere alone, but had to admit later, that serious practical preparation was going on. Because of the secrecy that was maintained, a certain amount of tension arose between the »uninitiated« and the comrades from »*Der neue Weg*«. The Secretariat's attitude was particularly complicated, first because it involved comrades whom one could not simply expel, and secondly because fundamentally it was a question of a task which in the end was pioneer work. Naturally, most of the *Hachscharah* looked on these comrades as romantics, but they understood very well that the realisation of

188

such a plan could involve great danger for the whole *Hachscharah*, when after careful investigation it became clear that their way through Germany and the Balkans would lead to Erez Israel. No doubt this plan sounds fantastic to you, it is beyond discussion that it is so, also for us. You must, however, take into consideration the fact that for them it was not a question of flight from Denmark to Sweden, but of the possibility of coming to Erez Israel, and the only way there lay through Germany, since it was well known that no one – not even from England – went to Erez Israel. It is hard to believe what detailed preparations were made for all eventualities, during which it was possible to reconnoitre parts of the route. So, since the end of December, Bertl Grass is no longer in Denmark. We presume that he wished to return, but did not succeed. I have mentioned that many of the comrades looked on these preparations with anxiety, as they believed they contained the danger of arrest of the *Hachscharah* by German or Danish authorities, and this obviously increased the comrades' nervousness.

»The more or less sudden change of government in Denmark in the autumn 1942 underlined for many of the comrades the insecurity of their position. They saw what had happened to the Jews in Holland, and especially in Norway, and they saw that even in Denmark, the same thing could happen one day. We told ourselves that we, as pioneers, dared not let our actions be overtaken by events, but must use our present good position in Denmark to prepare ourselves for all eventualities. This standpoint was not shared by all the *Hachscharah* by any means, as such preparation cut deep into the private life of the individual, and also demanded personal initiative. At the next committee meeting in January, we spoke for the first time openly about all these problems, and tried to give support to the comrades in their preparations, partly also because we realised that these things were not only a task for a small group, but for the whole movement. It was obvious, however, that if any possibility could be found, one must make use of it immediately, as such a possibility could become an open question from one day to the next.

»All this can perhaps be better understood if I go into the political situation in Denmark in somewhat more detail.

»However strange it may sound, th Jews' position in Denmark has hardly changed since the German occupation on 9 April 1940. There is not the slightest (anti-) Jewish legislation, and Jews still hold their political and economic posts. It is a fact that the Danish Government, in spite of the German occupation, possesses extensive autonomy, and that in spite of repeated demands on the part of the Germans, they have refused, successfully, to introduce any (anti-) Jewish laws. The Jewish question, for the Danish Government, has become a direct question of the existence or non-existence of an independent Denmark, and it has – and this applies also to the King – refused to be daunted by threats of withdrawal. As a result of this, the Germans have shown the greatest consideration towards Danish independence from the start, and even militarily have received quite special instructions in this respect. Nevertheless, the reaction in the Danish population is quite different from what the Germans expected would result: especially since the sabotage which has been happening lately has not yet resulted in any counter-measures by the Germans. One thing is clear to us, however, and that is that a continuation of these actions must necessarily bring German reprisals, sooner or later. During the three years under German occupation, Denmark has been able, it is true, to maintain her independence, but as total war develops, it can be necessary for Germany to introduce a different state of things, here too.«

This detailed report, which contained both true and false evaluations, was at least correct in its concluding passage: that developments in Denmark were nearing a crisis, and that in a crisis it would be the Danish Jews, both the home Jews and the immigrants, who would be among the most threatened. It is evident from the report, that this terrible fact was clear to all.

Flight and Imprisonment

The German Action against the Danish Jews

With most of Europe under Nazi rule, it is understandable that Jews everywhere had to cling to even the slenderest hopes. For the Danish Jews, the hope was vested in the Government's possibility of the keeping Germans in check. Everything else must seem unrealistic. Smaller groups like the c.50 young people who were attached to »Der neue Weg« could seek desperate solutions, but even in the most favourable circumstances and with the greatest possible luck, such ways could only be open to very few. They certainly could not include the entire Danish *Hachscharah*, and there could be no question of their helping the c. 7,000 Danish Jews, who were deeply integrated into Danish society, in many cases for several generations, and who were only in exceptional instances personally engaged in the Zionist idea. Very many of them were sympathetic to the idea, and they could give economic and moral support to the young people from Central Europe, who sought to realise their vision, but by far the greatest number were so deeply rooted in Danish society, that the idea of themselves finding a future in Palestine was quite foreign to them.

There remained the hope that the Danish Government would be able to hold the German authorities back, so that measures against the Jews were not imported into Denmark, and for the first three years of occupation, the Jewish leaders in Denmark received categorical assurances from the Government that it would in no circumstances agree to special legislation or other measures against the Jews. This assurance, which was both honestly meant and kept to the full, did, however, contain the undeniably fragile elements that no one could know whether the Government would have power to carry out its intentions throughout the time of occupation, or whether the Government could remain in power as long as the Occupation lasted. There were government crises enough for this question constantly to bore into the consciousness of Jewish circles in Denmark. And if the Government had to go, what would happen then? It is quite understandable that the Jewish leaders, during the first three years of occupation, took the stand of urging their fellow-Jews to refrain from any hasty decisions or acts, and that similar appeals also went out to the members of the Danish *Hachscharah* – the *Hechaluz* group as well as the *Alijah* group.

The thought of flight could never be exorcised altogether, however, and looked at realistically, in the event, there could only be a question of flight to Sweden, to seek temporary asylum there. But the leaders were also against this thought. Individual attempts could create unrest and danger for thousands, and no one could foresee that flight could succeed for more than a few people, or unimportant small groups, and besides, no one knew what the Swedish attitude would be. All previous experience, up to the autumn 1943, indicated that flight to Sweden was both dangerous and almost impossible to carry out. When, therefore, the flight from Bornholm, already mentioned, succeeded as it did, the undertaking did not arouse any hopes – only fear in the Jewish circles. The vice-chairman of the Mosaic Religious Community, Karl Lachmann, has expressed their standpoint with the words:

»There was unanimity that one should refrain from it. 6–7,000 people could not be hidden. Any action would demand help from non-Jewish countrymen, demands which one could not make, and could not expect to be fulfilled. No one dreamed that Sweden would receive such a large contingent. All that one could achieve would be both to create panic and give the Germans an excuse. The question of rescuing the children received the same reply.«

This was the attitude in the Mosaic Religious Community. Was it also the attitude of the young Jews in the *Hachscharah*? There was after all a question of two quite different groups, in quite different situations, only with the essential addendum that their acute situation was the same. Both groups were threatened, and equally threatened, by possible anti-Jewish measures. They were thus in the same boat, but on quite different premises. What was thought and decided in the one camp, need not correspond to the ideas in the other.

It is worth remembering, here, that the direct line of communication between the two groups was rather slender, for geographical reasons alone. The great majority of Danish Jewish society lived and worked in greater Copenhagen, while the c. 550 stranded members of the *Hachscharah* were dispersed over the whole country, North and Central Jylland and South Jylland excepted. Of course, many of the young people came to Copenhagen at intervals, and had personal contact with members of Danish Jewish society, but contacts of this kind were haphazard. Economically and socially, as well as professionally, the differences were also noticeable, with established town occupations in one group, and improvised occupations in agriculture and horticulture etc. in the other group. There were differences also as regards age: in one group a mixture of ages, corresponding with the normal family pattern, in the other group exclusively young people. One important point of contact was the fact that the Danish Jewish community had supported the trainees in the *Hascharah* again and again, and that the Jewish leaders, with sympathy and varying degrees of commitment to the Zionist cause, had followed the work in the *Hascharah* and had also participated in its construction. Nevertheless, the *Hascharah* remained an enclave within an enclave.

There is no doubt, however, that the fatalistic attitude of the Danish Jewish community, the belief that one should cling as long as possible to the Governments assurances, and enjoin calm and passivility, generally speaking also penetrated the *Hachscharah*, and perhaps especially the *Alijah* group. As we have seen, it was only a small minority that were initiated into the plans for »*Der neue Weg*«, and even in this group, in the end, after the unsuccessful escape attempts, members were left free – and this in reality meant giving up organised plans for mass flight. The realities showed themselves to be harder than the dreams, and the great majority of the members of the *Hachscharah* chose to wait and see, and hope for the best, influenced in that direction by many impulses, the Government's appeals for law and order, the Jewish leaders' appeals for the same, the influences in the foster-homes, and not least the realisation of the hopelessness, for the time being, of any other solution.

Up to the summer 1943, all this was a matter of speculation, or perhaps »let sleeping dogs lie«, without actual immediacy. But then things suddenly began to happen, and snowballed much faster than anyone could have foreseen. As late as July 1943, the Danish Government's position seemed quite secure, but events in August toppled the policy of negotiation, and with that, the Government's possibilities for blocking anti-Jewish measures. On 29 August, the Government had to resign.

Now the way was open to a German action against the Danish Jews, and this came on the night between 1 and 2 October 1943. Even in September, the leaders of the Mosaic Religious Community clung to the last, thin straw, that the Under-Secretaries' administration, which to a certain extent and in certain circumstances, continued to negotiate with the German authorities, could restrain all the plans for German intervention against the Danish Jews, but also this hope was crushed. The

German action against the Jews will not be described here. It is narrated elsewhere, for example in Leni Yahil's book, »Test of a Democracy« and in my own book, »Til Landets Bedste«, vol.I, ch.5 and 6.

Here – for the sake of coherence – a very few of the most decisive developments will be outlined. The action was started by a telegram, which the German Reich plenipotentiary, Werner Best, sent to the German Foreign Ministry on 8 September 1943, asking to what extent, in the state of martial law which was one of the results of the German take-over on 29 August, it would be expedient to consider the Jewish question in Denmark, requesting a decision on what Best in the given situation was to take as regards the Jewish question. The telegram found its way upwards in the German hierarchy and let loose an order from the Führer for an action against the Jews in Denmark, and their deportation. While the Germans were dealing with the matter, in the period 8–18 September, the German shipping consultant in the German Copenhagen headquarters at Dagmarhus, G.F. Duckwitz, became aware of the notorious telegram. He reacted immediately and energetically, to prevent the catastrophe he foresaw. First he tried to stop the telegram on its way to Hitler's headquarters. This failed. He then alerted the Swedish authorities, to get them to intervene, which they did, first by making a diplomatic démarche in Berlin, which was of no effect, and then by informing, amongst others, the Jewish leaders, that Sweden was open to all Jewish refugees. Finally – when it was quite clear that the action was imminent and could no longer be averted – Duckwitz took his decisive step. On 29 September he informed the Social Democrat politicians, Hedtoft-Hansen and H.C. Hansen, of the plan and the time for the action, and thus prevented the full catastrophe. His warning was passed on, the same day, to the Jewish leaders, after which it was spread by all imaginable channels, for example at the morning service in the Jewish synagogue on 29 September. Whit that, the Jews whom the warning reached in time received the chance of going underground, and finding an escape route to Sweden, and with that there began a mass flight without parallel in occupied Europe. It was possible for many reasons. One of the chief reasons was Sweden's attitude. Another reason loses itself in individual actions, taken by the Jews themselves and their many Danish helpers. But their most important deliverer was Duckwitz.

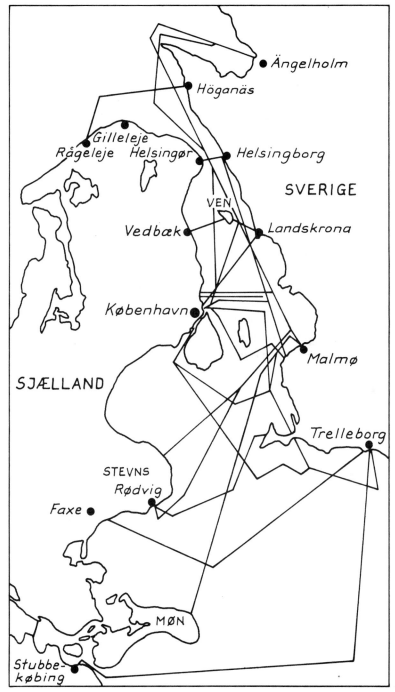

Rescue routes criss-crossing the Øresund.

The bare Figures

The mass escape, which Karl Lachmann and with him all the other leaders in the Jewish community had not considered possible, became a reality. The flight began gradually, during September, when two German raids on Jewish offices gave warning of a new course, following the resignation of the Government, and it grew to a general mass flight, when the omens in the last days of September were sent on to larger circles. A description of its kaleidoscopic course is given in the book mentioned, by Levi Yahil, in Aage Bertelsen's book, »October 43«, and in a great many other works, both Danish and foreign. Here I shall simply refer the reader to the bibliography in the handbook, »Besættelsen 1940–45, Politik, Modstand, Befrielsen«, (»The Occupation 1940–45, Politics, Resistance, Liberation«).

The fugitives were, first, pure Jews, but there were also a number of half-Jews and spouses of Jews. The total number of those threatened, who reached safe harbour in Sweden, can therefore be difficult to calculate, as the number must vary, depending upon what categories are included. Julius Margolinsky, in his work, »Statistiske undersøgelser over Alders- og Kønsfordeling m.m. blandt Flygtninge fra Danmark« (»Statistic Research in Differences of Age and Sex etc. among Fugitives from Denmark«), reached the following conclusions:

Number of Danish Jews, living in Sweden 1945		7,906
Died in Sweden 1943–45		101
		8,007
Deducted:		
Born in Sweden 1943–45	265	
Escaped because of marriage with Jews, and therefore included on the list	686	
	951	951
		7,056

After this, it must be a matter of opinion, whether one chooses the one or the other of the two figures.

But not all escaped to Sweden. There were those who did not receive any warning, those who ignored the warning, those who physically or practically were unable to reach safety, and those who were caught during their flight. Here we have to do with smaller, and yet tragic numbers.

During the night of the action itself – the eve of 2 October – 202 Jews were arested in Copenhagen, while another 82 were seized out in the country or during 2 October – in all 284 – who were taken, in 2 transports, to the concentration camp Theresienstadt. In the weeks that followed, this number increased, when, exceptionally, the Germans succeeded in arresting Jews during an attempted flight. These last, after a short stay in the North Sjælland camp in Horserød, were then taken to Theresienstadt. A few did not survive the transport, and a very few, after the Danish authorities demands and pressure, were sent back from Theresienstadt; and the Danish authorities succeeded in preventing the transport to Theresienstadt of a smaller number of Jews.

Leni Yahil gives this calculation:

The 2 transports on 2 October	284
The 2 transports on 13 October and 23 November	190
In all	474
Missing en route and returned	10
Number of Jews deported from Denmark to Theresienstadt	464

Of this number, there were 28 *Hechaluz* trainees and 38 *Alijah* children, and 35 other Jewish refugees, who were staying in Denmark at the time of the German action, in all 101 persons.

If we deduct this number from the 464, we have 363 deportees out of the Danish Jewish community in Denmark. If we estimate the number of persons in this group – very roughly – at c. 7,000 persons, we come to a percentage of those arrested as c.5%, perhaps slightly lower. As regards *Hechaluz* trainees and *Alijah* children arrested, the corresponding percentage is decidedly higher, c.7.5% and 20% respectively.

The conclusion from this must be that these two groups, and particularly the group of *Alijah* children were considerably more exposed than the Danish Jewish community.

The explanation is probably simple. They were living farther away from the warnings and the embarkation points, and they had fewer personal contacts to draw upon, than the established families in the Copenhagen area. Their line of escape was longer, and could involve complications before they could reach the Øresund coast or other embarkation places. Possibly some of them, out in the country, felt themselves more protected than they really were. However, the reason was not that everything that could be done was not done from Copenhagen, to get into contact with them and warn them, and as far as possible try to help, but there was and remained a difference between a telephone and a personal contact. The leaders of the organisation in charge of contact with them, and with responsibility for them, remained at their posts during the critical weeks and did what they could to help where they could. This applied, amongst others, to the Jewish leaders, Slor, Margolinsky, the leaders of the *Hechaluz* office and Mélanie Oppenhejm, who did not seek a way of escape until there was no longer any prospect of being able to help. For Mélanie Oppenhejm and her family this came to mean arrest and deportation to Theresienstadt via Horserød. But the help to these groups was more difficult, because of distance and dispersal, and because the two groups, to the extent that warnings reached them and were believed, dissolved in the attempt to find independent escape routes, and for that reson could not be traced by the leaders at the centre. The numbers establish the fact. The trainees' accounts contain memories of individual sequences of events.

Just one Route

»After the Germans' 'seizure of power' on 29 August 1943, we always reckoned on being forced to flee once more from the Nazis. In a way we were 'spiritually' prepared ... Our postman 'Willy' called early in the morning after the night (1–2 October) and was surprised to find us (my wife and our little daughter, born on 21.8.43 ... and I) still in our little house, which we could rent in the neighbourhood of my place of work at the research farm ... I rushed to the farm and asked for help in a hard and difficult situation. The head showed himself without understanding or unwilling to understand. Cast down, I had to leave the farm, but on the way home to our little house I was already accompanied by a number of our neighbours, who must have heard of 'the action'. Grocer – baker – tobacconist – porter all came with me and tried to comfort and all wanted to help us. My wife decided that we should go to Odense ... In the summer 1943, my wife had had to ask for extra clothes coupons because of the expected child. She had to apply to the social welfare office in Odense, and on that occasion mentioned her terror of a possible attack from 'the Germans' against us Jews. The ladies at the social welfare office thought that could never happen. But if – yes if – then my wife should just come to them and they would give all the help they could ... Now this offer was like a gift from above.«

The account describes the journey to Odense, a telephoned warning to a Jewish friend, who immediately went underground, to escape later to Sweden, the visit at the social welfare office, the telephone contact from the office to the Mothers' Help in Bogense, and two days' temporary stay in Odense with the local district chairman of the Women's League for Peace and Freedom, until the family were installed in Bogense.

»In no time I was also installed in the Mothers' Home, and with our own room, with my wife and our little child. It was the first time in the History of the Mothers' Home, that a man had received shelter. And how could one explain to all the feminine 'guests' that one was forced to make an exception? It must not be disclosed to anyone that we were fleeing, still less that we were Jews.«

This was managed with a story that the couple had bought a farm in the neighbourhood, and now were just waiting to move in. In the mean time, the directress of the home worked to establish the contacts which could bring the family, and one more Jewish woman with her one-year-old son, who were kept hidden in a nearby children's home, to Sjælland, and from there on to Sweden. What happened here is beyond the knowledge of the writer – and the historian. The problem – one of the problems – was whether the children could go too, but repeated offers to take care of the children in Denmark were categorically refused. The families intended to keep together, if necessary to the bitter end. And finally the reconnoitering succeeded, after hours and days between doubt and hope. An anonymous man with further contacts announced himself in Bogense.

»Late in the evening there was a ring at the door, and in came a gentleman and burst out with a 'JA'...Even today, it is impossible to describe how happy we *all* were – tears of joy flowed, and in that moment, it was joy that overshadowed all else... We were told that we should soon drive by car to Odense, later to go on to Copenhagen, but first the directress came with gifts – and more than 1000 crowns, which her family and their friends and acquaintances had collected as a 'little' help for us, which could give us the possibility of paying, if necessary, for our crossing to Sweden. We were quite overcome, and everything was like a dream. In the car there was already a lady, who only introduced herself by her first name, and she was to be 'our' nannie the whole way to Copenhagen.«

The account describes the journey in detail, by Odense – Nyborg – Copenhagen, with a couple of hours' wait in a forest because of air raid warnings, the »nannie's« and the ferry personnel's help during the passage past the German military police, and the »nannie« being relieved on Copenhagen main railway station by still another anonymous »nannie«, and in by the back door to a room in the Industrial Council's building, near the Town Hall Square, where an anonymous young man »Hans« took over as leader.

»In the house there was constant telephone traffic, and we moved as though in a dream world, and did not grasp much of what was going on around us ... we were told that we were to go on from here on the morrow or the next day, either to a new hiding-place or else direct to Sweden. The time of waiting was long for us, in spite of brave attempts on Hans's part to make our stay as pleasant as possible.«

The family did not come to Sweden the next day. The tour went to a flat in Frederiksberg, and yet one more two-days wait, until a courier arrived with a mesage to the family to hold themselves ready on the following day at a certain hour.

»At the given moment the courier came with a big bouquet of flowers, which I sitting in front in the taxi, was to hold up so that it could be clearly seen. As said so done, and so the trip went out in the afternoon to the 'funeral' at Bispebjerg hospital. Arriving there we were directed at various crossroads by nurses stationed there, to the chapel. There a sight met us, which we shall never forget. About 100 people were collected. A mountain of flowers and wreaths in the choir. The situation was sinister and frightening. Young people walked about with large postmen's bags, and with milk jugs, and also with baskets filled with sandwiches. What the bags were for we soon realised. They went from person to person and said: »If you have cash, leave it here. We can use and need money, whatever there is. Your Danish crowns are not worth much in Sweden ... What does one do in such a situation? We felt ourselves rich and happy ... Everything we owned ... we gave in the hope thereby also to have contributed to a humanitarian help of the first order.«

During the afternoon, the many refugees were divided into three groups, each with its destination. In the third group there were older people and people with small children, who had to be driven in Falck's ambulances from Bispebjerg.

»It was a long day's expedition in the night. From Copenhagen we steered northwards, and in clear moonlight reached a little place with some fishermen's huts. Here we had to wait – and wait – and wait for many long hours. We were told that small boats would take us on board and sail us to larger fishing cutters, which could manage the crossing. Everything was arranged with various fishermen. After a long – a very long wait – the message came: Everyone into the waiting cars, and away from here as fast as possible. What had happened? Yes – the whole group had been betrayed ... In the disturbance and confusion which ensued, we three became separated from each other, all search was in vain. I left the place as the last man, and no one could give me an answer as to where the two

200

Jewish refugees on their way to Sweden in October 1943. (Frihedsmuseet)

beloved people had disappeared to. With the only car which was left, to wait, the tour went back to Bispebjerg hospital. Neither the chauffeur nor our 'orderly' had been told where we were to go. This drive to the hospital was a nightmare. Many times we were stopped by 'assistants' and redirected to narrow little sideroads, because the Nazis had stopped some cars on the main road to Copenhagen, and now it was a question of being very careful. None of those questioned had seen any sign of a mother with a child a few weeks old. I was seized more and more by desperation – did not know what I was to do or believe. Were they already in safety? Should we meet at Bispebjerg? Had the Germans taken my wife and little Ruth? My companions tried to give me courage and hope. At last, after an endlessly long tour, we reached the hospital again, and I was received in the private flat of an older nurse, who had already been told that I had been separated from my wife and child. All contacts were used. The conversations had to be camouflaged – but no one could give an answer as to what had become of the mother and child. Now I was almost breaking down. The nurse gave me a tranquilizing injection, and I fell into a deep sleep. The next day I was woken, carefully, and told that one had had contact with a forester, in Gjørlev, in whose house a mother and child were staying. I was not informed of any name – no name could be named – but now there was hope again. But how was I to come to Gjørlev? A little lorry was requisitioned, equipped like a Red Cross car – there was no lack of crosses, either on the sides or the roof – and in this auxiliary column, both doctors and nursing personnel accompanied us. Many large milk pails, large baskets with food stowed on board, and so we started off to the forester's house ... After some hours' drive we at last reached the place mentioned – and never have so many tears of joy and happiness been shed as at our happy reunion. We had actually been parted for 3 days and nights. Ah! so cruel.

»But there was still a long and difficult way to the desired peace-and-quiet-freedom. Late in the evening the same day, we had to start – as it was said – the last stage in the journey to Sweden. The taxis drove forward and all who got places went with these, and the rest of the people were to drive in Falck's ambulances. There were old people, and we two relatively young with our youngest of the whole group. In the darkness of the night, but well protected and guarded by men armed with pistols, it went by express speed to one of Denmark's 'south sea islands' (Møn?) and there a fishing cutter awaited us, which was boarded by 200 people, and at 2 o'clock at night the craft left the Danish fishing harbour, and after 9 hours at last, at about 11 in the day-time we reached Trelleborg.«

A tragic Course

»In the summer 1943, I was staying with three friends in the neighbourhood of Tølløse. Immediately after 29 August, we decided to try to escape. The agreement was that two should go to Copenhagen to find a possibility for flight, whilst the two others, among them myself, for the time being should stay in the country, and try to raise some money, as we had heard a rumour that one should pay for being sailed to Sweden. After a couple of weeks we heard from our two friends that we were to come to Copenhagen with the money we had borrowed in the mean time.

»It turned out that these two had found a fisherman who was willing to sail to Sweden with four persons. He had however already promised a Danish officer one of the places, so there were only places for three of the four of us, in the first round. We agreed that the two who had found the fisherman had first priority, and we two others drew lots, after having decided that whoever was left behind should come over on the next trip, and that the three should wait for the fourth, as it was our intention from Sweden to go on to England, there to join the Czechoslovakian Army. I won the bet, but the loser asked me to let him come too, the first time, with the other two, amongst other things on the grounds that those three had grown up together, were from the same town, had gone to school together, while I was from a neighbouring town in North-west Bohemia. I consented to this, and by agreement kept half the borrowed money. We bade farewell to each other, with the arrangement that I would be contacted by the fisherman at a particular address on Østerbro, after his return from this tour.

»Two days passed without my hearing from the fisherman or from my friends, which disturbed me, although I could do nothing, as I knew nothing about the fisherman. I tried, therefore, together with some other friends, to find new escape routes. About 1 October I came into contact with the director of a well-known firm (hearing aids) who gave me the name and address of a naval policeman, where we were to present ourselves the same evening before curfew time. That day we were two friends, together, there was not much time to waste. We fetched our 'escape bags' with the most essential things, and drove to the address given, on Amager. We did not arrive, however, until after curfew time, the policeman had already left, but his brother-in-law knew where the meeting-place was, and was willing to help us, inspite of the curfew, by accompanying us there. Later we were told it was the Acid Factory in Kastrup. Just before we came to it, there suddenly came out of the darkness (a coal-black October night) two men, who warned us against going on, as 'the Germans had surrounded the place and caught all those who had collected there to flee'. The brother-in-law thought he was in the least danger, and would therefore investigate matters himself, but he quickly returned and confirmed that the Germans evidently 'dominated' the place. Then he disappeared, telling us not to disclose anything about who had brought us to the place, and left us to ourselves. We two then crawled over a barbed wire fence, and waited for several hours, for the area to quieten down. We heard the Germans come with several cars and dogs to collect all those they had caught, and for a time we were afraid that the dogs would find us. When it had all quietened down, and between 1 and 2 at night it was moonlight, we decided to get away. We crawled over the fence again, followed a railway track for a little (the Amager line) and then went into an allotment garden area to find shelter. There we met a man who had succeeded in getting away from the Germans, when they surrounded the meeting-place.

»The next morning at the beginning of the working day we separated, and I took the train back to Bellahøj, where I was staying illegally with a student whom I knew from my time on the land.

»In the afternoon we met again at Østerbro with 5 or 6 other friends, but we 2, who had been in the attempted flight the night before, had almost decided not to try again. I had the promise of a clergyman, that I could come to the vicarage and stay there for the rest of the war. However, the others had in the mean time found a new escape route via Gilleleje, and we let ourselves be persuaded to join in again. We agreed that we should take a certain train, but not to get on together from one station. I was to get on at the main station, the others at the following stations. I think our departure was to be the following day.

»We parted, and the next day in the afternoon, I got on the train as agreed, at the main station. While I waited for the train to start, I could see that four men came along the train on the platform, two in German SS uniforms, two in plain clothes. A little later, the two plain-clothes men came back in the train itself, and when they came to me, demanded my identity card (the two SS men walked back at the same time on the platform). I showed my membership card from the Danish Hiking Club, but they asked whether I was a Jew, which I confirmed, and then ordered me to go with them, and pointing to their revolvers, warned me not to try to run away. The two plain-clothes men were evidently Danes, the two in uniform Germans.

»The way led to Dagmarhus. There I was interrogated by the SS, had my money and my camera taken away (on the grounds that I was certainly out spying!) I was in Dagmarhus for c.24 hours, and after the interrogation, with two other Jews who were also brought in the same afternoon, put in the room which the German police who were on guard at Dagmarhus, used as a sitting-room between watches. One of the police officers, who was in command at night, was unusually helpful, and showed definite opposition to the SS. He helped me, for example, to hand over some valuables (ring, watch) to my girl friend, whom he allowed me to ring up from Dagmarhus, to ask her to come and visit me, which made the SS men furious, when they heard later in the day that I had had a visitor.

»From Dagmarhus the road led to the West Prison, also hardly 24 hours there, and thence to the Horserød camp. After a few days there, the journey in a cattle truck to Theresienstadt, less than 30 kilometres from the town where I was born and had lived most of my youth.

»In April 1945, together with all the other 'Danes' I was fetched by Count Bernadotte's 'white busses', and driven to a camp in Tylösand, near Halmstad. From there, on one of the first days, I contacted our organisation's office, and was told, among other things, that my three friends, with whom I should have escaped, had never reached Sweden, but the body of one of them had been washed up on the coast, near Höganäs, in the spring 1944. What had happened, whether the boat had capsized, or whether the Germans had seized it, so far as I know has never been cleared up.«

Ways to Sweden

Of the two groups we are dealing with, 56, as mentioned, ended in Theresienstadt. About 475 reached Sweden by circuitous routes. No ones route became everyones route, and the picture of the routes became chaotic.

A systematic historic description of a mass flight, which in the first weeks of October 1943 brought over 7,000 persons across the Øresund, is simply not feasible. There are no common denominators in a course of events which, generally speaking, were marked by accidental circumstances, luck and bad luck, daring initiatives and changing plans in the face of changing situations. Thousands were involved on the Jewish side, thousands became involved on the non-Jewish side. No one was prepared. Everything had to be improvised. No one had a comprehensive view. Each man created his own chances, and none could quite do so. Everyone – Jews and non-Jews – had to decide and act according to the possibilities and demands of the moment. Everything had to be altered from one hour to the next.

A historic description cannot build on contemporary documents. In the hectic weeks, where flight and the work of assistance forced its way forward to something which could resemble organisation, no diaries were kept, no letters were written or reports made. It was everything else, that had to be dealt with, and worried about. Once the Jews were in Sweden – or in Theresienstadt – it was possible for Margolinsky and the Danish authorities to register statistically how many and who had reached their goal, and who had failed to. This statistical statement demanded great care and a great deal of work, but it only posed the general question of »how many«, and never the complicated question of »how« for the individual. When posterity and the historians pose this question, it becomes evident that clear commom denominators are not to be found. Fundamentally, there are of course certain common elements: A large majority reached Sweden, a minority did not. For all those who reached safety, the route took them sooner or later to the coast, a harbour and a ship or boat. But before that, it was a question of broken routes, of help or self-help, of luck or ill-luck, of solo or collective performances. The variants dominate, and only behind the shadow of single events does one guess at the organisation, which in spite of all the improvisations grew up, only to be held fast in the construction of an illegal route network, the Jews' decisive contribution to building the Danish resistance movement's organisation, with its countless ramifications.

In the construction of this network of routes, there are institutions and groups of the population that stand out clearly and strongly – hospitals, doctors, nurses, ambulance men, taxi drivers and in the end, fishermen and skippers. But in the course of the route one glimpses others, women as well as men: farmers, foresters, innkeepers, policemen, students, clergymen, teachers, and first and last the countless anonymous men and women, who never let themselves be known.

Those in flight never sensed this correlation, with its mixture of the accidental with the planned. For them, every helping hand stood for a helping hand from »the resistance movement«, because in most cases, and regardless of how fluctuating was the course of the flight, it was given by people who in one way or another had their contacts in order. For the Jew, who one night after wandering from one address to another, ended on a foreign shore with a rescue ship, it must seem as though there lay a central direction behind it all. To some extent this became the case, during the action. But when the action began, a permanent route organisation had not been set up. The flight was only made possible because of a coincidence of scattered and tentative initiatives, from people all over the country, who often – perhaps most often – were not in any way familiar with resistance work, and perhaps only came into contact with it on this one occasion.

In the following pages, the flight will be described, as it is remembered and perceived many years later, by a score of those who with help, or in spite of refusals, found a way. Later memories can contain shifts in timing and miscalculations of details and the course of events. However, there is no doubt that those days and nights have etched themselves deeply into remembrance, and minor lapses of memory or misunderstandings have no great importance in regard to the historic value of these recollections. At all events: They are the only existing source as to what happened. They supplement each other. They allow themselves to be tested, again and again, as to time, places and persons, and every test serves as a guarantee for objective truth – subjectively experienced and never forgotten.

Out of the chaos of impressions, a picture materializes in black and white, which neither can nor shall be systematized.

Memories of Autumn Days and Nights

A number of the accounts are miserly in words and could – if they stood alone – give a false picture of a seemingly uncomplicated *dénouement*. The miserliness seems to arise from modesty: what part does my fate play in that great drama?

»Hid myself for c. 2 weeks in North Sjælland until flight was possible.«

»My flight from Denmark went via Copenhagen over Lolland-Falster. We came there by taxis, which turned up and asked no questions. Fishing cutters from Lolland-Falster took us later to Trelleborg.«

»Came on 8 October in a fishing boat from Copenhagen to Malmø. In the same boat there were another c. 20 men and women, and also children. The voyage was very full of fear and we covered ourselves with a tarpaulin so as not to be discovered by flyers. It was night.«

Bispebjerg hospital, which was an important collecting point for the fleeing Jews during the German action in October 1943.

»Then came October 1943. We went underground at Mrs. Ebba Rasmussen's in Farum, who found possibilities for travelling not only for us but also for half a score of other Jews in some way or other.«

»I left Denmark on 11 October with the help of a clergyman. I came with a steamer from Copenhagen to Sweden, where I landed at the Falsterbo Canal. From Fyn to Copenhagen the tour went in an ambulance. In the middle of the night we left the steamer – it was DFDS – and were fetched at the Falsterbo Canal by Swedish soldiers.«

»On 7 October I fled with the help of a Danish fisherman to Sweden. We sailed out from Redhavnen in Copenhagen, and he 'put me down' a little way from Barsebäck harbour, as he dared not sail into the harbour.«

»On 29.9.43 'underground' after telephone from Copenhagen to the group's liaison man with an agreed code word. (My wife and the 5-week-old daughter in Køge hospital, I with the blind organist in Køge church.) On 10.10.43 with large transports from Strøby (2 stone dredgers) to Sweden.«

»(Fled) on 10 October 1943 in a little rowing boat. Lived illegally with the family Poul Andersen in Vedbæk, who obtained the boat and a flight opportunity for us. First attempt some days before failed. We waited with c.60 other Jews on the shore near Humlebæk. We gave all our money – but no boat came!«

»In October 1943 I was searched for by the Gestapo at the places where I had lived earlier. The Danish resistance organisation arranged for me and some comrades a well-organised escape route, where in the end we were landed on the island of Ven by a Danish revenue cutter.«

207

»Between 6 and 9 October I received a personal warning from a patient at Næstved hospital whom I visited. Left Næstved with a comrade to Copenhagen. We contacted a friend, who was also our teacher. He sent us to a Mr. Hansen, who lived in Ellebæksvej. The day after we were driven to Køge and from there with a mass of other Jewish refugees we fled to Sweden.«

»One of my last days in Vinding, it was in October 1943, we were warned about the 'razzia'. I escaped – with a friend – first to Askov High School, where we stayed in Mrs. Fenger's house ... and then at Richard Andersen's – they were wonderful people who kept us there for two weeks until it was possible to get away to Sweden.«

»Heard rumours and talked with the *chawerim*. Travelled to Copenhagen. After some days to Gilleleje, where first crossing did not come off. Some found night's lodging for us in a summer house c. 30 persons. Next day around mid-day went – ran to the harbour and came c.200 persons with a schooner. Can remember that people in Gilleleje stood on the street and showed us the way.«

»The flight itself was dramatic, but on the other hand, no more dramatic than for all the others.«

A good many of the accounts are fortunately more detailed. In them the reality of those October days stands out.

»We heard that the Germans had taken away the files from the police in Roskilde. So one knew that 'the clock had struck'. Our little group had rented a room in Roskilde, and here I spent a couple of nights before I went to Snekkersten in the hope that from there I could go on to Sweden, but it did not work after all. Some comrades and I went to Copenhagen, where we got contact with, among others, Knud Damgaard and others, who found a night's shelter for us and arranged for a contact to be able to come to Sweden ... From Køge I then came to Sweden on 7 October 1943, more nearly, to Skanør.«

»I was helped by the Danish underground movement (with special help from students) in October 1943 to excape to Sweden in a Danish fishing boat. I remember the night in an empty summer villa, where underground helpers supplied us with sandwiches and beverages. When one saw that the coast was clear, we sailed across to Sweden.«

»I left Denmark on 13.10.43. The Danes from Gilleleje and its neighbourhood were very busy that night, because they were to make sure that no undesirable guest turned up, while we were on our way down to the shore, where a small fishing boat waited to take 33 persecuted refugees. Among them there were people of varying ages, for example there were two little girls, one of 6 and another of 8 years, and then there was a man of 50, who came straight from hospital after an operation and could not walk. A Dane and I took him under the arms and together brought him down to the shore ... The warning came to the farmer and his sister, and after consultation with the vicar a collection of money was started to make our flight to Sweden possible.«

The innocent-looking fishing cutter – Gerda III – belonged to the Lighthouse and Buoys Authority, and sailed post and provisions daily to Drogden lighthouse. It proved possible, however, to change the sailing route and landing places, so that the cutter could be used for the transport of escaping Jews – without attracting attention.

»When it was known that the Germans would deport the Danish Jews, and also us agricultural trainees, a young resistance man came one day and sent us to another farm nearby, where we went 'underground' for a week. After that week another man came, who took us at night to Faxe harbour with all our comrades. There we stayed for another day. The next night we were taken by a fishing boat which sailed us to Trelleborg. It was a night with storm and rain, and we were all seasick.«

»I left Denmark on 13.10.43 with my husband. We were brought with a whole group to Gilleleje, where at night we went down to the shore and on board a fishing boat, which brought us to Swedish territorial waters. A Swedish warship took us up... We lived at that time on a farm near Ringsted. My husband drove the next day up to Høng, where he knew a farmer in Løve, who lived there with his sister. They agreed to hide both him and me, although they were clear as to the risk, if they were discovered... The farmer was also the one who received telephone and warning from the resistance movement, and he also paid a lot of our flight.«

»On 6 and 7 October, Jens P. Jensen enquired for us two sisters by telephone. He... asked us immediately and in no matter what way to come to Smerup. He would pay all possible expenses. From Smerup he drove us the same day to St. Hedinge or a village in the neighbourhood. A farmer near Stevns Klint collected us all, and at his home we waited for an opportunity for flight. We were a score of people there, I only knew one or two. There were both foreign refugees and Danish Jews. We waited two nights and then were brought to the coast and sailed over after a couple of hours' wait in the darkness... Naturally we had no information about the people who took us over. As far as we could see, they were fishermen. Nothing was asked of us. If people had money they gave, but we came to Sweden without money.«

»In October 1943 I worked on a farm... near Odense. Here one day I received a letter from a Jewish friend... who had now 'hidden' himself in Middelfart mental hospital. He advised me as soon as possible to leave Denmark. I dared not stay any longer on the farm, but hid in Seden Apprentices' Home, where the warden was a very understanding and perceptive man. I was helped away from there at night by people I did not know. But I trusted them. I came by train to Copenhagen and was billeted in the Communal Hospital's 6th Department... On 27 October I was brought by underground passages up to a waiting gas turbine taxi. It drove me... to Copenhagen Free Harbour, where a little fishing cutter with the name »Forward« lay moored. From there we chugged away out into the Øresund. We arrived at... Barsebäck.«

»The farmer«, »the young man«, »Danes«, »people I did not know«, »a Mr. Hansen« – they will all turn up in the following, more detailed accounts, which, like the previous ones, come from fugitives in the *Hechaluz* or *Alijah* groups.

»In October 1943 we received a telegram from *Hechaluz*: If the child was not well, we should send it on recreation. We understood the warning and travelled immediately to Odense, and there really was a children's home to receive the child. One day... the farmer received an internal call from the police, that the Germans would come and arrest us... He told me, and I ran across to my wife. We decided to go to our room on the 1st floor to fetch some things and flee. We were still in the room when we heard someone come up the stairs. We were terribly frightened when we heard him ring, and then it was a police officer from Odense. He advised us to leave the flat at once, and told us that the index cards with our names had been destroyed. We ran to the station and went to a friend who was married to a Dane. He was cowman on a farm near Nyborg... Through our friend, where we hid for some days, we received the instructions to get in touch every day with Kragh-Petersen in Ringe. He was contact man with the resistance movement. After about one week he told us that they would try to bring us to Sweden... and we should come to him with our child. There we met some comrades, and spent the night there. Next morning we were instructed to take the train to a station outside Copenhagen. Here one would expect us. On the street stood a man with an empty perambulator, and we were entrusted to the care of various contact folk, until we came to a hospital, where we only stayed a short time, as they were afraid of a *razzia*. We were taken to another hospital, where a fairly large number of refugees were concentrated. The next morning we received tickets so that we could take the train to Lolland-Falster. The train was full of German soldiers. We were afraid every minute of being arrested. All went well, and we were taken to a farm near the sea, spent some hours until it was dark. A fishing boat came which took as many people as possible on board. Many older people and small children. We sailed in the direction of Bornholm, to mislead the Germans and after 8 hours reached Trelleborg.«

»The *Hechaluz* organisation and Margolinsky in Copenhagen were informed direct, through Hedtoft-Hansen's secretary, and people were sent out immediately to the various centres. To Faaborg there came a *Hechaluz* friend to me on Hvedholm (I was centre chairman), 2 days before the Jewish persecution began. I left my work at once... bicycled to the other 'centre members' who were on the various farms, and all were informed in the course of a few hours. In the evening we held a meeting and it was decided that everyone should leave their farms and go to Bøjdenskov, which is quite out of the way, with some summer villas. We had some Danish intermediaries who arranged for supplies and information. I myself – after unanimous decision – went to Copenhagen, and through my friends in Copenhagen I at once was put in touch with resistance people, and special people at Bispebjerg hospital. An ambulance (Falck) was sent to Bøjden and some of our people were then transported by ordinary ambulance to Copenhagen. At all events, when the Jewish persecution began, the day after, none from the Faaborg centre were taken by the Germans. All got to Bispebjerg hospital, and from there – after some days – they were sent to Sweden, partly from Gilleleje and partly from Humlebæk. None of our folk had to pay for the crossing and all arrived intact in Sweden. I myself remained for a while with my friends in Copenhagen, to help with finding more of our folk in the various places in the country, and getting them to Sweden. But when it became more and more dangerous I too crossed over to Sweden from Vedbæk to Landskrona, at the beginning of November.«

»In the autumn, the general situation became very acute and we received from *Hechaluz* a first warning that something could happen to the Jews. We decided, when the moment came, to leave our places of work and meet on a certain beach. We organised contact with the individual comrades, and when the final information came, it all worked well. We disappeared from our places and met on an out-of-the-way beach, where there were some large summer villas. We broke into one of these houses and hid ourselves there. As the country was under military law, it was very difficult to get in touch with people, and particularly with the underground movement. I can remember that we came into contact with the vicar in Aastrup, and he with the resistance movement in Odense. In addition we received food from some people in Horne. After some days our position became too dangerous, and we decided to leave the summer villa at night and divide into small groups of 3 ... I went with a young man and a young girl to a teacher on a nearby agricultural school. The next day (or night) we were fetched to Odense, where we met each other again near the town at a veterinary surgeon's. It was very early in the morning, and the veterinary surgeon explained that we must travel to Copenhagen on our own, but that everything was arranged, and we need not be afraid. We spoke perfect Danish in those days, and he thought all would be well. But one had not taken the American and British planes into consideration ... There was an air raid warning, and everyone had to go to the air raid shelter. Normally 3 trains went to Copenhagen every day, but because of the air raid warning none of the trains left until the afternoon ... In Copenhagen we were brought to a hospital. There was a whole wing arranged for Jewish refugees alone. The same night we were taken out in the neighbourhood of a harbour in a port, from where we would be brought two at a time on board a boat. When it was my turn, a message came that the boat was fully loaded, and we had all to return to the hospital. There we stayed for the night, and next morning it was explained to us that the boat that night was the last from Copenhagen, so that we must try and get across the Sound farther south. We travelled in the Danish coach of the German express to Falster. There was a school near the water with a fishing boat to Trelleborg. We were 15–20 men on board and came in the morning to Sweden.«

»In (the October days) I was in Copenhagen for a few days' holiday. Felt at once the strained atmosphere and sorrow in the Jewish community. Made telephone contact immediately with my then place of work in Vedbæk with a gardener family to say that I was returning at once. Before I got back ... (I had) contact with a Jewish family in Vedbæk, who knew that they were to flee to Sweden the same night in a small fishing boat. Quickly got contact with this Jewish family. We left their home about 8 in the evening and hid in one of their Christian neighbour's. Precisely 9, we began our flight and went down to the little fishing harbour. The way there was patrolled by Danish coastguards who helped us, in that by signs and agreed passwords, they let us understand that the road was free of possible German military patrols. We reached the harbour in peace, but had to wait 1½ hours till the boat was ready to sail. We hid behind the trees in the harbour and were guarded by Danish resistance people. During the wait, other resistance people came with another Jewish couple and 2 Jewish men. With the fisherman and his helper we were 12 persons, including 3 children. We sailed away at 10.30, and the voyage across the Øresund passed almost without danger. When we were out in the middle of the Sound, a German warship crossed our path, but luckily for us we were not observed by it. At about 11 we reached the little island of Ven in safety.«

»From the courthouse in Odense ... I was informed of a transport to Sweden. We were to collect on the railway station in Odense at a certain time. Apart from some of my comrades I noticed some other private people – Jews who lived in Odense and its neighbourhood. According to our orders – a man appeared with a certain finger mark – we were distributed in a train. It was a regular train connexion with direction: Copenhagen. At Valby station one drove with an

ambulance – which was standing ready at the station – to Bispebjerg hospital . . .
There we had to give up our ration coupons. Then we were again driven by
ambulance to Valby station. After that again by train to Nykøbing Falster. From
the station in Nykøbing we were driven in one of the police's 'Black Marias', to the
police station. It was in the middle of the night when we arrived at Nykøbing. An
ambulance drove us to Stubbekøbing. At 2 o-clock at night we began to sail with a
fishing boat – we were c.20–25 persons – in the direction of Trelleborg. At 14
hours the next day – sailing in stormy weather – we were received by the Red
Cross in Trelleborg.«

»In 1943 we heard of the Jews' fate in Norway . . . I managed with some others
to smuggle ourselves into one of the German army's ammunition trucks, which
drove from Helsingør with the ferry across to Helsingborg and on to Norway.
The plan was to jump off in Helsingborg. Everything went according to plan.
After the German soldiers' check-up, we managed to jump on to one of the
railway trucks, and the ferry started across to Helsingborg. A few minutes later
there was an air raid warning. Allied Flying Fortresses were on their way to bomb
Germany. The ferry had had orders to go back into the harbour. I dared not
jump off. So we lay there for a day and a night . . . The Germans inspected once
more and I was arrested . . . I was in prison in Kalundborg for 4 months. After I
came out (30 August 1943) it was clear that the Germans would change the
conditions in Denmark. With the help of a Danish fisherman we 3 *chaluzim* . . .
came to the island Ven – Landskrona.«

There were rumours in circulation that one intended to deport the Jews. It was
after 29 August 1943. I went with my child to Copenhagen . . . while my husband
stayed on his farm until I telephoned to call him to Copenhagen, after I had
found a safe hiding-place and further transport to Sweden. I was warned by
comrades in *Hechaluz* . . . I stayed with the child in Tivoli nearly the whole day in
the 'Palladium' (cinema), where a kind lady, who evidently saw what was wrong,
but said nothing, played with him in the playroom. We took a room at a hotel
behind the main railway station, where almost only German officers stayed. It
seemed the safest to me, and it was, too. After some days 2 Danish students came
and fetched us out to a summer villa in Bagsværd. We were there a week, could
not leave the house in daylight, and at night we might not have light, so that no
one could see that the house was inhabited. There was nothing to eat. In the dark
we crept out into the garden where some apples still hung on the trees. That was
our only food for a week. We already thought that we were forgotten, but
suddenly a taxi turned up, and we were brought to Kongens Lyngby to a Mrs.
Strandbygaard, who was an important figure in the . . . resistance movement. We
spent 2 days of rest in this house, where other fugitives were also placed, amongst
others a parachutist . . . for whom a search was going on. We all had to leave the
house as fast as possible, after Mrs. Strandbygaard had received a warning. We
were at the house of some friends of Mrs. Strandbygaard's, a highly placed civil
servant in the Ministry of Education. This splendid house lay in Sorgenfri, near

the palace where the Royal Family were interned. The lady of the house was a friend of the Crown Princess Ingrid, as she then was, and could visit her. She told the Crown Princess about us, and we received greetings and best wishes for a safe flight to Sweden, with deep regret that because of the German guards, she could not hide Jews. That is something which I shall keep as a good memory, as long as I live, apart from the fantastic performance of many unknown Danes, who finally brought us to Nivå and Humlebæk, where we were hidden in the tileworks, until a stone dredger, on the eve of 6 October, brought us across the Øresund to the Swedish territorial boundary, where a craft from the Swedish Navy waited and took us on board. On the boat there were c. 200 refugees.«

»When the Jewish persecution started, I was on a farm on Sjælland. I knew nothing of transports to Sweden. I packed my things, and had them sent to Flemløse, where I had spent a year . . . I drove there myself, to be certain. My idea had been to come to England . . . My previous farmer in Flemløse thought of a good friend, who lived near Esbjerg. He got in touch with him immediately – and he agreed that I could come. It was not so easy to come to Esbjerg at thàt time, because it was a military zone. I had to go to the police in Odense to get a pass. On my arrival in Esbjerg the – for me – first air raid warning. Some people went to the shelters, others not, nor I. Everything seemed strange to me. Thousands of German soldiers in the streets. (In the country we saw no German soldiers.) So I hurried out of the town, I had 2 addresses with me of clergymen near Esbjerg, where I could if necessary pass the first night. The first clergyman refused at once. So I tried my luck with the next clergyman, after about 1 hour's walk. But here I was just as unlucky. He would neither let me sleep nor give me anything to eat – and I was hungry and tired. It was already dark. I went out and saw some German soldiers and became a little frightened. I plucked up courage and tried again with the same clergyman. I said that he could not, in propriety, push me out into the dark and uncertainty. That helped! – – – He changed his mind and gave me something to eat, and I was allowed to sleep on the loft – – – Next morning early, away to the address I had been given, where I was cordially received. Here I stayed c. 10 days. He tried everything possible with fishermen for a possible sailing to England, but it did not succeed – – – Then one evening we heard on the radio that the Jews were escaping with fishing boats to Sweden. The next day I again drove to Flemløse. My previous farmer put me in touch with a clergyman's wife in Odense. The day after, we met in Odense on the railway station, to go to Copenhagen. The ferry was full of German soldiers . . . We came to a school in Valby, where there were quite a lot of people, waiting for an opportunity for flight . . . The next morning c. 4.30 we drove by taxi to the South Harbour, where we were stowed like herrings in the fishing boat. I think we were about 15. When we got across the territorial boundary, the skipper opened the hatch and said: Here you are, now you can come up and get some fresh air.«

»10.10.43 I left Denmark . . . One Wednesday afternoon after work had ended, I bicycled to Næstved out to the little house near Fladsø. On the way I met my

214

comrades, who said that now we must try and escape to Sweden, as they had had news that the Germans would arrest the Jews in Denmark. At that point, I had not spent the night in my room for a week, but with one of the dairymen at Næstved Dairy, as I had had a hint from one of the milk drivers, who evidently had contact with the resistance movement. I went on working at the dairy until I had a letter from a friend . . . who had gone to Copenhagen to find an escape route. I was to visit Eva . . . who was in hospital in Næstved. There I was given the address of the parish officer, Jensen, in Smerup near Karise, and the day after, I bicycled . . . there. When I knocked and opened the door, I saw 6–8 comrades and one or two from *Hechaluz* sitting there cosily in the living room. We did not sail from what had been the port of embarkation on Stevns that night (it must have been 9.10.43). We were told that the German soldier who had been bribed was not on guard at the harbour, and also it was full moon. So we had to be billeted round about . . . I was sent to a small-holder family. It was a young couple with two small children. Because of my accent, the man told me that if anyone should ask who I was, I should say I was one of his friends from Iceland. He had actually spent some time there. The next morning, I was helping him a bit with the farmwork, when the schoolteacher's little son came to say that I must hurry away to the parish officer. We were to leave. And there were 2 big private cars from the Zone rescue corps. They were requisitioned for ambulance service, and we drove over the new Alexandrine bridge to Møn, and from there sailed with the ferry to Falster (the ferryman told us that he was to sail with fugitives the same night), where we were told that we were to go to Næsgaard Agricultural School. There was a gathering of c.50 coming refugees already, well, some had tried it before. We were given a meal, and the school staff entertained us till midnight (we were also encouraged to give up our Danish money, as it was said that it was not worth anything in Sweden). Then we drove in haywagons to the ferry-place between Stubbekøbing and Møn, crawled into the hold in 2 fishing cutters, and sailed to Sweden, where we arrived rather exhausted but safe and sound 1½ hours later.«

»The warning did not come until *after* the action against the Jews. My place at the time was as gardener on the estate of Axel Jarl near Hillerød, and was evidently not included in the files which were used by the head-hunters. The Monday after the Action I was in touch with Inga . . . via her father, the head telegraphist of the Fire Service in Gentofte. She got me to come to town ('take care you don't catch cold, there are so many that can be infected'). In Vangede I received some information on possibilities for escape. Inga believed that an attempt was to be made in Sletten. If that did not succeed, one should go to Møn. Back again at Strødam I told . . .the head gardener Viggo Brøndal that I meant to leave the next morning. He arranged for me to receive 1000 crowns next morning from Axel Jarl, and also gave me some hundred crowns himself. The bicycle I took with me, that is, I cycled to Sletten, but it soon proved that the Sound was no longer safe. I (and the bicycle) bought a ticket to Vordingborg . . . On arrival at Næstved, it turned out that the train did not go any farther that day.

At night at the Mission Hotel as Peder Ravn from Haderslev. Tried to get in touch with some of the children from the so-called »*Jugend-Alijah*«, who I knew had lived in the town . . . The next day: Via Vordingborg and bus to Stege. Purchase of map of the island. Bicycle ride to Ulvshale to try to get across to the island Nyord, where I hoped to get a 'lift' from the fishing hamlet to Sweden. The ferryman, who was to put me in a rowing boat across the narrow channel between Møn and Nyord, soon got wind of what I was after and warned me: After the 'Jewish action' the Germans had released the interned Danish Army people, and some of the officers from Næstved had 'borrowed' a fishing boat and had sailed to Sweden. After this people on Nyord rang up the police at once, whenever a strange face showed itself on the island. The ferryman advised me to cycle to Klintholm harbour. For most of the day I stayed there and chatted to the fishermen on the possibilities (while a Danish policeman held guard on the other side of the harbour entrance, and knew quite well what was going on). A fisherman offered to sell me his boat for 10,000 crowns. He would sail it to a jetty at Haarbølle, where there were no guards. There he would empty the boat for equipment, stock up with fuel and give me instructions on using the motor. One couldn't miss the way to Sweden. A 15-year-old boy, who was used to sailing, wanted to come too, he could quite well manage the technical side. All that was lacking was the 10,000 crowns. Towards evening the above boy came running to tell me that there were some people at the saddler's, who also wanted to go to Sweden. So, off to the saddler's – a lovable old couple, both over 75. It turned out that it was true that there had been some folk, but they had gone again. The two old people were rather confused at everything that was happening around them, but both were deeply religious and felt it was their duty to help. In the end, the old woman said: 'You must ring to the baron.' He must be able to give them good advice. It turned out that the saddler had always worked for Baron Rosenkrantz of Liselund. Rosenkrantz asked him to send me up to the castle. Here I was received by the old baron and his wife, for whom I identified myself without being asked. The two old people were just as touching towards me as the saddler couple. The baron took the telephone and rang up someone or other, asked me to wait a little, and soon after I was fetched by a young man who simply asked whether I *too* was to go to Sweden. It was the assistant estate manager, who led me to a barn. On the hay loft there were also some people who were waiting for transport. It was, I think, the Students Intelligence Service that had transported them to Liselund. Their contact man on the spot was the young Baron Rosenkrantz. After a night on the hayloft, the flock was installed in the pensionat wing of the castle to wait for transport. I believe a warning system had been organised which could give the alarm if Germans should show any curiosity. We waited until Friday. At dusk, we were taken to a little house on the cliff. Some people from the estate had with herculean efforts carried a rowing boat the whole way down the steep path to the shore. At about 7, we 12 were led down to the beach. Along the path stood guards with machine guns. I received a 'blowing-up' because I had a light-coloured

216

trenchcoat on, which could be seen far off, in the clear moonlight. Just off the beach a cutter lay at anchor and the rowboat punted us out, two by two. The operation did not take long, and then the boat sailed with direct course towards Trelleborg in Skåne. The first hour, the skipper was nervous, and we were all stuffed down into the narrow galley. But after that, feelings calmed down – we were in international waters, and those who wished could come up on deck. It was as calm as a millpond. We seemed to be sailing in the centre of a moon-bridge. I sat up beside the steering house and 'enjoyed' the spectacle. Rostock was being bombed. The tour took 5 hours – quite without drama.«

»I came to the Workers High School in Roskilde, and there got in touch with the circles who would soon be of help in the flight to Sweden, to me and to many of my friends. Before our flight from Køge to Skanør succeeded, we had some unsuccessful attempts behind us, the tour from Gilleleje was probably the most dramatic. There we were c.25 persons in a toolshed, and suddenly were told that the Gestapo was on the way. We were 3 men who decided to try to get to Hillerød on foot, and from there take the first morning train to Copenhagen (the idea was, that this train had no connexion further north, and therefore could not bring any escaped victims). After 2 hours' tour over sopping wet beetfields, we arrived at last at a signpost which told us that we were 2 kilometres from Gilleleje. So we had walked in a circle. After that we kept near the road through Gribs forest, and reached the train in Hillerød. When we came to our hosts on Nørrebro, the lady almost fainted: At 12 p.m. they had toasted, 'Now they are across'.«

»We succeeded in coming to Sweden on 13.10.1943. During the summer 1943 I stayed at a farm on Thurø. (On Thurø we were 3 'boys' and 1 'girl'.) We had a telegram (end September) from Copenhagen with the following text: 'Father ill – come at once – tell the family.' Sender? We presume that the telegram was sent by *Hechaluz*, as on previous occasions we had discussed the possibility of Jewish persecution in Denmark, and it was agreed that in one form or another we would probably be informed when it was time to go underground. We went from Thurø to Korsør, where some Danish friends hid us for c.10 days. One night one of our comrades 'came... and told us that we should go to Copenhagen, where we should apply to Bispebjerg hospital (the nurses' college). From there we could come to Sweden. In the afternoon (11/10) together with c.150 others, we were divided in various vehicles (lorries, ambulances, taxis, etc.) which drove us around on the Sjælland roads for several hours. At night we were lodged in a shooting hut (where?) where we also stayed for most of the next day. Towards evening the next day we left the shooting hut and finished up on Møn, where, in a kind of storehouse, we waited for a chance of sailing to Sweden. After 6–8 hours' sail in a fishing cutter, we reached Trelleborg on 13.10.1943 (exactly 166 persons in the same boat).«

»On 28.8.43 I received news from a comrade that something was brewing among the Germans, but one did not yet know what one should do about it, but in the mean time, one should go 'out into the Country'. When I passed through

217

Copenhagen main railway station, I saw many Jews who were already leaving the town, for example, for Kalundborg. I went to Sdr. Jærnløse, as one thought everything would clear up after a few days. On the Swedish radio, one could hear that the night before, 500 Jews had crossed over to Sweden, south of Malmø and 500 north of Malmø. This was a clear signal, of which we could understand the meaning . . . The next morning I began to test 'how things stood'. At Rungsted Coast Inn I received a 'tip' from the waiter and went out on to the coast road. At Humlebæk station I came into contact with the underground's folk, who told me to cycle to Gilleleje (I only rode my bicycle to avoid the railway). In Gilleleje we were collected in a dark railway coach. Those who had money paid voluntary sums, and after a time we went down to the harbour (under the eyes of the police). When there were about 150 people on the fishing boat, we sailed across to Sweden . . . All my things and those of many others were sent after us to Sweden in 1944. The Resistance movement arranged this too.«

»On 16.10.1943, I was rung up at my place of work, which at that time was . . . in Bjert – from Copenhagen. He told me that my comrades and I (we were 5) should leave Denmark as fast as possible, as otherwise we could be arrested by the Germans. On 17.10.1943 we took the train to Copenhagen, to be exact Valby station, where we were fetched by a younger man with a white carnation in his buttonhole. The tour went in a taxi to the Copenhagen neighbourhood. We were lodged with a youngish married couple in a quite ordinary flat. Next morning c.5 o'clock, we were fetched by a taxi, which drove us to a Copenhagen harbour, where a fishing cutter lay and waited for us. The sail across the Øresund lasted for 4½ hours, and before we reached Malmø we were discovered by a Swedish torpedo boat.«

»At the end of September 1943 we went to Glamsbjerg, we were 5, where we had many Danish friends and could be hidden, which very soon became necessary, when the action against the Jews started. We lived in various summer villas, changed our billets at night, as our Danish friends advised. It was they who established contact with the Hospital Group in Odense hospital. We were driven to Odense in small cars, and outside Odense fetched by an ambulance which was to take us to Copenhagen. We were each given a lot of money, and were told that if anything went wrong we should try to bribe people. Otherwise we should give them back in Copenhagen. The ambulance had a permit for a patient for the neurological department, and I can still see the ambulance men standing on guard at the doors to the ambulance on the ferry. The Germans were around us and we lay down flat, so as not to cast shadows. We did not speak to each other. We reached Copenhagen at the end of the afternoon, changed over into small cars, I think it was Istedgade, and had been told that there would be a lady with a little dog on her arm who would receive us. We were to ask after the dog: Gandhi! We gave the money to her and were taken out to Bispebjerg hospital and must have been installed in some nurses' quarters. One could not say when we could come further, but if the telephone rang and a voice said, 'Genforeningsplads', we should be ready in 0.05 seconds. At that point I had become separated from my friends. The same night the telephone rang, and we were driven in small cars to the Free Harbour and went out to a boat, which was to sail the next morning. We lay in the coal cargo, buried in coal, and had been told that when someone stamped 3 times on the deck, we should be deathly quiet, as then there was German inspection on board. All went well. The Germans were both bribed and plied with drink, as we were told later by the crew. We could feel when the motor was started, and when we were close in to Swedish waters, we were allowed to come up. We were c.20 people between 3 and 70 years. The smallest had had sleeping medicine.«

»From Svendborg in October we received a telegram from Hechaluz, that we must leave home ... I left the farm and went to Odense ... As it so happened, I had met a Danish family from Odense in the summer 1943. The lady was a hairdresser. After I had received the telegram, I told my comrades, who were living in the neighbourhood of Skårup, that we must move, and I decided to drive to Odense to this family ... The family got in touch with a lady, whose name was Petra Petersen, who was very active in the resistance movement. Petra arranged ... faked papers in Danish names, and she sent us to Aalborg, where there was a connexion for Danish saboteurs, who had to go underground, so that they could come over to Sweden ... From there I went to Aalborg and had contact with the contact man from Aalborg. He arranged that I could come over to Sweden with a coal steamer, which sailed coal from Aalborg to Copenhagen, and on the way nipped across to Sweden.«

»The warning reached our group while we were gathered for the Jewish New Year's feast, through a courier from Copenhagen. We were advised that we should leave our homes immediately and try and come over to Sweden. We were a group of 4, who took the road, on bicycles, to North Sjælland. We had not eaten much on the way, so when we came to Liseleje we decided to stop at an inn and have lunch. It proved to be very lucky, for the innkeeper, who saw who we were, obtained contact for us with the resistance movement. We were taken to a house near Rågeleje, where we were hidden with a number of Danish Jews, until we went together in a boat to Högenäs.«

»Someone rang from Copenhagen and warned us not to stay at home. Although my foster-parents did not think there was reason for panic, I cycled to Vinding High School, where I met a girl friend who was a pupil there ... Afterwards we were both at the pastor Richard Andersen's in the vicarage in Aagaard. He accompanied us to Copenhagen and took us to Bispebjerg hospital, from where, the next day, we were sailed to Barsebæk.«

»I worked on Als until the autumn, when local, private people gave us – a friend and me – shelter and help in our 'underground' time, before we could come to Copenhagen, with the aim of further transport to Sweden. After 3 weeks' nightly wanderings on Als, where kind people gave us shelter, the resistance movement found us. It was a young schoolmaster from Askov High School, who came cycling at night from Askov to Fynshav on Als. He had traced us to Danebod High School, where Frede Terkelsen and his wife did a great deal for our rescue, and made contact with our 'underground' lodging, at the time at Normark vicarage ... We came ... to Valby, where the resistance movement people awaited us and took us to a workshop near Valby, where picture frames were made. From here, the same evening (23.10.43) we were driven by taxi to the then students' college, of the Communal Hospital, in Gammeltoftsgade, where the warden – Miss Clara Feldthaus – took care of us in an unequalled way. After thorough instructions from a young man from the resistance movement I came the next day with the 'coastguard cutter' from Tuborg harbour to Ven in Sweden.«

»On 30 September we met in our little house outside Kalundborg to celebrate the Jewish New Year. At midday one of our comrades came ... in suddenly to us. In Copenhagen he had heard that deportation of Danish Jews was to start the same day. He had at once taken the train to tell his comrades this. After a short discussion among us on 'tactics' we divided up into small groups to take our bicycles and try to get to North Sjælland, and from there to Sweden ... We left the same evening. We were 2 boys and 2 girls, who went together. The first night we slept in an open strawstack. The following nights we asked at farms to be allowed to sleep on the haylofts. We were lucky enough to end up with people who understood what the problem was ... We reached North Sjælland and met one of our first contacts in Rågeleje. A Danish policeman who guarded the beach at night promised to help with a rowboat. As it happened, the weather was too bad for us to dare take it on. Some days later we at last made contact at Græsted Inn with (the man) who would finally help us across. We were glad to hand over our money for the effort which we hoped could rescue us (and bicycles) to Sweden. The crossing started from Gilleleje in the middle of the day of 6 October 1943 ... The night before, there were Jews hidden in the whole town. At about 12, the 'all clear' was given. From all the small houses in every direction, folk ran down to the harbour. Farthest out on the quay beside the boat, a man was standing with lifted hands and shouting: Come all of you! Afraid that some groups had not received the message. Who was the man? I only know that he was a schoolteacher and led the work with the flight, in the neighbourhood of Gilleleje. The crossing went well ... I will mention that many of us, in connexion with the flight, received large sums of money, which were to help us to come over the Sound.«

»Also we young people in the provinces received a message from the Secretariat through our local leaders, to 'go underground'. I hid in various haylofts – awaiting further instructions ... Not long after, I saw from my 'look-out' a mounted German policeman visit my farm. It was the 'green light' for me to leave and reach the Swedish coast on my own ... (I received) an address in the neighbourhood of Copenhagen. With the first train the next morning I left, with a small suitcase – among other things there were blue overalls and rubber boots, as I planned to get to the Helsingør coast as a fisher-lad. After a short and risky visit at (the address) and an address in Helsingør, I went on by the train – full of

German soldiers – to Øresund. On the station I could distinguish a number of people who had the same aim as I, but they quickly disappeared, before I was able to get any information. After changing my things I went down to the water in the darkness. Before me the fully lit Swedish coast greeted me, and the Sound separated me from a beautiful free world. An unforgettable experience. But the area was swarming with German soldiers and I had no papers. So I beat a retreat. I remembered the address I had been given in Copenhagen. Late at night I was given shelter by the Lykkebo family. At dawn I was driven to Mr. Axel Erting's house. He adjured me to take it easy, and said he would look after me. The whole day the telephone rang, and there was talk of countless 'boxes of fish'. The 3rd evening, transport was in order, also for me. There were some frightening episodes during the transfer to the fishing boat, and during the voyage, when we discovered a German patrol boat, but at last it went well, and when we reached Swedish waters we were taken over by a Swedish patrol boat.«

»At the rumours of the start of a Jewish action at the beginning of October 1943, I hid on the hayloft of my employer's farm, where I was given food. My employer rang to an acquaintance in Køge, who arranged contact with a fisherman there. I and my fiancée bicycled from the Roskilde district to Køge, practically without luggage, not to arouse suspicion. In Køge we spent 2–3 nights in the fisherman's home, as he would not sail across the Sound for fear that his boat would be confiscated by the Swedes. He suggested that I should steal a pram, which he would take in tow, and in which I and my fiancée should manage the last part into a Swedish harbour. In spite of the dangerous situation, I refused the idea. The crossing took place on 5 October at 20 hours, after the Swedish Government (?) had dropped the decision on confiscation of refugee boats. The fisherman told us we were to go by a larger boat, and with c.20 Danish Jews from Copenhagen in a party. We paid with all we had, c.1000 crowns and our bicycles.«

»At the beginning of October 1943, I was rung up one afternoon and told that I should contact some others and then just get away from the farm where I was . . . There were several of us who went back to our first starting-place on Stevns, and stayed some days at a farmer's. He not only hid us, but also some people from Copenhagen, all in all we were c.12 people. There was no discussion about anything whatever. We were in need, and it was a matter of course, that he and his family were at our disposal. The second day in the evening, a man suddenly came and just said: My name is Jørgen, we must go now . . . We said good-bye to the family, some of them went with us, we had to walk through the forest down to the shore. We had to be absolutely quiet and must not speak to each other. What happened, I shall never forget. It was full moon, and when we came down to the beach it was as light as it can be on a quite still night at full moon. And there on the shore stood a mass of people from the town. No one said a word, and it was deathly still, but they were there. A little distance from the shore, lay a fishing boat, it could not go right in as there was low tide. So we were rowed out to it, a few at a time, and when all were aboard it sailed . . . I know with absolute certainty that neither I nor my comrades had any money, and not a word was said to us about money. We had to go below decks and down into the hold, which was so low that one could not stand upright. How many people we were it is impossible to remember, but we were many. At one point, the hatch up to the deck was shut because we were near the German patrol boat. And I was so seasick that I did not care what happened. We sailed to Trelleborg, I have no idea, today, how many hours it lasted, but I think it was 7–8 hours. An old man had a heart attack, but survived. Suddenly the hatch was opened, and we were in Swedish waters, could see the lights of Sweden.«

Arrests

Not all were to see the lights of Sweden. The German arrests also hit the young Jews up and down the country.

»At my new place on a gentleman farm, I stayed until 3 October 1943. The same morning at 6 o'clock I was arrested by the Gestapo . . . They showed me a list of the comrades living closest, and with a pistol in my back I was forced to show they way to them. In that connexion an episode which could well have formed the coming 1½ years for me in a different way from what I experienced. On the way from the farm – I sat in the Gestapo car, other comrades in a closed lorry behind us – I remembered that because of the shock I had forgotten to pack my shoes in the suitcase I was allowed to pack with necessary things. I said so to one of the Germans who was an army soldier. He arranged that I was allowed to run the 400 metres back to the farm to fetch the above. It was still dark, I could have hidden myself, I could have run to neighbours who would have helped me to organised flight. No, I came back like a trained dog. My thoughts were these: If I fled, what would happen to my comrades, would one as a reprisal set the farm on fire, where I was arrested? – – Had I known what I was to go through, the next 1½ years, I would only have thought of myself. We had received no warnings at all, nor information on coming arrests, either from Copenhagen or the authorities in Assens.«

»There, in October 1943, we were surprised by the Germans and deported to to Theresienstadt. Unfortunately we had not received sufficiently sharp warnings from Copenhagen, and many of our Danish friends did not consider such an action possible, and nor did the policeman in Assens, who was well-disposed towards us, as he believed, with good reason, that our addresses could only be found in his (files). We ourselves, who had no experience of such a lightening action, were also too naive. It is true that we had taken our 2½-year-old child to one of our previous farmers, but stayed, after the evening milking, at his request, at the house of the farmer whose stables we looked after. After our arrest, under pressure we gave the address of the farm where our child was placed, in the hope that we could keep him with us in that way. We could not know that the Danes had already started a rescue action, and as we heard later, had already, on the following day, been to the farmer to take our child to Sweden.«

»Three days before the hunt started, we had a telegram from Copenhagen: 'Father very ill, go at once.' I could not do this, of course, but got on my bicycle at once to ride round to the farmers to warn and ask them to hide the young people. Unfortunately they did not take me seriously. Most of them thought I was exaggerating, and the League's chairman . . . rang me up with reproaches. The farmers had even told the Alien Police about my doings, and I had great difficulty in explaining to them that I could not keep to the curfew at night . . . It took some time, as we all know, before the police had learned their lesson. Without going into details, it can be said that my wife and I were taken prisoner . . . During the interrogation (I) discovered that they had a list of my young people from the German Consulate in Tønder. Thank God, a lot of the addresses were out of date, which saved some of them.«

»When I was working on a farm in Holmstrup, I had a telephone call from my 'foster-parents' in Hjallese. They told me that the Germans had been to them and were looking for me. They told them I had left the farm a year before. In fact: they warned me that the Germans would come sooner or later to arrest me, and that I should come to them, they would hide me at one of the neighbours'. This warning took me so much by surprise, and besides, I was afraid of the Germans, and in my childish imagination I saw them everywhere, so that before I had stopped to think, they came to the farm and took me with them.«

»While I was there, we heard one morning on the English radio that now the Germans were going to begin deporting the Jews from Denmark. When we heard it, we decided to leave the house the next morning and hide with some Danish friends. Then, the same night, the Germans came and took us.«

»In September 1943 I was warned by many. During a lesson of Axel Ahm's. One of my fellow-students – Søren Stauning – hid me for a couple of days (amusing memory: slept in the Prime Minister Stauning's pyjamas!), later at a nurse, Helga Ettrup's, where the Bohr family traced me. Flight was arranged – Amager, the acid factory, where we were taken, amongst others the university rector Harald Adler. (Quite clear memories: met Karen Callisen (geologist) and Paula Strelitz (emigrant actuary, Salmonsen's singlevolume encyclopedia) in Horserød. Then Theresienstadt.«

The arrests seem to have been concentrated most in the Assens district, and the reason, here, seems to be lack of warning, but also disbelief and lack of resolution could play a part. One of those caught tells how, the evening before the action, he received a warning of the rumour from the leader of his course, who offered to house him for the night, but he ignored the warning and next morning was arrested at his place of work.

In two instances the arrests only lasted a short time. There were some escapes:

»I meant to slip across to Sweden at that time – June 1943 – but TB was discovered, followed by immediate hospitalization in Øresund hospital. From there attempted flight October 1943 via Gilleleje, caught on church loft and 24 hours in Horserød. With help of nose bleed, which I explained as TB, express to West Prison German infirmary, but the forest vehicle stopped in front of Dagmarhus, to drop some people. There I saw my chance, jumped out, a taxi saw my flight, took me up, with address Øresunds hospital. Hid at the chief physician Blegvad's, and in the middle of October, off via the warehouse from Christianshavn to Barsebäck in the harbour Customs boat.«

»The warning reached me by telegram from Copenhagen via the group's visiting teacher. I went underground temporarily in South Jylland (Als) with people who were attached to the high school, and with whom I had also become good friends during the term at the high school. Some of these were active resistance people, and they helped me about the middle of October to Sjælland and Copenhagen, where by agreement I was collected by the students' resistance organisation, and placed with others in the same situation, in a flat belonging to the Communal Hospital. Most of the inmates came after 24 hours with a boat from Tuborg harbour to Ven... As there was not room on this transport, I stayed in the flat till the next day, when I, together with a new group, took the train to Nykøbing Falster, where, at an agreed spot, 2 taxis waited, that were to bring us to Stubbekøbing, from where we should sail to Sweden. We had been informed on, and our taxi was stopped on the main road by the Germans. We were taken to Vordingborg barracks by army lorry, from there next day on to Dagmarhus (interrogation) and Horserød camp. After about 5 weeks' stay there we were put in a train to Germany, with a lot of other inmates, of whom several had been caught during attempts at flight. The train stopped outside the West Prison to take on more prisoners. However I and two fellow-prisoners succeeded in jumping out of the windows outside Roskilde, where we managed to disappear in the darkness of the night, and after dramatic episodes and with the help of private people, the police and Falck, we ended up again at the communcal Hospital – or I ended up there again, the others had not been there before – from where after some days on a boat belonging to the then naval police, were brought over from a garden facing the Sound in Helsingør and Helsingborg. The affair – naturally in brief – was reported a few days later in the BBC's broadcast to Denmark, and also several Swedish newspapers and weeklies published shorter or more detailed (and over-dramatized) accounts.«

When the c.460 young Jews had reached safety on Swedish soil, a reorganisation began immediately of the Danish *Hechaluz*, with the election of a *Merkas* assembly and the establishment of a *Maskirut* governing body, Their first task was to make a survey over who had come across, and who had been hit by arrest. As a number came in scattered groups during the autumn, and the young Jews were divided, according to where they had landed, and the Swedish authorities' decision, among various camps, quite a time had to elapse before a comprehensive idea of the total had been worked out. Even at the beginning of December 1943, in a letter to the *Hechaluz* leaders, Margolinsky could send a list of the agricultural trainees, about whom he had no information. The number then was 17, and only applied to the 341 agricultural trainees, who came as regards organisation under Margolinsky's secretariat, and of whom 28 had been arrested. At that stage, Margolinsky had the names and addresses of almost 300 of the secretariat's people. Others were soon added to it, as a 'refugee office' was set up under the Danish Legation, with Professor Stephen Hurwitz at its head. With the aim of helping all Danish refugees – not only Jews – and with a view to later return, etc., this office procured information on names, addresses and possible employment of all who might have got across the Sound or who were arriving constantly in Sweden.

With their escape to Sweden, the rather artificial division, which had still remained in September 1943 between the *Hechaluz* and *Alijah* groups, disappeared. With their arrival in Sweden, all the young Jews from the two organisations had but one organisation to rely upon – the *Hechaluz* organisation.

In the new conditions, this now tried to take care of the members' general interests, and particularly to re-establish the education and the cultural work which had been its task in Denmark and remained so in Sweden. The aim was still the same: Emigration to Palestine.

On 18 October a preliminary *Mercas* meeting was already being held in Hässleholm, where a number of the questions arising from the flight were dealt with. Here it was agreed that *Jugendalijah* should be incorporated into the *Hechaluz* organisation, so that if new centres were formed, there should be no differentiation between the two groups, but that a much closer contact should be established between them, or preferably, a total merger. At the same time, a discussion began of the Copenhagen *Maskirut's* arrangements in the critical weeks up to 29 August and in the period between that date and the action against the Jews in October, and a preliminary judgement was passed on the question of whether these leaders and visiting teachers had acted irresponsibly, whether they had relied too much on the assurances of the Jewish community in Denmark, and whether they therefore had omitted

225

to make the necessary preparations, and lay concrete plans for the eventuality of a possible anti-Jewish action. The discussion on this was brought about by critical voices from a number of the fugitives, who did not think that the Copenhagen leaders had handled the situation correctly, and that they had omitted to make the organizational preparations for building up an illegal apparatus, and the critics demanded a commission of enquiry, set up to test this question in detail.

The hearing took place on 12 December 1943. The conclusion of the hearing was that a number of coincidental causes had brought about the catastrophe. On the one hand, the long stay in Denmark, with its scattered placing and the constant changes of location, had led to a number of the Danish *Hachscharah* members distancing themselves from the organisation, so that it had been difficult to keep this together and maintain sufficient contacts. On the other hand, one had been under strong pressure from the Jewish community in Denmark, which, especially after the flight to Bornholm, had demanded that the *Hachscharah* be strictly disciplined and laid under an obligation to prevent the repetition of individual flight, so that a state of panic could be avoided. In addition, via Slor, one had received an assurance that in the event of threatening changes, one would receive a warning of 4 to 6 weeks, a promise which – as it turned out – could not be kept. On this background, the leaders had acted in the conviction that one served *Hachscharah's* interests best, if one did not, by provocative single actions on the part of *Hechaluz* endanger the rest of the Jews in Denmark. When, nevertheless, the action took place more suddenly than foreseen, the leaders had done all that they could in the circumstances to warn and help, and they had not left Denmark until it was clear that there was nothing more that they could do. The conclusion of the long hearing was that there was no question of cowardice, negligence or irresponsibility, but that the real cause was a misjudgement with its roots in Danish-Jewish society's unrealistic evaluation of the political situation.

It was stated, nevertheless, that in the period between 29 August and 1 October one had neglected to convene a *Merkas* meeting, and that one had not after 29 August formally released the *Hascharah* members from the duty to refrain from individual flight, and also that one had neglected to destroy the files, when one had left the office in Copenhagen. These were later burned, however, so no harm was done thereby, and another set of files was brought to safety in a bank box. All-in-all, the 7-hour long hearing led to an acquittal of the leaders and visiting teachers.

One might have expected that in the autumn 1943, it would have been joy at the prepondantly successful flight, which would have dominated Jewish minds and feelings. This was not the case. The dominating feeling was sorrow for the comrades who had not crossed the Sound and were now either in the concentration camp Theresienstadt, or on their way there.

Theresienstadt

The concentration camp, Theresienstadt, will not be described here. It and the Danish Jews' fate in the camp is described elsewhere, for example in M. Friediger's book: »Theresienstadt«. Mélanie Oppenhejm, in her book »Menneskefælden« (»The Man Trap«), has recently described her experience of the camp, and her son Ralph Oppenhejm, in the form of a novel but based upon his diaries from the camp, has depicted the 1½ years of terror which awaited the deportees. Other accounts are listed in the bibliography in the handbook, »Besættelsen 1940–45. Politik, Modstand, Befrielse«.

But we cannot drop the 28 *Hechaluz* trainees and the 38 *Alijah* children, who landed in this hell, without a short explanation of the circumstances which contributed to the survival of nearly all of them. Only one trainee, Ruth Nebel, died of illness. They themselves made the most important contribution, by their will to survive, but multitudinous Danish desires and determination also watched over their fate. They were not forgotten either by the authorities, the organisations or the foster-families.

Unlike the Jews from the Danish-Jewish community, they were all stateless. A number had already been so, before they came to Denmark, and those who had German or Austrian citizenship had been robbed of their rights in 1941, by a unilateral German decision. They could therefore be in greater danger of further deportation or oversight than the Danish citizens. But that did not occur. Right from the Danish authorities' first protests against the deportation, and their repeated demands, at least to be constantly informed of the names and addresses etc. of all the deportees, no differentiation was made between the two groups. They were all implicitly regarded as being under Danish protection – as far as such a thing could be realised at all in the form of concrete measures – and in the camp the Danish leaders achieved at least a tacit acceptance of this standpoint. Here a small victory had already been won.

In my book »Til Landets Bedste« I have described how the Danish authorities, from the first to the last day of the deportations, unceasingly sought to protest against these, and how this attitude of protest showed itself, for example in the demand constantly to be kept informed on names, addresses and conditions, and how this activity would quite soon be expressed in concrete relief measures, particularly in the supply of Red Cross parcels. Regardless of the fact that the authorities constantly ran into a blank wall, that the protests were brushed aside, and that much of the help did not reach its destination, there is little doubt that all this had an effect, perhaps often overlooked. The German authorities were not left in doubt for a single day that from Copenhagen the Administration tried to follow everything that concerned the Danish deportees, and at all times held the German authorities responsible for what might happen to people who had been deported from Denmark. The effect of this cannot, of course, be measured, but it seems undeniable that the regular protests, the ceaseless demands for return and the constant intervention – whether it took the form of notes or verbal objections – had a restraining effect on German behaviour. The German authorities knew that they were under constant observation, and even though Danish authority was tragically limited, it was persistently used, and this stubborn pressure finally led to concrete results. If one only takes into account the Red Cross parcels and the return of the deportees under Count Bernadotte's name, and with Danish-Swedish personel and materiel, which took place in the spring 1945, one is perhaps forgetting the quiet effect of the many months' bombardment with protests, notes and enquiries and an unceasing demand that the fate of the deported was a Danish responsibility.

The first condition for any help to the deportees was naturally to know their names, addresses, and if possible conditions. The Danish authorities, as mentioned, immediately demanded this information, but the young deportees from the Alijah group themselves helped. As early as 5 October, some small insignificant lettercards were sent from the camp in Theresienstadt to Danish foster-families. In the League's archives, 7 letter cards have been preserved, written on that date and addressed to 6 homes and one district chairman. They are all written in German. They are all short. They all had to pass the German censor. They are all written in an optimistic tone. They would all, of course, be closely read. When they all stated that the writers were in good health and well, this was

The entrace to Theresienstadt concentration camp. (Frihedsmuseet)

probably dictated. At all events, they were under forced circumstances. The most important information was probably that they gave their carefully precise addresses. These were immediately noted in the foster-homes, organisations and ministries. But all the cards begged, directly or indirectly, for letters and parcels – as long as all letters were written in German. Here is just one example, slightly more detailed than the others, and given in translation:

»My dears!
We arrived here about an hour ago and in the circumstances we are well. Miss Bomholt has promised me to look after my things. For the time being they can remain with you, as I do not yet know where I am to live, work, and what I shall need. We are in a town with only Jewish inhabitants and Jewish selfmanagement. We may only write German, but I hope father or Erik can read it. Could you send me some food some time? Please write soon. With hearty greetings and a kiss to mother.«

And then, quite against the rules a little Danish: »Thank you for everything«.

This was the start of a series of lettercards to the homes, district chairmen and Fanny Arnskov, who had taken over the management of the League office. From the first months of 1944, cards were mostly standardized and printed simply with a »Dear X. I confirm with thanks receipt of your parcel« – and then normally only the recipient's name. In between, little greetings, most often a line expressing gratitude. And again and again carefully written the sender's address. In all, 80 such cards are extant in the League's archives, sent to many addresses, which shows that these cards ended in the League's office, for close reading, and in support of the relief work which started at once. But many more got through. On 11 December 1943, the League counted 510 cards that had been received. If the cards themselves said little or nothing, they cried aloud for contact, and they revealed, in their uniformity that nothing was allowed to be said.

Not much could slip into the lines, but a little could be deduced from nothing. In those days people had cultivated a sharp sense for reading between the lines. On 4 November 1943, Mélanie Oppenhejm – now a deportee – wrote a card to Fanny Arnskov. It reached Denmark on one of the first days of December:

»We four are together and are all well. Do write at once. Do tell your daughter she must write to us often. We will be very glad to hear from her. Have you a lot to do at the office? We think much of you. With many kind regards, Yours Mélanie Oppenhejm.«

Here the most important sentence was certainly: »Have you a lot to do at the office?« For the German censor an innocent question of care for the conditions in Copenhagen, but without much doubt a hidden question: Is relief work going on?«

It was! The foster-families reacted immediately by sending first clothes and later food parcels. To begin with, it was a question of single parcels, but during the autumn 1943 the work was centralized, so that the Red Cross took over the practical work of obtaining papers and parcels. On 1 December 1943, Fanny Arnskov could send a number of district chairmen a note with details of the new procedure for sending parcels through the Red Cross. News had then been received that the first parcels had got through, but also that there was still only permission for clothes parcels. The notes mention that up to then, it had not been possible to get permission to send food, and that it was not certain that that sort of parcel would get through. But they added that it was worth trying, and gave instructions in that case how to do it, and what could be sent by way of an experiment: »In all 4½ kg may be sent: cheese, 1 kg meat, sausage, marmelade and fruit. It does not matter how the amounts

Meine Lieben!
Wir sind vor ungefähr einer Stunde hier angekommen, u. geht es uns den Umständen gemäß gut. Frl. Bomhold hat mir versprochen für meine Sachen zu sorgen. Vorläufig können sie wohl bei euch stehen bleiben, da ich noch nicht weiß wo ich wohne, arbeite u. was ich brauche. Wir sind hier einer "Stadt" von nur jüdischen Einwohnern, u. einer jüdischen Selbstverwaltung. Wir dürfen nur deutsch schreiben, ich hoffe aber daß Vater oder Erik es lesen kann.
Könnt Ihr mir mal etwas Lebensmittel senden? Schreibt bitte bald. Mit herzl. Grüßen u. einen Kuß für Mor von Eurer Ruth.
Tak for alt!

One of the first letter cards sent from Theresienstadt by one of the deportees, Ruth Salm, on 5 October 1943.

of the goods are distributed, except for the meat.« These instructions were based on experience with parcels to other camps and prisons.

The first acknowledgements extant, for receipt of parcels, are dated January 1944, and in the course of the spring 1944 the number of standardised cards of thanks, usually with only a signature on a form increased, and in January it was still only a question of clothing parcels. But from February 1944, the food parcels also began to get through, and on several printed cards a few word crept in, of thanks for receipt of sausage and cheese. I have previously described this relief work in my book »Til Landets Bedste«, Vol.I, ch.12. Here I will only add that neither the foster-families nor the League leaders felt themselves released, by the deportations, from any kind of responsibility. In the letter mentioned above, from Fanny Arnskov to the League's district chairmen, dated 1 December, this was expressly emphasized:

»Several of the foster-homes have received an enquiry about the children's clothes, etc., from Bishop Fuglsang Damgaard, Professor Ege and Doctor Brandt Rehberg. This has very likely confused them. The committee that is looking after the other Jews has sent the note to our children's foster-homes in error. We have told them that we look after our 'children' ourselves.«

The committee mentioned, which took care of »the other Jews«, had the *Hechaluz* trainees on their list, as a matter of course.

That all this aid to all the deportees was centralized quite soon in the Social Ministry under the Permanent Under-Secretary' H.H. Koch's authoritative direction, is another matter. The foster-families and the League agreed at once to do what, for the time being, could be done, and in this work of relief could rely upon the central authorities' efforts to pave the way for the work of relief.

In these efforts, the demand for getting permission for an inspection of the camp in Theresienstadt was also included. The authorities pressed stubbornly for months, and were met with German postponement tactics, where grudging promises were waved aside week after week. The camp had to be »polished up«, and it was, extremely thoroughly, as Mélanie Oppenhejm describes in her book »Menneskefælden«. But in June 1944, »Action Beautifying« was finally complete, and Frantz Hvass, head of department in the Foreign Ministry, and the chief surgeon Eigil Juel Henningsen of the Red Cross, at last received permission to see the camp as it appeared that June day, during a watchful German conducted tour with fixed routes and prepared replies. For the Danish Jews, the visit was actually a disappointment, as the Danish visitors were apparently taken in by the carefully arranged German conducted tour. However, they saw and caught considerably more, of course, than the interned Jews could know, and considerably more than they could express in their »official« report. If they were not able to see everything behind the outer facade, the could not avoid perceiving that it was only a smooth surface that they were shown. That alone was a recognition. What was decisive was that on their return they could report verbally in the Foreign and Social Ministries, and the knowledge obtained made it possible from then on, for the Social Ministry to organise the parcel shipments much better than had been possible before. What is seen depends upon the eye that sees it. The Jews in the camp saw scenery being set up before the visit, and were grieved, but it was impossible for them to know what happened afterwards in the Copenhagen offices, where the Permanent Under-Secretary Koch from now on was a good deal better informed, and therefore better equipped for the relief service, he and his assistants in and outside the Ministry organised. There was relief service before the visit. Now it entered a more reliable framework.

In Copenhagen, full knowledge of the conditions in the camp were never obtained. One had to guess at a good deal, and all guesswork must

Facsimile of a letter card which Mélanie Oppenhejm wrote to Fanny Arnskov at the League office from Theresienstadt on 4 November 1943.

always lie far below the cruel reality of hunger, cold, illness, toil and inhuman treatment. The parcels could at best alleviate, and the main thing was then to bring the deportees home. This work is also described in my book »Til Landets Bedste«, volume II, chapter 2. For the deportees in Theresienstadt, this work bore fruit in the middle of April 1945. On 30 April 1945, the Foreign Ministry could address the following letter to the League:

»The Foreign Ministry informs you that the persons entered on the list of so-called League-children, given in the League's note of 10 November 1943, by arrangement of the Swedish Red Cross in co-operation with the Foreign Ministry and the Social Ministry, on 15 instant have been released from Theresienstadt and tranferred to Sweden, where they arrived on 18 instant, excepting only Herbert Kain, born 26 September 1923 in Cologne, who during his stay in Theresienstadt has been arrested, as far as is known on account of illegal trade, and interned in the concentration camp Kleine Festung near Theresienstadt. It is further pointed out that the Gerhard Löb, entered in the above list, according to information received by the Foreign Ministry, at the time of the deportations to Germany, avoided deportation.«

Both addenda were correct. It was Gerhard Löb who in the autumn 1943 had jumped off a prison train outside Roskilde, and who via the Communal Hospital came to Sweden. As far as Kain was concerned, it was correct that he sat in prison under a death sentence in Kleine Festung, outside Theresienstadt, the day that the »white busses« fetched the comrades he had tried to help through his smuggling trade in the main camp itself.

How did his path to Kleine Festung take form, and what was his path out of the condemned cell?

Kain's father was a merchant in Cologne, had performed military service during the First World War, was liberal by conviction, quite wealthy, and felt himself completely assimilated in German society. With 1933, this was changed. His parents were exposed to persecution and their business to boycott, and during the »Crystal Night« their home was razed to the ground. His parents were later liquidated. In these conditions, the 15-year-old Herbert made contact with *Hechaluz* and came under strong Zionist influence. On 4 September 1939, he came to Denmark as a »League-child« via Gedser-Warnemünde, and was allotted his first foster-home with a Home Mission farming family on Mors. When Mors became a security zone, he was moved to the Odense area, where on his own initiative he found a new home/place of work, on a farm in Skalbjerg. Here, in August, he enrolled in a matriculation course in evening classes, and received a warning, based on rumours, of an action with an offer of lodging in Odense. He ignored the warning, and on one of the first days of October 1943, was arrested and via Koldinghus was taken to Theresienstadt. Here he claimed he had an engineering training, and was made use of on a work gang which was to build a railway from the camp to the nearest railway station. This made contact possible with Czechoslovakian gendarmes, and so the smuggling into the camp of, for example, foodstuffs – a transaction which was repeated undetected until January 1945. After being searched, he was tortured and transferred to »dark prison« in Kleine Festung, in an underground cell of c. 1½ square metres.

The death sentence pronounced was never carried out, perhaps because he instinctively refrained from answering when an SS man called him out. In the darkness and isolation, all sense of time disappeared, and he had hallucinations.

Liberation came, when the Russian troops occupied the camp, and when Kain went back to his comrades in Theresienstadt, he was told by a Dutch lady that they had driven away in white, Swedish busses, shortly before. He then found his way on foot to the Danish Consulate in Prague, where the Consul gave him a sealed packet to deliver to the Head of Department Franz Hvass in the Foreign Ministry, if he could manage to get to Denmark. The Consul drove him into the American-occupied zone. From here, by various means of transport, his travels brought him to the Danish Consulate in Brussels, where the Consul obtained a lift for him on an American plane to Kastrup. The packet was delivered to Hvass, who obtained a set of clothes for him, a small sum of money, and a ticket to Skalbjerg.

The circle was closed.

Just one of the 1,850 fates which an attempt has been made here to describe from a common fate, which never could be common.

Thirteen years had passed, since the *Hechaluz* office in Berlin had asked Niels Siggaard about the possibilities for placing Jewish agricultural trainees in Danish farming homes. The possibility had been there. The question is only, whether the possibility had been sufficiently exploited?

Subject and Source Material

In the 1960's, while I was working on my two-volume book, »Til Landets Bedste« on the Danish Permanent Under-Secretaries' Administration, from 1943 to 1945, and in that connexion wrote two chapters on the German action against the Danish Jews in October 1943, as well as a description of the Danish relief work for the Danes who were deported to German concentration damps, I noticed from the ministerial documents, that the deportation of Jews did not only include Danish Jews, but also a number of young Jews who, during transit in Denmark, had been stranded here as the result of the German occupation, and now had to share the fate of the Danish Jews.

The construction of the book, with the weight concentrated on the central negotiations between Danish and German authorities, excluded, temporarily, a more detailed study of the special background of this group, its situation and fate. Since then it had stood as a desirable historical task, for me to investigate this section of Danish Jewish history. In 1980, I started on such an investigation.

A few conversations with one or two of the Jewish and Danish persons who, in the 1930's, were active in the work for the group's – or the groups' – arrival in Denmark and placing in Denmark, and some introductory approaches to the State Archives and institutions, led me to suppose that important source material concerning these young Jews' history could have been destroyed in connexion with the German action against the Jews in 1943.

The supposition bore the mark of probability, and it closely resembled the situation I faced in 1947, when I began my work of collecting material for the history of the Resistance Movement. This time, too, the general impression was that not much, if any, source material could still be in existence. I imagined at that time that to fill in all the lacunae, I would have to try and obtain reports from surviving participants in the work, as material, and I approached as many of these as time and circumstances allowed, with the result that I both obtained a collection of important material in the form of accounts, and also discovered a large number of private archives, which contrary to all expectations, had been filed and preserved.

This was also the case, here.

Owing to the fact that both in Denmark and in Israel there were societies which to some extent kept the earlier Jewish agricultural trainees, and the so-called »League children« together, and were in possession of a considerable register of addresses, in the autumn 1980 I could write to a large number of those in question, with the request that they would write personal accounts, or else reply to a questionnaire which was enclosed. The result of this was a quite unique collection of accounts, some brief, but most of them, fortunately, detailed. In all, the collection came to comprise 86 accounts, of which 55 were from earlier *Hechaluz* trainees, and 31 from earlier League children. In addition, 7 accounts came from Jews who had been marginally in contact with the 2 groups. Most of the accounts came from Israel, a number from Denmark and Sweden, and a few from Australia, England and the U.S.A. As the reports gradually came in, it was possible to supplement them in subsequent correspondence. The whole collection, supplemented with the correspondence, is now in the State Archives in Copenhagen.

This individual contact with surviving members of the two organisations, and personal meetings with a number of them, brought me further than to the collection of accounts. It turned out, in spite of the original information to the contrary, and the negative answers to enquiries, that a very considerable mass of archives had actually been preserved, emanating from organisations and individuals, and as the contact surface of research gradually broadened, archives – some hidden away and some fragmentary – came to light. These were sent to me, concurrently with the personal applications, and became a quite decisive side product of the collection of accounts. Each group only contained elements which illustrated the Jewish sojourn in Denmark, but together and sorted, they proved to contain an extremely solid foundation for describing it. In addition, the two ministries, the Foreign Ministry and the Ministry of Justice, which were directly involved in the sojourn, very kindly gave me permission to study the documents relevant to the research. In this way, the work gradually took on a different form from that originally conceived. With the appearance and discovery of large archives, it became these, rather than the accounts, which had to become the main basis for the book, although it should be added that the accounts, by virtue of their elements of personal experience, partly in areas where the

The association »Dengang i Danmark« – photographed in Israel, with guests from Denmark, in the twenty-fifth anniversary year of their escape across the Øresund (1968).

archives must necessarily be silent, maintained their independent value, supplementing the copious archive material.

As I have wished to spare the reader for notes, which would only contain monotonous references without supplementary texts, I will account rather more precisely in the following pages for the records which have been used, and try briefly to describe them as to size and contents:

1) The Foreign Ministry archives
2) The Ministry of Justice archives.

The ministerial archives have been especially valuable for the work as regards their information on the decisions of the ministries and authorities, and on the basis for these decisions, before the resolution, was taken, in principle, on permission for immigration and its procedure. This applies particularly to the decisions leading up to the immigration of the League children, whereas the immigration of the *Hechaluz* trainees could be based on the practice, already accepted, of exchange of agricultural

238

trainees with foreign countries, administered through the Agricultural Travel Bureau.

3) The Agricultural Travel Bureau's archives.

These records, which cover 1 file of minutes of directors' meetings, 4 journals and 21 files of carbon copies, were stored in the Trade Archives in Aarhus. As it was the Agricultural Travel Bureau which, based on current practice, dealt with all negotiations with the authorities, foster-homes and organisations relating to immigration and placing/moves of *Hechaluz* trainees from 1932–39, and partially also in the first months after the outbreak of war in 1939, these archives were the most important source for the account of immigration during that period. The start, procedure and extent of immigration could be established on the basis of the documents in these archives, all drafted by Niels Siggaard.

4) The Danish Women's National Council archives.

5) The Women's League for Peace and Freedom's archives.

The archives of the two women's organisations which, separated from the »normal« archives of the organisations, concern the work with the League children alone, came to light during research, mostly in unsorted condition. It is difficult, if not impossible, to separate these from each other, as the two women's organisations' activities, especially as regards the start of the work, overlapped each other. Both sets of archives, which cover several thousand pages in extent – divided and arranged in about 10 cases of files + a number of loose-leaf folders – cast light on the details of the League children's immigration. The documents span the period from the first plans for such an immigration in 1938, to the return of the children from Theresienstadt and Sweden in 1945. A number of essential documents, now collected in a special group, cast light on the negotiations in 1938–40 with German, English and Danish authorities, with enclosures from other countries which took part in the international relief work, but the main bulk of the archives consists of correspondence between the Copenhagen headquarters and children, homes, district chairmen, authorities and organisations, etc. The archives thus show the start of the work, its organisation and development, and the thousands of documents provide an insight into the countless individual and general problems which arose for the League children and homes, not least when the Occupation brought the majority of the children a sojourn of years. The archives of the two women's organisations have been handed over to the State Archives.

6) Julius Margolinsky's Archives.

These archives, too, which were believed for a time to have been lost, also came to light during research. They contain 12 portfolios, kept by Margolinsky, as well as a large collection of unsorted correspondence, now sorted chronologically in 3 cases of archives, covering the years 1940–43. The portfolios mentioned cover the same period, and it is not apparent what caused Margolinsky to let the unsorted part of the archives be excluded in the portfolios. The contents in the two groups of archives are identical: Margolinsky's extensive correspondence from the years 1940–43 with the authorities, the Mosaic Religious Community, organisations, the *Hechaluz* office, and hundreds of *Hechaluz* trainees etc. The archives cast light particularly on the *Hechaluz'* problems and changing situations after the outbreak of war in 1939. At that stage, Margolinsky's Committee for Jewish Agricultural Trainees, which changed its name after the occupation to the Secretariat for the Jewish Agricultural Trainees, took over the organisational work from the Agricultural Travel Bureau, as the link between the trainees and the Danish authorities. His secretariat also acted concurrently with the *Hechaluz* office, as the trainees' spokesman and advisor in many directions, and in countless cases. A number of loose sheets in the archives are difficult to arrange in chronological or thematic order. The most important find here is a short summary, »Den tyske *Hechaluz' Ausland-shachscharah i Danmark* 1933–45« prepared around 1960 to support an earlier report from 1953 on the same subject. The first report, which is not in the archives, is made for Professor Hugo Valentin and used in his thesis, »Rescue and Relief Activities in behalf of Jewish Victims of Nazism in Scandinavia« (Yivo Annual of Jewish Social Science, vol VIII, New York, 1953). The later report from about 1960 is used by Leni Yahil in her work »Et Demokrati på Prøve« (»Test of a Democracy« (Copenhagen, 1967) and seems to have been written for use in her research into the fate of the Jewish community during the Occupation.

7) Max Bezalel Ellberger's archives.

Ellberger acted during the years 1940–43 as visiting teacher for a large group of League children. His archives, which also came to light during research, contain, in 3 duplicated books + 1 portfolio, a good deal of educational material used in the teaching of the League children, and it demonstrates both the character of this teaching and the teacher's opinion of its importance; and it also contains a number of pupils' assignments, extracts of which are quoted earlier in this book. By agreement with Ellberger, the archives have been handed over to the State Archives.

8) Ernst Laske's archives.

Ernst Laske acted as visiting teacher in 1940–43, and was closely connected with the *Hechaluz* office's staff in general and Bertl Grass in particular. The archives, which came into my hands during my research, contain in 3 portfolios, a considerable number of circular letters from the *Hechaluz* office to the *Hechaluz* trainees, the *Merkas* group, and to immigrating *Hechaluz* trainees (summer 1939 to 29 October 1942). In addition there are a number of letters from the *Hechaluz* leader Bertl Grass, who was in change of the visiting teacher system, to Ernst Laske (8 April 41 to 4 April 1942) and a number of documents concerning the reorganisation of the *Hechaluz* organisation in Sweden after October 1943. The archives makes insight possible into the trainees' internal debate, of which only fragments appear in the rest of the material. At Ernst Laske's request, these archives have been handed over to the State Archives.

9) Mélanie Oppenhejm's archives.

These archives contain both a complete register, giving dates of birth, dates of immigration and possible dates of emigration for all the League children, and also a list of all the League children who have returned to Denmark from Sweden or Theresienstadt, giving the place of residence from 1943 to 1945. The archives have been handed over to the State Archives.

10) A single document, from the British Foreign Office archives, dealing with the flight from Bornholm mentioned earlier.

11) Some Swedish material has been put at my disposal by Doctor Svante Hansson, including an unpublished paper by Anna Besserman on an episode in the Swedish *Hechaluz* history, referring for example to the Jewish detention in Hässleholm. Also material relating to the escape boat »Julius«.

12) The use of newspaper material and other printed material will appear in the book.

13) In addition to the contemporary archive material mentioned, there is also the material in the accounts quoted. As this has been used to a great extent, or quoted direct in the book, a few lines on my opinion of this memoir material must be appropriate. Although these accounts have been written after 40 years or more have passed, I have had no hesitation in using them as a source on the actual events, especially as regards the young Jews' intense experience of their temporary host country. The events described were so intensely experienced, but in general are so soberly described, mostly of good, but now and then of bad memories, that I do not find any reason to take weighty considerations into account

of the danger of rationalization after the event, or lapses of memory. Impressions bit deep into the young, receptive minds, in the most tragic and dramatic circumstances, and not only have the poignant impressions from those times been deeply rooted in memory, they have also proved, by occasional tests, to hold, under check. In a great many instances, chance or direct enquiry have given me the opportunity to note the coincidence of the reminiscenses with the actual conditions of the times, and when the reminiscenses have been compared against all other knowledge, they have proved to be true. It goes without saying that there would be lapses of memory, and particularly misinterpretation, owing to lack of insight into the background for actions, and there can probably be a risk that good memories make up for bad, even though these are seldom forgotten and are often mentioned. But given these possible weaknesses, the personal accounts possess such a first-hand quality, that much genuine reality comes to expression through their honest state- ments on what was once their experience. Often it is a question of grass-roots experiences, which would never come to expression in archive material.

Students of history are traditionally taught to show some scepticism towards personal accounts, especially when these are prepared long after the events. In certain circumstances, which are present in this instance, I do not share this scepticism. For me, such first-hand material is often more realistic than comtemporary documents. It seems to me to be the case here. As regards the reports on the flight to Sweden in October 1943 – or the arrests in the same month – the accounts are primary sources, as the improvised work of escape did not leave any form of archives.

In conclusion, a few words on a question of language. It is the case, both for the archive material and the accounts, that they are written in various languages. It is obvious that letters to and from Germany are written in German, and letters to and from England are in English. The trainees' internal correspondence in the circulars to the *Merkas* assembly and hundreds of letters from trainees to the central offices and organisations in Copenhagen were written in German, although it is surprising how relatively quickly many of the trainees went over to the use of Danish. In many letters from out in the country, one can measure the rapid adjustment to Danish conditions, first a faltering half-Danish and then often pure Danish. Internally, German – or Czechoslovakian – has been the language used, alongside Danish, which had to be spoken in the homes, at places of work and with Danish inhabitants. There have been many variations. It is odd to meet an example of a girl, who had quickly learned Danish in North Jylland, only to discover, during a term at Askov High School, that her Danish was broad dialect and far from »high« Danish, so that she had to learn the language anew. That also French, and now and then Hebrew appears in the correspondence is mentioned for the sake of completeness. In addition, Jewish expressions are scattered in a large number of letters and circulars.

Faced with this linguistically variegated spectrum, now and then also gibberish, I chose to translate all the texts into Danish – now, with the exception of the English texts, translated into English – but retaining some quite simple and recurring Jewish words. I am aware that a certain atmosphere is lost in this way. On the other hand, I hope that the reader will appreciate this solution.

The accounts are a chapter of their own – perhaps in themselves a striking proof of an emotional relationship with their temporary Danish homeland. A number of the accounts are written in German, some in Swedish, and a few in English, but by far the greatest number have chosen to write in Danish, often a somewhat half-forgotten Danish, which must have given difficulties. These accounts seem, however, to whisper between the lines, that the writer has by no means forgotten his Danish, the language which was once a daily requirement. Here it has been easy, by keeping the whole text, to translate its words to normal Danish by slight alterations in orthography and syntax. It is also significant that all who have chosen to write in German or English, often do so with some form of apology, stressing that the one in question both reads and understands Danish, but they obviously thus feel freer than when using a Danish form of speech.

In all requests for accounts, I made it clear that the choice of language was quite free. When so many have chosen the difficult solution, to write in Danish, it must be the expression of an attitude to the old host land, which in itself says a good deal for an often strong attachment – retained after nearly half a century.

Postscript

During the preparation for and the writing of this book, I have met enormous helpfulness from countless people at home and abroad. This help has come in the form of archives, accounts, letters, pictures, and a myriad of small and large references. I owe all those who in one way or another have given me help and trust, my hearty thanks. It has hardly been easy always to give up archive material, or speak of tragic memories. As the number of those who in some way have assisted and often brought me a step forward runs into hundreds, I must refrain from expressing my thanks to them by name, and simply send them all the assurance of my gratitude for every list of addresses and every reply. Let me, then, here send to all those who have written, the greeting which concludes the thousands of contemporary letters:

Shalom

Jørgen Hæstrup